BRANDS

BRANDS

AN INTERNATIONAL REVIEW BY

INTERBRAND

MERCURY

Mercury Business Books
Published by Gold Arrow Publications Ltd
in association with
Interbrand Group plc

First published in 1990 by Mercury Books
Gold Arrow Publications Ltd
862 Garratt Lane, London SW17 0NB

Designed by Bridgewater Design,
Hove, East Sussex
Typeset by Central Southern Typesetters,
Eastbourne, East Sussex

Printed in Great Britain by
Clays Ltd, Bungay, Suffolk

British Library Cataloguing in Publication Data
Brands: an international review.
    1. Marketing. Role of brand names
    1. Interbrand
    658.827

ISBN 1-85636-000-8

CONTENTS

PREFACE

THE 1990'S HAS BEEN CALLED 'the decade of the brand'. The brand is a concept which has become of central importance to companies in a wide range of industries – consumer goods, toiletries, soft drinks, foods, franchising, services and industrial products. Yet it is a concept which has only been developed over the last century or so. However, interest in brands is now so intense that they are being presented on company balance sheets, are the cause of massive takeover bids and are now of increasing interest to boards of directors, investors and bankers, and not just to brand managers and marketing specialists.

A brand is a simple thing: it is in effect a trademark which, through careful management, skilful promotion and wide use, comes in the minds of consumers, to embrace a particular and appealing set of values and attributes, both tangible and intangible. It is therefore much more than the product itself; it is also much more than merely a label. To the consumer it represents a whole host of attributes and a credible guarantee of quality and origin. To the brand owner it is, in effect, an annuity, a guarantee of future cash flows.

Consider the Coca-Cola brand. Coca-Cola is a brand of soft drink with a distinctive (and protected) brand name and 'get-up'. The brand offers consumers taste and refreshment plus an assurance of quality. The brand also offers assurance as to price, value and origin. But Coca-Cola offers far more than merely a tasty, quality product at a fair price – it offers a host of intangible benefits and it is the brand's intangible attributes, not its tangible characteristics, which so clearly set it apart from its competitors.

Coca-Cola is not, in product terms, highly sophisticated. It would be relatively easy for any well-resourced company to produce a carbonated, cola-flavoured soft drink. Indeed, in countries such as the UK and USA major and well respected grocery retail chains such as J Sainsbury, Safeway and A&P all offer for sale 'own label' colas produced for them by outside suppliers. These own label products are of high quality and, it could be argued, offer consumers most of the tangible benefits of the Coca-Cola drink at a lower price. They also offer the assurance

of high quality and the reassurance of a 'big name' company standing behind them. What they fail to offer, however, are the intangible elements of the Coca-Cola brand and for this reason such own label products are outsold by Coca-Cola despite their lower price. And this is in a truly open trading environment where consumers have complete freedom of choice and are spending their own hard earned money.

The intangible attributes of the Coca-Cola brand have been developed and nurtured over time and, even though it is essential that the tangible or product benefits delivered by a brand are appealing and of high quality, it is often the emotional, intangible attributes which have the greatest appeal for consumers.

This book focuses on brands and branding and looks at over 300 of the world's great national and international brands. These cover a wide range of industries from automobiles to financial services and a wide number of countries – branding is clearly a concept which can be applied to a wide range of products and services in all countries of the world.

In this book we describe, on a brand by brand basis, what makes each brand powerful and how each brand is differentiated from others. We also explore branding trends in different industries and different countries.

In selecting brands for inclusion in this book we first made a compilation of many thousands of brands drawn from published surveys and industry sources. We also used Interbrand staff members in the UK, USA, Japan, Australia, West Germany and Italy to draw up a checklist of major brands in their markets based upon the Standard Industrial Classification. From all these sources we produced an initial shortlist of brands which we then considered for inclusion in this book.

We next reduced this shortlist to a working list of some 500 brands having regard to the key characteristics which, in our experience, constitute brand strength. These include factors such as leadership, stability, trend and support as well as the markets in which the brands operate. Generally we focused on brands with a strong and distinctive brand personality; we have therefore tended to favour free-standing product brands rather than more generalised corporate brands as these often cover a wider range of products but in a less distinctive way. Having produced our initial working list, we then conducted a simple 'audit' of each of the 500 brands; we also prepared a 'profile' of each brand. This led us to our final selection, although, inevitably, we also had to have regard to such practical considerations as the availability of information and the wish or otherwise of brand owners to co-operate. Also, the logistics of gathering brand data from hundreds of brand owners around the world and the need to keep to timetables inevitably meant that last minute adjustments needed to be made to the shortlisted brands.

One important factor which struck us powerfully during the preparation of this book is the singlemindedness which the owners of important brands have for their brands. Brands are not, to their owners, amorphous, insubstantial things; they are very specific assets with distinct characteristics and personalities which demand meticulous management. Indeed, the owners of famous brands are intensely 'brand centric' and almost all owners of brands would share the views of John Stuart, Chairman of Quaker, when he said:

If this business were to be split up, I would be glad to take the brands, trademarks and goodwill and you could have all the bricks and mortar – and I would fare better than you.

or support the makers of LEGO bricks in their view that:

Trademarks and brand names are among the few familiar points that consumers have to guide them – they are therefore among the most valuable assets of the manufacturer.

We trust that, through our analyses of the world's leading brands, some broad rules of branding will become apparent which will lead to a greater appreciation of these valuable assets and to still better and more effective brand management.

We would like to thank the many brand owners who have provided information and illustrations for this book. We should also point out that all the brand names featured in this book are someone's property; we hope we have shown all such brand properties the respect they deserve.

Within Interbrand much of the analysis was conducted by Paul Stobart and the collation by Debbie Kitson and Sue Ridley. The analyses of national branding trends and the brand synopses were largely the work of John Murphy, Mike Birkin, Tom Blackett, Raymond Perrier, Alison Rolfe, Chuck Brymer, Terry Oliver, David Andrew, Roger McHardy, Bernd Adams and Marco Gualdi. Nick Dale-Harris and Tony Finn of Gold Arrow Publications developed the concept and co-ordinated design, production and the syndication of international rights.

Though many people were involved in the preparation of this book, responsibility for it ultimately rests with Interbrand. We recognise that, to some observers, certain of our selections and comments may appear idiosyncratic; we also recognise that not everyone will agree with all our observations. As we intend periodically to publish new, updated versions of *Brands: An International Review* by Interbrand, if you feel that we have excluded brands which deserve to be included, or if you have insights into brands which you feel we should be aware of, please let us know – you can contact us in London or at any of our overseas offices. We would be glad to hear from you.

Meanwhile we hope that you find this book on brands and branding both stimulating and enjoyable.

INTERBRAND
LONDON, 1990

INTRODUCTION

BRANDS AND BRANDING

BRANDING HAS BEEN USED since the earliest times to distinguish the goods of one producer from those of another. Indeed, the word 'brand' derives from the Old Norse word *brandr* which means to *burn* and brands were, and still are, the means by which owners of livestock marked their animals. From branding his livestock early man moved on to branding his wares — a potter for example would identify his pots by putting his thumbprint into the wet clay on the bottom of the pot or by making his mark — a fish, a star or a cross, maybe — and the good potter would expect customers to seek out those products which carried his mark. But of course it also worked to the benefit of the consumer — the brand or trademark allowed the consumer to avoid products which did not bear the required mark or, if a branded product had proved unsatisfactory, to avoid it.

Interestingly, even from the earliest times trademark infringement and counterfeiting flourished. It became common practice, for example, for producers of inferior products to apply the marks of reputable producers in order to deceive the buying public; the world's museums have plenty of examples of early counterfeit goods.

THE DEVELOPMENT OF BRANDING

It was, however, only in the second half of the Nineteenth Century that branding in its current form evolved and indeed many of today's great brands, among them Kodak and Coca-Cola, are around 100 years old and owe their origins to the explosion of economic activity which resulted from the new, fast and efficient communications systems brought about by railways and steam driven ships.

Until the advent of the railways it was difficult for manufacturers to distribute goods very widely, except by using ships or barges. Some trade in branded goods did exist between ports and their immediate *hinterlands* (raw cocoa, for example, reached Cadbury's factory in Bournville, Birmingham by barge and the finished product returned the same way) but such distribution systems were extremely limited in scope.

The railways changed all that. In the United States, for example, Mid Western producers could reach markets throughout the Mid-West and the Eastern Seaboard and even the Pacific Coast. The result was that certain branded products achieved an ascendancy over their competitors and grew on a regional, a national and, eventually, an international scale. Mr Procter and Mr Gamble's soap-making business in Cincinnati and Mr Kraft's new cheese processing business in Chicago both prospered at the expense of less resourceful, determined or skilful competitors and their high quality, branded, differentiated products drove out competition.

This process was repeated all over the world. In the UK, for example, in the mid-Nineteenth Century every village and hamlet had its own brewery distributing its products over a radius of only a few miles. The advent of the railways and, later, the internal combustion engine allowed the more powerful breweries to extend their influence over much wider areas; today leading beer brands are distributed worldwide.

Even though modern branding is little more than 100 years old the use of branding has developed considerably over that time:

1 legal systems have recognised the value of brands to both producers and consumers. Most countries in the world now acknowledge that intellectual property – trademarks, patents, designs, copyright – is property in a very real sense and therefore confers rights on the owners of such property. Indeed, rights in brands and trademarks are every bit as powerful as rights in more tangible forms of property such as land and buildings.

2 the concept of branded goods has been extended successfully to embrace services – in the last thirty years in particular some of the greatest branding successes have been in the area of services.

3 perhaps most importantly, the ways in which branded products or services are distinguished from one another have come increasingly to embrace non-tangible factors. The brand qualities which consumers rely upon in making a choice between brands have become increasingly subtle and even, at times, fickle. Cigarette A may be virtually indistinguishable from Cigarette B yet outsell it ten to one; a fragrance costing £5.00 a bottle may be outsold by another fragrance with very similar physical characteristics but which sells at £50.00 a bottle.

Modern, sophisticated branding is now concerned increasingly with a brand's *gestalt*, with assembling and maintaining in a brand a mix of values, both tangible and intangible, which are relevant to consumers and which meaningfully and appropriately distinguish one supplier's brand from that of another. The art of successful branding lies in selecting and blending these elements so that the result is perceived by consumers to be uniquely attractive and influential on the purchasing decision.

THE REWARDS OF BRANDING

The process of branding 'adds value' to the basic product: if the brand is successful the producer can frequently charge a premium and benefit from his or her ingenuity. Alternatively, the brand owner may choose to be rewarded by higher volumes, leading to economies of scale, or by the greater security of demand afforded by brands. Brands therefore are valuable to their owners because they represent a means to develop sales and profits which can, to varying degrees, be protected against competitive attack or trespass; brands are valuable to retailers, or suppliers, because strong brands can command higher prices and stimulate customer flow; and brands are valuable to consumers because they facilitate choice.

Brands can therefore acquire considerable value. Examples of brands which over the years have remained true to their promise are:

UK BRANDS			
Brand	Market	1933 position	Current position
Hovis	Bread	1	1
Stork	Margarine	1	1
Kellogg's	Cornflakes	1	1
Gillette	Razors	1	1
Schweppes	Mixers	1	1
Colgate	Toothpaste	1	1
Kodak	Film	1	1
Hoover	Vacuum cleaners	1	1
Source: Saatchi & Saatchi			

US BRANDS			
Brand	Market	1923 position	Current position
Eastman Kodak	Cameras/Film	1	1
Del Monte	Canned fruit	1	1
Wrigley	Chewing gum	1	1
Nabisco	Biscuits	1	1
Gillette	Razors	1	1
Coca-Cola	Soft drinks	1	1
Campbells	Soup	1	1
Ivory	Soap	1	1
Goodyear	Tyres	1	1
Source: Adapted from *Advertising Age*, 19 September 1983			

THE NEW HOOVER CLEANER advertisement. The Hoover Company · North Canton, Ohio. Hamilton, Ontario, Canada.

These examples demonstrate that many good brands, for all their complexity of product and consumer appeal, are not only capable of surviving for extraordinarily long periods but are capable of maintaining their market position despite fierce competition and changes in fashion. How can this be? Let us take two examples, Coca-Cola and Kodak.

The Coca-Cola formula has remained much the same since the 1880s, but its image has been updated constantly to keep its appeal fresh and youthful. This factor alone has helped the brand retain market leadership in the teeth of competition from Pepsi-Cola and many retailers' own brands. Coke, therefore, has maintained its position essentially by investing in and developing the non-tangible elements of its image.

Kodak's products, on the other hand, have changed dramatically over the last 100 years. The brand has enjoyed continuous leadership and stability because it has been quick to adapt to changing technology and has exploited this to the benefit of the consumer. Kodak has done more than any other manufacturer to popularise photography. Through its investment in product development and its commitment to mass marketing, it has helped bring photographic competence to millions at prices everyone can afford.

Thus, brands offer a guarantee to consumers of quality and value; if this guarantee is honoured by the producer then consumers will reciprocate with their loyalty.

TRENDS IN BRANDING

Over the last few decades we have seen the application of branding techniques to a number of new areas and the growth of retailers' own brands is one interesting and important example. At one time, of course, most of the products sold in shops were the retailers' own (manufacturers had frequently not yet learned that by branding their products they could 'talk' directly to the consumer and thus modify the power of the retailer) and, paradoxically, the growth of manufacturers' brands owes much to the inability of retailers to provide customers with the variety and quality of products they wanted.

In the last two decades, however, we have seen a gradual reversal of this trend with the balance of power shifting once more in favour of the retailer. In the UK, for example, where five or six grocery chains now account for around half the country's sales, approximately one third of all their sales are of retailers' own brands. In the United States too the big grocery retailers are investing in own brand development and are beginning to sweep away the cheap-and-cheerful image that has for so long characterised such brands and which has, in recent years, placed them at a competitive disadvantage.

Thus, retailers' own brands are no longer the inferior generic products of the 1960s and 1970s; they are brands in their own right and are every bit as good — and often better — than manufacturers' brands. The signs are, therefore, that retailers' own brands will continue to grow in popularity at the expense of manufacturers' brands for as long as they satisfy consumer requirements.

Another area where branding is increasingly used is financial services. The freeing-up of financial markets has led to a growth of competition between providers of financial services which is coupled with an increasing diversity of products. This has resulted in the need for branding to endorse, clarify and differentiate the new products coming on to the market, as much for the consumer's benefit as for the vendor's.

Similarly, many manufacturers of high technology products have also turned to product branding in order to help consumers understand the bewildering array of choice that is now available to them. Few manufacturers, however, have managed to emulate Steve Jobs' brilliance in naming his micro-computer Apple.

Apple, at a stroke, rendered obsolete the decades of technical gobbledegook and industry jargon that had characterised computer branding and replaced it with the concept of the 'brand personality'. So, as the purchase decision filters downwards to less technical staff in large organisations, and computer technology begins to encroach more and more upon our personal lives, the use of branding to demystify what traditionally has been the preserve of the expert is bound to increase. Apple's success is therefore due as much to its user-friendly brand image as it is to the user-friendly product.

In complete contrast is the market for pharmaceutical products. This is an area where names have, for a long time, played an important role in helping to guide the selection and prescribing of medicines. The pharmaceutical industry is, however, relatively unsophisticated in its use of branding (a factor which is largely explained by generic substitution and the part which governments and regulatory agencies play in drug purchasing) and it is only recently that drug manufacturers have begun tentatively to use some of the branding techniques that have for so long been applied elsewhere. But while the use of branding — with the brand name, graphics, advertising and targeting all working in concert to produce a well defined 'proposition' — is still in its infancy, the successful promotion of such 'wonder drugs' as Zantac and Tagamet has shown the industry the way in which strong branding can help manufacturers reap the benefits of innovation.

BRANDS AS ASSETS

Most brand owners now readily acknowledge that their brands are their most valuable and enduring assets. During the 1970s Jaguar Cars suffered badly from changes of ownership and a serious neglect of product quality. However, the company eventually recovered its market position and was recently purchased by Ford, mainly because of the power of the brand. Throughout the 1970s the Jaguar name — if not, for a while, its vehicles — continued to enjoy enormous prestige and this factor on its own contributed greatly to the survival of the company.

The extraordinary resilience that good brands display represents a unique attraction to investors. Thus an important issue surrounding brands today is not just how to create and market them, but how others perceive their success and, ultimately, their financial worth. Buying a major brand nowadays is often more attractive, and makes more financial sense, than building it up through marketing, advertising and promotion over a number of hard, non profit-making years. Brands are now increasingly regarded as tradeable assets of worth, and this has created an epidemic of acquisition fever, with major household names changing hands for staggering sums. For example, in a few brief months in 1988, almost $50 billion was paid for brands in just four deals:

1   RJR Nabisco, the tobacco, drink and food manufacturer, was the centre of a $25 billion fight between its own management and various predators all of whom wished to buy the company. Nabisco's European brands were later sold to the French food giant BSN for $2.5 billion by 'leveraged buyout' specialists Kohlberg Kravis Roberts, the victors in the takeover battle.

2   American food and tobacco giant, Philip Morris, bought Kraft, the maker of cheese products of the same name and a host of other brands including Miracle Whip toppings and Breyers ice cream. The price was $12.9 billion, four times Kraft's 'tangible' assets.

3   Grand Metropolitan, a UK food and drinks company acquired Pillsbury for $5.5 billion – a 50 per cent premium on the American firm's pre-bid value and several times the value of its tangible assets.

4   Nestlé paid $4.5 billion, more than five times Rowntree's book value, to acquire the York confectionery firm that makes Kit Kat, After Eight and Polo Mints.

The reason why the prices paid for these businesses are so high is that good brands produce profit streams that are highly tangible. Also, at least in the overcrowded consumer goods markets, it is extremely difficult to grow brands like Kit Kat, Winston cigarettes and Green Giant from scratch. So the value of such brands is twofold: first, the net value of future earnings; second, a premium for the sum a competitor would spend trying to create an equivalent brand.

Thus branded goods companies are increasingly the subject of takeover bids and this factor has contributed to the large number of companies now seeking valuations of their brands. In certain cases these valuations are for balance sheet purposes. Much more frequently, companies are using brand audit and evaluation techniques to understand their brands better, assess returns on capital on a brand-by-brand basis and determine the allocation of scarce resources (e.g. advertising expenditure) between brands. Such techniques are also being used in the area of mergers and acquisitions (e.g. identifying target companies, selling unwanted brands and in defence against hostile bids), fund-raising, internal brand licensing for fiscal purposes and external licensing to third-parties.

SUCCESSFUL BRANDING

The relationship between a brand and the consumer is, in many respects, something of a 'pact'. The consumer recognises that the benefits he or she gains when purchasing the brand are both tangible and intangible and rightly expects the brand owner to deliver full and fair value in both of these areas. Thus the purchaser of a Rolls-Royce or Lexus motor car will expect the car to perform reliably, to be designed and manufactured to a high standard, to have an appropriate service network and so on. The consumer will also expect that the intangible, emotional benefits he or she is buying are maintained. The owner will, therefore, expect that the promotional literature put out by the company is of a high quality and does not vulgarise or devalue the brand; he or she will expect too that the Rolls-Royce or Lexus name is not applied to products which might debase the brand name, for example bin liners or condoms. Similarly, the consumer will expect that the company controls unauthorised third-party use of the Rolls-Royce or Lexus name because misuse of the name could debase the imagery of the brand he has purchased lessening both its esteem and the intangible benefits of ownership. Careful management of the intangible attributes of a brand is therefore not merely in the interest of the brand owner, it is a specific responsibility which the brand owner owes to its customers.

Brand owners must therefore constantly ensure that the qualities and values of their brands are maintained. They must continue to appeal to the consumer and should be developed so as to maintain their attractiveness in a changing world. In other words, except in the short term, the brand can seldom shield the brand owner from his own failure to maintain his brand in good repair.

Successful brands are therefore far more than ingenious notions which appeal to the consumer only at one point in time; they are dynamic and changing assets which must retain their consumer appeal in a constantly changing world. And international brands, which need to appeal to consumers with a wide range of cultural, religious, language and ethnic backgrounds are particularly rare, extremely valuable and require the highest level of brand management skills and the closest possible care and attention.

INTERNATIONAL BRANDS

An important characteristic of many major brands is that they are international in scope — Opium is as likely to appeal in Brazil as it is in Hong Kong. The developed countries, whose inhabitants are the major consumers of branded goods, have shown in this century an enormous 'coming together' of consumer tastes and expectations. Regional and local tastes, attitudes and preferences remain and these must be taken into consideration. Nonetheless brands which are successful in one market are increasingly likely to have appeal to consumers on an international basis.

The reasons for this are many and include improved communications, increased travel and greater language tuition in schools (particularly of English). The most important reason, however, is that wherever we live, whatever our colour and whatever our culture

we are all very much the same. Coca-Cola tastes as good to a teenager in Kowloon as in Chippewa Falls, Wisconsin. A couple in Tokyo take as much pleasure in looking at their Kodak wedding photographs as a couple in Nairobi.

Equally important, however, is the fact that international brands provide companies with a coherence to their international activities. This is because international companies which permit, or are forced to accept, a proliferation of local brands often find a fragmentation of their activities. In theory each of these brands should be more ideally adapted to particular local conditions; in practice the appeal, coherence and power of competitive international brands makes it difficult for the local brands to compete in the market.

But while this form of 'commercial hegemony' may be entirely feasible for the large multinational companies, how can smaller businesses with more modest resources benefit from the wider opportunities that international markets provide? The answer frequently is through 'niche' marketing. Consumers throughout the world are becoming increasingly sophisticated and brands which offer a measure of exclusivity — or even eccentricity — are inceasingly sought after and valued because such appeals are universal. Many niche businesses like Burberry, Crabtree and Evelyn, and Dunhill have developed successful international brands by nurturing a quality image and promoting this selectively to carefully chosen target consumers.

For many companies international brands are the passport to international business success — strong, locally based brands can provide their owners with powerful benefits, but international brands allow companies to cross borders readily, making it possible to develop brand focus and coherence otherwise impossible via a local market. Developing international brands does, however, require considerable care.

SUCCESSFUL INTERNATIONAL BRANDING

What then makes up a successful international brand? It is possible to identify the following features:

a) at the core of the brand must lie strong intellectual property rights to which the brand's owner has clear legal title. Registered trademarks protecting the brand name itself are usually the key property rights in a brand but design rights, copyrights and patents may also contribute powerfully. (Kodak, for example, is a trademark of Eastman-Kodak which is registered on an international basis; the machines or the processes used to manufacture Kodak products may be protected by patent; the artwork on the packaging may be protected by copyright; and the shape of the container or general appearance of the product may be protected by design.) In the absence of intellectual property rights, brands cannot exist — they will merely be undifferentiated generics.

b) the brand must be meaningfully differentiated; it must stand apart from its competitors such that consumers recognise that the branded product has particular characteristics, both tangible and intangible. Unless brands are differentiated no brand personality exists and the consumer has no reason to select any one brand in preference to another.

c) the brand must be appealing; the consumer must recognise in the brand qualities and attributes which are desirable and which prompt recommendation and repurchase.

d) the brand must be consistent; it must continue to deliver satisfactions and must not let the consumer down.

e) the brand must be supported through advertising and other forms of promotion and through distribution; the consumer must be aware of the brand and its qualities and it must, too, be available for the consumer to purchase.

f) the brand must address consumer needs which exist internationally; no brand can become international if the satisfactions it delivers are purely local in nature.

g) most importantly, the brand must be meticulously managed over an extended period of time: quality must be maintained, distribution ensured and competitive challenges met. And, as mentioned above, appropriate and appealing advertising is required, modified to suit changing needs and conditions, and consistent and appealing packaging must be used to help existing purchasers recognise the product as well as to attract new purchasers to it. Brand extension may also be required to exploit the 'equity' in the brand and keep the brand relevant and appealing but this, too, needs careful and skilful management.

What distinguishes the world's leading brands, both international and national is the care and attention which are lavished on them by their owners. Good brand management requires singlemindedness, even a streak of fanaticism and all the great brands listed in this book display an attention to detail which sets them apart from the normal.

THE EUROPEAN SINGLE MARKET

One of the key factors assisting the international aspirations of all businesses is the dismantling of tariff barriers between all member states of the European Community. This move offers the single biggest opportunity ever likely to confront brand owners, European and otherwise. Satellite broadcasting is making pan-European advertising a reality, international distribution systems now exist and over 350 million consumers – a large proportion of whom are affluent – await the 'Eurobrands' of the future.

But companies have much to do to ensure that they fully grasp this major opportunity. American brand owners like Procter & Gamble, General Foods and Kodak, who have long been a force in European consumer goods markets, and many skilful Japanese brand owners, excel at mass marketing. Such companies will be seeking to dominate those sectors where consumers expect high standards of quality and value, and where such standards can be achieved irrespective of the scale of production.

It is also clear that Europe is by no means an easy market. It is tempting to equate the market opportunities in the new united Europe with the market opportunities which exist in the US though in many respects the two markets are entirely different. For all its size the US market is remarkably homogeneous: the same language is used across the entire country (though the importance of Spanish as a second language is growing fast) and the same basic culture is in place across an entire continent. Thus in many respects the Californian consumer is remarkably similar to the Massachusetts consumer and this relative homogeneity provides remarkable marketing opportunities and economies of scale.

The European market is, in branding terms, quite a different proposition: local tastes and preferences vary markedly from country to country as do languages, distribution systems, advertising media and so forth. Italy, for example, is dominated by owner-managed stores ('momma and poppa' stores) so the retail infrastructure is exceptionally fragmented. In Germany and Britain, on the other hand, major retail chains pre-dominate and the ability to reach consumer markets with a new brand by striking a deal with a major retailer are much greater. In Europe too there are no real Europe-wide newspapers and Europe-wide satellite TV is still in its infancy.

Even though, therefore, the experience of branding over the last 100 years is that branded goods drive out unbranded commodities and that powerful international brands drive out local brands it is likely that the process of brand harmonisation across Europe will be a long one and that enormous brand diversity will exist in Europe for decades to come. In many ways, however, this pool of brands represents an asset for Europe which is unique. European brands have been highly successful on an international basis in such areas as luxury goods, speciality foods, alcoholic beverages, fashion and so forth. Some of the most remarkable brand successes in Japan and the United States have been achieved by European brands such as Louis Vuitton and Perrier which were formerly confined to their home markets and this process seems bound to continue.

NATIONAL BRANDS

What, then, of the contention that international brands simply cannot have the close adaptation to local conditions and the flexibility and sure-footedness of local brands? This argument is not convincing because it is based on a false premise: namely that international brands are not, or cannot be, adapted in local markets to suit local conditions. In practice, one of the key skills involved in international branding is to maintain an international coherence but, at the same time, to adapt the brand to suit local conditions. Coca-Cola containers, for example, are smaller in Japan than elsewhere because Japanese consumers do not consume the same quantities of fluid as consumers in Europe and the United States. The cans, too, although they contain the identical product and have the same overall design as elsewhere, carry much of the detail in Chinese script and in *katakana*. The Coca-Cola Company does not, therefore, try to force on the Japanese consumer the identical product as is sold in Atlanta, Georgia.

The slogan of many owners of international brands is therefore to 'think global, act local'; in other words to seek the benefits of international branding but, at a local level, to be sensitive to local needs and nuances.

DEVELOPING NEW BRANDS

Companies follow quite different strategies for developing new brands. The most common is that of developing 'me too' products. Every successful new brand attracts a flock of imitators similar in concept, get-up, brand name and function to the original. Such 'me too' brands frequently have little chance of competing seriously with the original brand unless, for example, they are able to offer a substantial price advantage. They do, however, offer a producer a low-risk opportunity to enter a market at low cost .

Another common problem faced by brand developers is the over-emphasis often placed on research. Every possible attribute of a new brand is measured, whether it is relevant or not and whether such measurement provides data of any value to the brand owner. Moreover, such research is frequently done among consumers whose experience is limited to the existing brands on the market. They tend, therefore, to react most favourably in a research situation to the familiar and, frequently, the banal and this can lead to unexciting and uninspired brands. Such research does, however, provide good excuses in the event of failure!

Other organisations, especially those in areas such as fashion and fragrances, frequently view branding almost entirely as a creative or artistic process largely unfettered by research considerations.

Perhaps, however, the most appropriate and successful approach to the development of new brands is the pragmatic one — try to identify new brands with some measure of distinctiveness and consumer appeal and which are not simply 'me too' products. Use appropriate research techniques to measure the brand's likely market success. But recognise also that branding does have a strong creative element and therefore encourage creativity and flair.

In a sense, branding consists of thinking ahead of consumers, of anticipating and shaping their needs and wants. But branding is not a cynical activity. The consumer is part of the process. He or she does not have to buy the brand. If they really do not like it, if it does not perform well, or if it offers bad value, they will reject it. In other words, the brand must deliver — even if some of the delivered value is not directly measurable.

It is estimated that seventeen out of twenty new brands fail. The reasons for failure can sometimes be attributed to product problems, at other times to distribution problems, to changes in legislation, to bad luck or to bad management. Most commonly, however, the reason for failure is simply that the new brands do not offer the consumer anything of interest that he or she does not have already — they are not differentiated meaningfully from existing products. Most new brands are simply approximate facsimiles of existing brands — they are as close as they can be to existing brands within the constraints imposed by trademark law, passing off, copyright and corporate pride.

Innovative, differentiated brands however can offer potent advantages. Not only can they offer the consumer real benefits and thus give the consumer a reason to change, they can also serve to outmode existing brands. The new brand not only offers the consumer a new set of values, it wrong-foots the opposition and shows it up as being unexciting and staid. In the 1950s in Britain the culture of car branding was largely 'British' in style — cars had names like Westminster, Cambridge, Herald and Oxford. Ford then introduced the Cortina. The post-war boom was getting underway, consumers were starting to take organised Mediterranean holidays and Britain's earlier insularity was beginning to dissolve. Cortina hit the mood of the moment. It was fresh, exciting, different and a little foreign and sophisticated. Not only did the brand name assist in positioning the new car in an interesting and fresh fashion, it also wrong-footed competitive products and made them look somewhat dull and old-fashioned.

WHAT'S IN A NAME?

Of course, with many products the main means of differentiating one brand from another is the name. After all, if you are introducing a new mass-market, traditional beer you cannot do a great deal about the colour, taste, formulation, even about the basics of packaging or price. The brand name and the product 'get-up' are the main means of differentiating one brand from another. The brand name performs a number of key roles:

1 it identifies and helps to differentiate the product or service, and allows the consumer to specify, reject, or recommend brands.
2 it communicates messages to the consumer.
3 it functions as a particular piece of legal property in which a manufacturer can invest and which is protected from competitive attack or trespass. Through time and use a name can become a valuable asset.

The brand name is therefore not only important but it is also complex. It must satisfactorily perform a number of quite different roles involving aspects of communication and it also has an important legal role.

So how do you develop effective brand names — names that will not only help position the new product or service but are attractive, memorable and protectable and will stand the test of time? Brand name development necessarily involves a careful refining process — a great deal of ore has to be fed into the hopper in order to produce a small amount of pure gold: the attractive, strong, protectable brand name. There are four main stages:

1 development of a naming strategy — what sort of name is required? How many countries will the new name be used in? Should the new name 'fit' with existing company names? Should the new name fit within the existing naming culture in the sector or should it be entirely innovative? How will competitors respond?
2 development of names to fit the naming strategy. (Consumer groups, copywriters and computer techniques may all have an important role to play in the brand name development area).
3 shortlisting of preferred names, followed by language and consumer checks.
4 full legal searches, a process which can be both expensive and time consuming but which is of critical importance. (It is not uncommon, for example, for a

single name to encounter many apparent objections. These must all be checked, often the owners must be contacted and at times commercial agreements will be necessary. In other cases it may be necessary to conduct detailed confidential investigations to check independently if a trademark is being used and if so on what products. Sometimes it may even be necessary to threaten legal action to have a trademark cancelled so as to secure it in a particular country.)

Companies tend, when developing new brand names, to seek descriptive names. It is somehow felt that such names will help sales and scant attention may be paid to the longer-term implications. But why does the name need to contain an overt message? After all, the advertising, the graphics and the packaging all convey messages to consumers. So why use the brand name,

too, to describe the product? To hazard the success of the brand by adopting a descriptive name which is unprotectable is clearly absurd.

Brand names by no means need to be descriptive in order to achieve market success. Kodak, for example, has no element of descriptiveness whatsoever; it is a pure invention. So too is Exxon. They are both collections of letters which are short, memorable, strong both graphically and visually and yet have no 'core' of meaning that is instantly intelligble. Sunsilk is an attractive name for a shampoo. It has connotations of softness and associations with the great outdoors. It is by no means a pure invention but, rather, draws its strength from images and associations relevant to us all. Bitter Lemon, on the other hand, is purely descriptive of a lemon-based mixer drink. It has very little invention and hence is virtually unprotectable.

These brand names span the Brand Name Spectrum from totally free-standing names to completely descriptive names. All brand names fall somewhere along this spectrum. Schweppes, a name with delightful in-built onomatopoeia, conveys images of effervescence. Formica is mainly an invented name but has a core meaning. Visa is a name with associations of travel and crossing boundaries and Sweet 'n' Low is a name with a high descriptive content.

In general, the more descriptive a name the more it communicates immediately to the consumer. Unfortunately such names tend to be less distinctive and less protectable. In contrast, the more free-standing a name the less it immediately conveys to the consumer and the more the brand owner needs to invest in it to confer upon it the qualities of excellence and superiority he requires. Between these two extremes lie 'associative names', those which are distinctive and protectable and yet communicate some appropriate message or messages to the consumer.

This middle route, the associative route, can and does result in powerful, attractive and protectable brand names. Kodak might have fared as well had Mr Eastman adopted a name such as Vista but would hardly have been in as powerful a market position today if he had called his company Super-Pic or Easi-Foto.

The brand name is central to a brand's personality be it a product brand or a corporate brand. It is the one aspect of a brand which almost never changes and is an essential prerequisite of international marketing. It can become an asset of enormous value. Obviously it pays to get the brand name right, to select one which is legally available in all the countries of interest and to remove all third-party obstacles at relatively low cost before launch, and not at very high cost after launch.

Curiously, however, such a systematic approach is often ignored. Organisations select names with profound marketing and legal defects. They spend fortunes in litigation trying to resolve inherent legal problems. They even, not infrequently, have to withdraw products from the market.

In an age in which companies spend tens or even hundreds of millions of dollars or pounds per year advertising and promoting a single product or product line, when the clutter and noise in most sectors increases constantly and when those magical market share points can be worth hundreds of millions of dollars or pounds, the power of the brand name continues to grow. Within the brand name resides all that investment. And it is the one single most clearly identifiable aspect of the product that the consumer uses in selection and purchase.

BRAND EXTENSION

The costs and risks of new brand development have led many companies, despite the success of 'new' brands such as Apple, Benetton and Phileas Fogg, to focus for growth on the extension of existing brands rather than the development of new brands.

Brand extension offers the brand owner the possibility of endorsing a new product with some or all of the qualities of an existing brand. The company can thus enter a market more cheaply, establish the new product more quickly and increase the overall support and exposure of the brand. This strategy, safe though it may appear, is not without risk. By extending the brand to cover a new product the brand owner faces the possibility that all he is really doing is diluting the appeal of the existing brand.

In Britain, Cadbury's have, over the years, extended the Cadbury name to embrace not only chocolate and candy products but such mainstream food products as instant potatoes, dried milk, soups and beverages. It is arguable that in using the Cadbury name as an endorsement of quality, origin and value on non-chocolate products they have diluted its reputation for excellence and its power in the chocolate area. Recently Cadbury-Schweppes, having sold off many of its food brands, is trying to retrieve the position.

On the other hand brand extension (of both 'product brands' and 'house brands') has proved in many cases to be a remarkably successful strategy. It has reduced the risk and cost of new product launches, increased the exposure of brands, made brands more attractive and contemporary to consumers and, in many instances, has extended the brand's life. It is apparent, therefore, that brand extension is entirely practical but needs to be treated with considerable care and skill.

EVALUATING BRANDS

Brands are increasingly being viewed as rare and valuable assets and brand owners are working as never before at ways of improving the management of their brands and exploiting their value. Brand evaluation and audit techniques are increasingly being used in a number of very specific areas:

1 *In mergers and acquisitions,* particularly to identify and evaluate opportunities but also in disposals.
2 *In brand licensing,* both internally for tax reasons and to third parties.
3 *In fund raising.* Brands are increasingly being used as collateral on loans as they are freely transferable assets with clear title confirmed by trademark registration certificates. Brands are also starting to be the subject of sale and leaseback arrangements.
4 *For brand management purposes.* Brand evaluation techniques must necessarily be extremely methodical, highly analytical and very thorough. Such techniques analyse each brand's strengths and weaknesses and have proved to be management tools of considerable importance and value, particularly in the areas of resource allocation, brand strategy development and performance tracking.
5 *On balance sheets.* In recent years companies in certain countries have included acquired brands on their balance sheets as intangible assets; a few have even included both acquired and 'home grown' brands on the balance sheet.

Brand evaluation is a relatively new activity and one which has caused a great deal of controversy in

accountancy circles particularly when applied to company balance sheets. At Interbrand, brand evaluation systems have been carefully developed to give an accurate indication of a brand's strength. In this book we have taken the brand evaluation techniques developed by Interbrand (and which we have already applied to over 1000 leading brands both national and international in Britain, France, Benelux, Switzerland, Scandinavia, USA, Canada, Australia, New Zealand, Hong Kong and Japan) and applied them to our initial working list of the world's leading brands in order to obtain a measure of brand strength. The key factors we evaluate in determining brand strength are:

1 *Leadership.* A brand which leads its market sector is a more stable and powerful property than a brand lower down the order.
2 *Stability.* Long-established brands which command consumer loyalty and have become an integral part of the fabric of their markets are particularly powerful and valuable.
3 *Market.* Brands in markets such as food and drinks are intrinsically more stable than brands in, for example, high-tech or clothing areas as these latter markets are more vulnerable to technological or fashion changes.
4 *Internationality.* Brands which are international are inherently more valuable than national or regional brands.
5 *Trend.* The overall long-term trend of the brand is an important measure of its ability to remain contemporary and relevant to consumers and hence of its power and value.
6 *Support.* Those brands which have received consistent investment and focused support must be regarded as stronger than those which have not. While the amount spent in supporting a brand is important the quality of this support is equally significant.

7 *Protection.* A registered trademark is a statutory monopoly in a name, device or in a combination of these two. Other protection may exist in common law, at least in certain countries. The strength and breadth of the brand's protection is critical.

Our evaluation of brand strength based on these key factors goes far deeper therefore than merely measuring awareness, esteem or spontaneous recall, though such data is taken into account when judging brand strength. It will also be noted that a number of these key factors inter-relate. We have, however, found that taken together they provide an extremely useful framework within which to measure and compare brands and brand strengths.

When conducting a brand valuation exercise we normally use the brand strength score to derive a multiple to apply to brand earnings in order to calculate a valuation — the stronger the brand the more confidence one can have in future earnings streams and the greater multiple one can apply therefore to brand earnings.

All the brands featured in this book are strong brands. We have, however, scored each one on key attributes — leadership, stability, market, internationality, trend, support and legal protection — and we have also computed an overall score for each brand. This process allows us to identify the key aspects of brand strength, the main features of which have been summarised as follows:

- ● exceptionally strong
- ○ strong
- ▢ very strong
- △ problem area

We have also used this scoring system to identify the Top Ten and Top Fifty brands in the World and these are identified in the text as follows:

☆ ☆ indicates a Top Ten brand

☆ indicates a Top Fifty brand

As will be appreciated, the differences between, in particular, the major international brands are very fine indeed as they all cluster close together at the top of the world rankings — we are concerned with only a very few exceptional brands out of the thousands, perhaps even millions, which exist worldwide. Also, such major brands tend, by definition, to have few obvious flaws or problem areas though, clearly, brands such as those in the tobacco sector face particular problems due to changing attitudes to smoking.

The chart showing our Top Ten and Top Fifty brands can be found on the following page.

CONCLUSIONS

Branding has clearly come a long way since it was first used as a means of stamping an indication of origin on a product so that it could be better recognised by consumers. The central role which brands have played in mergers and acquisitions and the arrival of brand evaluation and audit techniques all show that branding has truly come of age.

In the post-war years, in particular, the explosion in the range and diversity of branded products available to the consumer has been enormous. Whereas forty years ago a British or American housewife might have performed all her domestic cleaning chores with only three or four branded products, now she may have twenty or thirty specialist products for floors, baths, windows, stubborn stains, tiles, fabrics, toilet bowls, even chandeliers. Brands provide consumers with a means of shopping with confidence, even when faced with bewildering choice. They also provide the brand owner with massive benefits. It seems clear that the phenomenon of branding will survive and continue to grow steadily in importance.

THE WORLD'S TOP BRANDS

BASED UPON OUR EVALUATION, THE WORLD'S TOP TEN BRANDS ARE, IN RANK ORDER:

1	COCA-COLA	6	IBM
2	KELLOGG'S	7	AMERICAN EXPRESS
3	McDONALD'S	8	SONY
4	KODAK	9	MERCEDES-BENZ
5	MARLBORO	10	NESCAFÉ

The following forty brands, arranged in alphabetical order,
constitute those which should be added to the top ten brands listed above
to arrive at the world's top fifty brands:

APPLE	ESTÉE LAUDER	PERRIER
BACARDI	GILLETTE	PORSCHE
BLACK & DECKER	GREEN GIANT	QUAKER
BMW	GUINNESS	ROLEX
BOEING	HEINEKEN	ROLLS-ROYCE
CAMPBELL'S	HEINZ	SCHWEPPES
CHANEL NO. 5	HERTZ	SMIRNOFF
COLGATE	JOHNSON & JOHNSON	TAMPAX
DEL MONTE	LEVI'S	TOYOTA
DER SPIEGEL	LOTUS (software)	VISA
DOM PÉRIGNON	MARKS & SPENCER	WALT DISNEY
DUNHILL	MARS	WRIGLEY'S
DURACELL	PAMPERS	
ESSO/EXXON	PEPSI-COLA	

It will be seen that the first seven of the top ten brands are all American, a tribute both to the boldness of the American companies in tackling world markets as well as to the size and importance of the domestic US market.

There can be little doubt that a strong base in the US has provided many US companies with an unequalled springboard for expansion throughout the rest of the world's markets.

American-owned brands also dominate the next forty brands but a number of European and Japanese brands, for example Chanel No. 5, Heineken and Toyota, are starting to appear on the list.

It is also interesting to note that even though packaged goods brands still predominate, financial services, computer products, software, retailing and movies all have at least one representative on the list.

McDonald's, Black & Decker, American Express, Dunhill, Kodak, BMW

INTERNATIONAL SECTION

DRINKS AND CIGARETTES

OF THE WORLD'S TOP fifty brands ten fall into the drinks and cigarettes category. Perhaps, however, this is not surprising in view of the size and stability of world markets in these sectors, the ability of manufacturers to reach such markets with large, free-standing brands which are not subject to fragmentation or rapid change, and the huge and sustained advertising and promotional expenditure put behind major drinks and cigarettes brands.

The drinks and cigarettes category therefore contains a wealth of powerful brands, both national and international. In recent years, however, there has been a rapidly growing 'globalisation' of branding in these sectors — Marlboro has taken on local brands around the world and has, generally, won; the world spirits market has become increasingly concentrated into the hands of a few key players and a few major brands; and major soft drinks brands such as Coca-Cola, Pepsi and Schweppes have continued their inexorable progress, often at the expense of local competitors.

Observers expect this process to continue — even though 'niche', closely targeted brands, including local brands will continue to flourish and new brands will come on the scene constantly to add interest and variety, it is believed that an increasing proportion of world markets will fall to major world brands controlled by strong, multinational corporations.

Is this a cause for concern? We think not. Governments are highly sensitive to the possibility of abuse by strong entrenched interests (the EEC, for example, keeps an eagle eye on the licensing of beer brands in Europe, the British Government's Monopolies and Mergers Commission has investigated the tied bottler and distribution system for soft drinks and virtually all Governments, even the Japanese, have intervened to restrict cigarette marketing activities) and the owners of strong world brands cannot use them to stifle competition or restrict access to markets for others. Rather, the powerful brands flourish, and will continue to flourish, by offering consumers the satisfactions they require and if they fail to satisfy consumer needs new, better adapted brands will take their place.

DRINKS AND CIGARETTES

BRAND	LEADERSHIP	STABILITY	MARKET	INTERNATIONALITY	TREND	SUPPORT	PROTECTION	TOTAL
BACARDI★	○	●	□	□	□	□	●	□
BAILEY'S IRISH CREAM	□	○	●	○	●	□	□	□
BALLANTINE'S	○	●	□	●	□	□	●	□
BECK'S	□	□	●	□	●	□	●	□
BEEFEATER	○	□	□	□	□	○	●	□
CAMEL		●	○	□	△	●	●	○
COCA-COLA/ COKE★★	●	●	□	●	□	●	●	●
DOM PÉRIGNON★	□	●	●	□	□	○	●	□
FOSTER'S	□	○	●	○	□	●	●	□
GLENFIDDICH	□	□	□	○	●	□	●	□
GUINNESS★	□	●	○	●	□	□	●	□
HEINEKEN★	□	●	●	●	□	●	●	●
JOHNNIE WALKER	□	●	□	□	□	□	●	□
MARLBORO★★	□	●	○	●	△	●	●	●
PEPSI-COLA★	□	●	□	●	□	●	●	●
PERRIER★	○	△	□	□	□	●	●	□
SCHWEPPES★	○	□	□	□	□	□	●	□
SMIRNOFF★	●	●	●	●	□	□	●	●

KEY ★★ Top Ten brand ★ Top Fifty brand ● exceptionally strong □ very strong ○ strong △ problem area

HEINEKEN

At the core of every great brand is a great product – branding is not a cynical exercise designed to make an indifferent product acceptable to consumers, it is a process for adding distinctiveness, personality and differentiation to products or services which are appealing in themselves and which offer the consumer quality, value and satisfaction.

Heineken illustrates this process well. Freddy Heineken, introducing his company, chooses first to talk of

'one of the strictest quality control programmes I have ever encountered, ensuring that Heineken products meet the same high standard, throughout the world'

The passion for product quality which characterises the Heineken brand, is also carried through into packaging, advertising and distribution. Great care has been taken, for example, to ensure that the distinctive Heineken label is periodically up-dated, but in a way which preserves all the existing brand equity and hence does not undermine brand loyalties. Heineken, the leading beer of Holland, is now one of the world's great beer brands and seems certain to remain so.

Many of the world's great beer brands are not so much international brands as local brands with a specialist cult following elsewhere. Heineken is an exception – it dominates the Dutch market but is equally at home in the US, UK, Indonesia or the Caribbean.

BALLANTINE'S

Ballantine's Scotch Whisky dates back to 1809. George Ballantine started selling whiskies through his small Edinburgh grocery emporium and successive generations of the family continued to blend and sell Scotch under their own name.

The brand's acquisition by the Canadian firm Hiram Walker in 1937 and, more recently, its inclusion in the Allied Lyons portfolio (alongside such brands as Teachers and Canadian Club) has enabled Ballantine's Finest to become one of the largest international whiskies, second only to Johnnie Walker Red Label in sales. This is despite it being virtually unavailable in the UK.

Ballantine's has a unique solution to the guarding of its bonded warehouses in

Dumbarton, Scotland. The 'Scotch Watch' is a hundred strong flock of white Chinese geese – inspired by the Ancient Romans – who patrol day and night ready to sound the alarm at the sight of an intruder.

A fine, traditional Scotch with particular strengths in export markets.

SMIRNOFF ☆ ●

The Smirnoff family's company was appointed Purveyor of Vodka to the Czar in 1886 but after the Revolution only one member of the family, Vladimir, escaped. He established a small distillery in Paris and in 1934 sold the US rights in the brand to his friend Rudolph Kunett. Kunett, after a hard struggle to establish the brand in the US market eventually sold out in 1939 to GF Heublein for $14,000 plus royalties. Compare that with the balance sheet valuation of £588 million which Grand Metropolitan put on the brand in 1988, having recently acquired Heublein Inc!

White spirits such as gin, vodka and white rum have increased greatly in popularity over the last thirty years – they are clean tasting and mix with almost anything – and Smirnoff is

now the world's leading vodka brand. In the US for example, vodka is the top-selling spirit with a 23.3 per cent share of the total distilled spirits market and Smirnoff is the leading US vodka with over 20 per cent of its sector. Factors which contribute to the brand's success include its authenticity and ancestry – consumers are remarkably conservative in their drinking habits; they like their drinks to have heritage and tradition and do not like to think of themselves as pawns being manipulated by faceless marketing people. Smirnoff possesses genuine heritage and reassurance and the balance sheet valuation placed on it by Grand Metropolitan is widely considered to be a conservative one.

Consumers appreciate heritage and ancestry in their drinks brands. Smirnoff is an authentic vodka brand which dominates the world's vodka markets outside the eastern bloc.

BAILEY'S IRISH CREAM

The Irish are great storytellers and nowhere does myth and reality get more joyously intertwined than in Ireland. It is mooted that Irish coffee, that delicious mix of fresh coffee, Irish Whiskey and fresh cream, was invented by a barman at Ireland's Shannon Airport in the 1950s to restore the vigour of passengers arriving after a long, trans-Atlantic flight prior to the introduction of the early jets.

Bailey's Irish Cream is a linear descendant of Irish coffee and draws brilliantly on its imagery and heritage – the labelling is attractive and distinctive, the use of a traditional Celtic-style typography reinforces its Irish origins and the overall brand proposition comes across as quintessentially Irish and entirely credible. It also benefits, of course, from being considered a delicious product with great consumer appeal.

PLEASURE SHARED...

BAILEYS

Establishing new spirits brands in notoriously difficult – marketing history is littered with failed brands. Bailey's Irish Cream is a rare success story and demonstrates that, even in this sector, a fine product combined with skilful marketing leads to success.

JOHNNIE WALKER

Johnnie Walker is the world's leading Scotch whisky brand. Owned by United Distillers (now a part of Guinness plc) the brand has been strongly developed through powerful international distribution.

The brand has three identities. The best known is Johnnie Walker Red Label – the 'standard' scotch. Johnnie Walker Black Label is the premium whisky variant competing with other aged variants and prestige labels such as Chivas Regal. More recently Johnnie Walker has launched Gold Label in Japan to cater for the ever increasing demand of the Japanese for top quality whiskies.

One problem which has resulted from market leadership is counterfeiting. Over the years Johnnie Walker has been plagued by scores of counterfeit products from countries as far afield as Bulgaria and Venezuela. These range from the out and out fake (often a

locally produced spirit with added colouring) to products which use the distinctive square bottle, the diagonal label and other brand 'cues' but which bear another brand name – Marshal from Thailand and Johnnie Hawker from Indonesia are examples – presumably because the producers believe, wrongly, that as long as they do not directly copy the name they will be immune from attack.

The world's leading whisky brand comes under frequent attack – and not only from other producers of fine, authentic Scotch whiskies.

Even where the Coca-Cola brand name is transliterated into other scripts the company has been careful to preserve the visual integrity of the brand identity.

 COCA-COLA ☆ ☆ ●

Coca-Cola is the quintessential international brand and displays virtually every characteristic of a classic brand:
● the brand dates from the late 1880s, a period when mass transportation was starting to permit the marketing and distribution of branded products over wide areas. Many other leading brands such as Kodak, Heinz, Quaker, Waterman, Sunlight and Sears Roebuck can also trace their history back to the same period of rapid commercial expansion and many developed countries, among them France, the UK and the USA, first set up formal trade mark registration systems around the same time.
● the basic brand proposition – 'Coca-Cola satisfies . . . Coca-Cola is a delightful, palatable, healthful beverage' – has remained unchanged for over a century. So too has the brand name, invented by Frank M Robinson, the book-keeper of the company's founder, and the basic logo, a distinctive wordmark written in flowing copperplate.
● the company developed a unique franchise system to support the brand – the emotional appeals of the brand to the consumer were

solidly underpinned by real benefits to the trade.
● it was recognised all along by the brand's owner that branding is not mere labelling, it is in fact the creation of a distinctive personaity . . . 'the reason for our success . . . is the atmosphere of friendliness we create . . . customers actually want to identify with the product'.
● the company has sought constantly to reinforce the brand identity through powerful and consistent advertising and promotion and through the careful use of packaging and visual identity, for example, the distinctive contour bottle introduced in 1915, and the Standardisation Booklet of 1931, a forerunner of today's corporate identity manuals.
● the brand has, nonetheless, been developed to suit changing tastes and conditions – as with everything else, the lesson is adapt or die. Thus new forms of packaging have been introduced over the years (e.g. cans and disposable bottles), special versions of the Coca-Cola logo have been produced to suit a wide range of languages and scripts and more recently, a range of different flavour and ingredient variants have been introduced to cater for different tastes and lifestyles – for example Diet Coca-Cola, Caffeine Free Coca-Cola and Cherry Coca-Cola.

Coca-Cola also has one characteristic which is quite unique – it has two brand names, Coca-Cola and Coke, both of which distinguish the same product, both of which are virtually interchangeable and both of which are registered trademarks.

To students of branding Coca-Cola is a textbook case of meticulous brand management and development over more than a century.

Coca-Cola is the world's Number One brand. Now over one hundred years old it has been meticulously managed and developed but in a fashion which maintains brand equities in full. Coca-Cola today is still quite clearly the same brand as that launched in Atlanta in the 1880s.

The last ten years have seen a rapid crystallising out of spirits brands into a small number of important international portfolios – Suntory, Pernod-Ricard, Guinness, Seagram, Brown-Forman etc.
Beefeater is now part of the Allied-Lyons brand portfolio and is one of the world's leading gin brands.

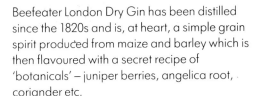

BEEFEATER

Beefeater London Dry Gin has been distilled since the 1820s and is, at heart, a simple grain spirit produced from maize and barley which is then flavoured with a secret recipe of 'botanicals' – juniper berries, angelica root, coriander etc.

On an international basis Beefeater competes mainly with Gordon's though both brands are now part of competing stables of powerful spirit brands including whiskies, vodkas, cognacs and so forth; Beefeater is now owned by Allied-Lyons and Gordon's by Guinness.

Strong labelling, a name which is clearly linked to the brand's London origins and an attractive bottle shape with a satisfying 'hand', are all elements in Beefeater's success.

BACARDI

The Bacardi name and the bat device are used to identify the world's first light, dry rum developed in Cuba well over a century ago. The brand has since survived revolutions, wars, depressions and frequent attacks on the trademark (particularly one in 1960 when the Castro government tried to confiscate it) and is now the world's best known rum and a leading international brand among all liquors.

The Bacardi company attributes its success to a single factor – quality – but this factor, while essential to success, does not tell the whole story. Bacardi has a large number of local and regional marketing organizations to support the efforts of distributors and dealers

The Bacardi brand enjoys such power that the name is sometimes preferred by consumers to the generic term 'white rum'.

and its success can be linked to its marketing muscle, wide distribution, massive production capacity, a quality product, strong packaging, a distinctive name and a worldwide trend towards lighter, mixable drinks.

DOM PÉRIGNON

Dom Pérignon is named after the Benedictine monk who, as cellarer of the Abbey of Hautvillers until his death in 1715, reportedly discovered the delicious, sparkling wine we now know as champagne. It is a high quality, vintage champagne brand produced by Moët & Chandon. It was first sold in 1921 in the United States and is only produced in those years when the grapes are particularly good. Supply is, therefore, strictly limited, a factor which adds to the brand's mystique.

It has been estimated that six times more wealth has been created since the Second World War than was created in the whole of history before it. In a world which is becoming rapidly wealthier but where the availability of this fine luxury product is strictly limited (in the case of Dom Pérignon by the climate and by strict rules as to the exact area from which 'champagne' can be produced) it is almost inevitable that the brand esteem attached to Dom Pérignon will continue to grow, provided, of course, that quality and exclusivity is maintained.

Fine quality exclusive products with limited supply always find a ready market. Dom Pérignon is the premium champagne brand of Moët & Chandon and is produced only in classic vintage years.

PEPSI-COLA ☆ ●

PepsiCo Inc, owners of Pepsi-Cola have annual revenues of more than $15 billion, profits of almost $1 billion and more than 225,000 employees worldwide. PepsiCo's fortunes, like those of Coca-Cola, have been built on a simple concept – a strongly branded kola nut-flavoured, carbonated soft drink sold through an exclusive network of distributors.

It is curious that such a simple, even narrow product proposition should have given rise to two of the world's greatest brands – Coca-Cola and Pepsi-Cola and two of America's – and the world's – highest profile and most successful business corporations. In fact, it seems clear that the intense rivalry which has existed between the two companies for generations has led to both of them being successful on an international basis.

Pepsi-Cola, like Coca-Cola, was born in a drug store in the Southern United States; in Pepsi-Cola's case in New Bern, North Carolina in 1902. Pepsi-Cola used powerful marketing and advertising, alongside a strong franchise system, to drive its business forward. In 1934, it embarked on a period of international expansion.

Pepsi-Cola International is now particularly strong in certain Latin American and Middle Eastern Markets and is also determined to be Number One in Eastern Europe, the Soviet Union and China. Indeed, as early as April 1973, Pepsi-Cola became the first American consumer product ever licensed for manufacture in the USSR and in 1981 it scored another first by forging the first Sino-American joint venture – to manufacture Pepsi-Cola in the Chinese province of Shen Zhen for consumption in Hong Kong.

Pepsi-Cola's owners are intensely aware of its 'brand image'. The company's literature bristles with references to 'brand values', 'brand superiority' and 'brand leveraging' – quite clearly, the central role of the brand is explicitly recognised.

Pepsi-Cola has been highly successful in introducing the brand to large new markets in the Soviet Union and China.

In international terms Foster's is a newcomer — only ten years ago it was little known outside Australia. Now 'The Amber Nectar' has carved out an important international niche position.

FOSTER'S

In the US the by-line for Foster's is 'It's Australian for beer' and in the UK Foster's is promoted as 'The Amber Nectar'. Foster's is Australia's number one selling beer brand with an 18 per cent share of the market, it is the No 2 lager in the UK and the No 6 import in the US.

Foster's is positioned as overtly Australian, a nation which takes pride in being a beer drinking nation and which holds dear notions of 'mateship' and camaraderie. The brand is heavily promoted through mainstream media as well as through world class sponsorship.

Foster's demonstrates how new brands can succeed in relatively stable markets with strong entrenched players, provided the product is of good quality and the brand itself is differentiated and properly supported — only a decade ago Foster's had just 5 per cent of the Australian market and was little known outside that country; now it is brewed in five countries, sold in eighty-five and is regarded as one of the major international players in the world beer market.

Counterfeiting and product adulteration have been present for millenia. In 1516 the *Reinheitsgebot* was enacted to regulate the quality of all beers brewed in Germany and it still applies today. Beck's is a tribute to Germany's strict brewing regulations.

BECK'S

Beck's beer is brewed only in Bremen, a seaport on Germany's North Sea coast. To many confirmed beer drinkers it is the classic Northern European-type 'lager' beer: a fine quality, tasty product brewed according to Germany's strict traditional brewing regulations; a memorable, incisive brand name; a distinctive label design incorporating the key to the ancient Hanseatic city of Bremen; an attractive flint bottle with a satisfying 'hand'; and a complete absence of hype.

PERRIER ☆ ☐

In early 1990 the Perrier brand suffered the kind of product quality problem which gives brand owners nightmares – independent testing in the United States detected minute traces of benzene, further tests in other countries confirmed the US findings and the company was forced to remove all supplies from the market for a period of several weeks. The cost to the company of withdrawing the product, of lost sales in the interim and of additional advertising and brand support has been estimated at over one billion French Francs (c £100 million). This may prove to be an underestimate as it will take the company much time and expense to regain its market

share (50–60 per cent in certain markets), if in fact it is able to do so.

Even though any appraisal of the Perrier brand is inevitably coloured by the contamination scare, the brand is nonetheless a remarkable success – who would have believed that consumers from New York to Melbourne, would be prepared to pay such a premium price for water? Of course, the brand is far more than merely the product – Perrier is chic and sophisticated, it comes in a highly distinctive and attractive bottle and it makes a strong statement about the user; a mere glass of water could not do this , a proposition which strong advertising supports.

The French *penchant* for mineral water owes its origins to the poor quality of the domestic supply. Now French mineral water is sold worldwide and Perrier, the brand leader in mineral water, is a household name. French tap water is now also of a high quality.

SCHWEPPES ☆ ☐

Jacob Schweppe was a Swiss entrepreneur who emigrated to London in the late Eighteenth Century and quickly set up in business selling pure, bottled waters to wealthy London society. And the market was huge – drinking water was almost all polluted and it was recognised (even if it was not proved until some fifty years later) that much disease originated from the appalling water supply.

Mr Schweppe was blessed with a delightful, onomatopoeic name (would he have prospered had he been named Reifenhauser or Uithoff?) and Schweppes soft drinks are now famous worldwide. Curiously, Schweppes has always found it difficult to compete internationally in the pop drinks sector against such brands as Coca-Cola, Pepsi-Cola and Seven-Up (though in many countries the company acts as distributor or joint venture partner with these brands). Schweppes' heartland is in the mixer drink area and even though the production and distribution of such drinks is identical to that of

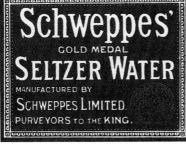

pop drinks, clearly the culture of branding in the two market sectors is quite different – whereas mixer drinks are adult, sophisticated and 'special occasion' and also require a wide range of flavours, pop drinks are younger, informal and more closely focused on a single product formulation.

Schweppes is the world leader in mixer drinks and the Schweppes name conjures up images of sparkling effervescent beverages. Indeed, the brand is sometimes used by consumers as a quasi-generic.

GUINNESS ☆ ☐

Guinness, a heavy, rich beer, is now undergoing a repositioning in its major markets as it searches for younger, more contemporary brand values.

Guinness is a rich, heavy, 'black' stout which was first brewed by Arthur Guinness at his Dublin brewery on the banks of the Liffey in the 1750s. It is now a major world brand which is brewed in Ireland, England (at Park Royal, near London), West Africa, Asia, even in the Bahamas.

It is not however a 'mainstream' beer product. Heavy, dark beers are, except in one or two countries, a minority taste and most of the world's beer market is taken up by light beers of the Heineken, Beck's and Foster's type. Fortunately for Guinness, however, it has

the world's dark beer market pretty much to itself though the brand's owners constantly have the problem of maintaining 'share of voice' and share of market in an extremely competitive, heavily promoted, brand dominated market. Only ten years ago many observers were predicting the demise of Guinness as anything other than an extremely narrowly based niche brand. Skilful marketing of the brand, whereby a gradual repositioning has taken place focusing on more contemporary values, has however, reversed the decline.

MARLBORO ☆ ☆ ●

Marlboro was originally launched in the United States in 1924 by Philip Morris and was positioned as a cigarette for women (it had a red filter tip and the company used the immortal catch phrase 'a cherry tip for your ruby lips'). It was not a major success but in 1955 the brand name reappeared on a man's cigarette complete with the lean, weatherbeaten cowboy and the Marlboro Country imagery.

Marlboro was targeted at Camel and shared an almost identical positioning – the brand for the strong, outdoor, independent man, the person who thinks for himself, lives his own life, does his own thing. The message was however communicated in a more up-to-date way and the packaging and advertising were also 'snappier' and more modern than Camel. These factors, combined with massive promotional support and the fact that Camel never altogether lost its association with old-fashioned untipped cigarettes, resulted in massive success and by the 1970s Marlboro had overtaken Camel as the No 1 brand in the US market.

The brand has, however, succeeded too in becoming a massively powerful brand on a world basis – Marlboro is now the world's leading international cigarette brand and with its distinctive red and white pack and cowboy symbolism, is instantly recognised round the world.

Curiously, the cigarette industry tends to be remarkably happy-go-lucky about new brand development. While most industries agonise over their new brands and painstakingly research them, refine them, research them again, test market them . . . and so on, the cigarette industry often takes the view, as one company executive put it, that:

'New product development is a crap shoot . . . or like putting money on a horse. You study form and try to do the right thing but most often you get it wrong, so you shouldn't get upset when you lose, and you should do it enough times to get the occasional winner'.

This philosophical attitude is, no doubt, brought about in part by the fact that tobacco companies are remarkably prosperous and devote some of the funds they would normally spend, were it possible to do so, on TV and other advertising, on new brand development. Under such circumstances, and provided one has the occasional success, who cares about a few failures? Particularly, of course, when the success can be a massively powerful brand such as Marlboro.

The pervasive image of the Marlboro cowboy makes Marlboro one of the most powerful brands in the world. As opportunities for promoting cigarette brands are increasingly restricted the established awareness of the brand will become an increasingly valuable property.

GLENFIDDICH

Glenfiddich is by far the largest selling malt whisky in the world. Owned by Grant & Sons, Glenfiddich can fairly be said since the 1960s to have virtually singlehandedly developed the public's awareness of malt whisky. The brand is now positioned somewhat differently from other malt whiskies – its marketing support and, in particular, its smart triangular shaped bottle place it firmly in the premium scotch whisky category rather than in the specialist malt whisky category *per se*.

As the premium and malt sectors are the fastest growing parts of the whisky market, Glenfiddich will continue to thrive although the brand is facing increasing competition from a number of well positioned and carefully supported specialist brands, particularly Glenmorangie.

In the 1960s and 70s, Scotch whiskies came under strong pressure from light, versatile spirits, especially vodka and white rum. Glenfiddich, in particular, led the fight back and is now the world's leading malt whisky.

CAMEL

Cigarette brands pose their owners a profound brand differentiation problem – they often look alike, taste alike and are priced alike so the intangible elements of brand personality and positioning are critical to success. Moreover, cigarette brands are quite visible in use – brands of fragrances or even of clothing are used in a discreet, even unobtrusive fashion, yet cigarette brands are often displayed visibly by users and provide not just subtle reassurance to their users but clear signals to onlookers about the user's values and tastes. Indeed, it could be argued that the very act of smoking now provides information to third-parties about the smoker – smoking is by no means an activity which is devoid of any emotional charge!

The Camel brand was launched by RJ Reynolds in 1913 and was consistently associated with a particular type of user – the square-jawed 'regular guy' sports hero. This positioning proved remarkably robust and Camel held the No 1 spot in the US cigarette market from shortly after the time it was launched through until the 1970s when the rugged weatherbeaten Marlboro brand and imagery took over.

The positioning and imagery which served Camel so well in the US domestic market also proved appropriate overseas, particularly in Europe. This is due in large part to the dissemination of such imagery by Hollywood but also to the much increased US presence in Europe as a result of the Second World War. The curious structure of the international tobacco business with its proliferation of cross agreements made it difficult, however, for Camel to succeed as a world brand though in parts of Europe, notably Germany, the Camel brand has made a remarkable recent comeback as the result of skilful and successful upgrading of the brand – the elemental values of the brand have been presented in an altogether more contemporary way through the Camel Trophy and Camel Adventure initiatives, national contests which give fresh values to the brand.

Even though advertising and promotional techniques have changed markedly over the years, the image of the 'regular guy' has been a consistent theme in the development of the Camel brand.

How MILD can a Cigarette be?

MAKE THE 30-DAY CAMEL MILDNESS TEST— SEE WHY...

MORE PEOPLE SMOKE CAMELS
than any other cigarette!

CHOICE QUALITY

CAMEL

TURKISH & DOMESTIC BLEND CIGARETTES

MAN'S IDEA OF A MOVIE HERO
And the women agree! 6 feet 4 inches, John Wayne has smashed his way to fame in dozens of knock-down-and-drag-out — hard-riding . . . glorious motion pictures!

"The roles I play in movies are far from easy on my voice— I can't risk throat irritation. So I smoke Camels — they're mild"

John Wayne

POPULAR, HANDSOME HOLLYWOOD STAR

"I've been around movie sets long enough to know how important cigarette mildness is to an actor. So when it came to deciding what cigarette was just right for my throat — I was very particular. I made a *sensible* test—my own 30-Day Camel Mildness Test!

"I gave Camels a real tryout for 30 days. The most pleasure I ever had from smoking. My own 'T-Zone' told me just how mild and good tasting a cigarette can be! I found out for myself why *more people smoke Camels than any other cigarette!*"

R. J. Reynolds Tobacco Company, Winston-Salem, N. C.

Make your own 30-Day Camel MILDNESS Test in your "T-Zone"

(T for Throat, T for Taste)

Not one single case of throat irritation *due to smoking*
CAMELS!

Yes, these were the findings of noted throat specialists after a total of 2,470 weekly examinations of the throats of hundreds of men and women who smoked Camels — and only Camels — for 30 consecutive days.

FOODS

IN CERTAIN SECTORS OF THE FOODS MARKET, for example breakfast cereals, pet foods and confectionery products, it is possible to build large, free-standing brands which are similar in scope and power to successful drink and cigarette brands, but in 'mainstream' food sectors this is seldom possible. In such sectors — soups, chilled and frozen foods, baked goods, canned vegetables, etc. — consumers demand enormous choice and variety and preferences are constantly shifting.

Inevitably, brands in this area tend to become umbrella brands covering dozens, perhaps even hundreds of different products. They are, therefore, quite different from tightly focused brands whose attributes and characteristics are developed and marked out clearly. Instead these brands focus on more generalised attributes of quality, value and reliability, with all the individual products sold under the brand being linked together by a shared brand name and a common brand identity, e.g. the Heinz shield and the Campbell's red and white format give brand coherence to a wide variety of food products.

Managing mainstream food brands is, arguably, a tougher job than managing specialist brands such as Tabasco, Wrigley's or Tic-Tac. These latter have positionings and characteristics which are relatively precise and unequivocal but the umbrella food brands are altogether less precise and, for that reason, need more careful management or otherwise their values and coherence could easily be lost.

FOODS

BRAND	LEADERSHIP	STABILITY	MARKET	INTERNATIONALITY	TREND	SUPPORT	PROTECTION	TOTAL
CAMPBELL'S ★	○	●	□	●	□	□	●	□
DEL MONTE ★	○	□	□	○	□	○	△	□
GREEN GIANT ★	○	●	□	□	□	□	●	□
HEINZ ★	□	●	□	●	□	□	●	□
KELLOGG'S ★★	●	●	●	●	●	●	●	●
LEA & PERRINS	○	□	□	□	□	○	●	□
MARS ★	□	●	●	●	□	□	●	□
NESCAFÉ ★★	□	●	□	●	□	●	●	●
PEDIGREE CHUM		○	□	○	□	□	●	○
QUAKER ★	○	●	□	●	□	○	●	□
SHEBA			□	○	●	□	●	○
TABASCO	○	□	□	□	□		●	
TIC-TAC	○	○	□	○	□	○	●	○
WHISKAS	□	□	□	○	□	□	●	□
WRIGLEY'S ★	□	●	□	●	□	□	●	□

KEY   ★★ Top Ten brand   ★ Top Fifty brand   ● exceptionally strong   □ very strong   ○ strong   △ problem area

NESCAFÉ   ☆ ☆ ●

Nescafé is a textbook example of good brand management extending over half a century and around the world, though with careful local adaptation to suit particular tastes, traditions and cultures.

Nescafé instant coffee made its first appearance in 1938. Nestlé had been working on the project since 1930, having been approached by the Brazilian Government who were anxious to clear a major surplus of coffee.

Nestlé has invested continuously in both product development and in brand support. Into the former category falls such developments as freeze-drying, agglomeration techniques to produce granules, aromatisation processes to enhance the taste of pure coffee and the development of special blends based upon high quality arabica beans and other coffee varieties (e.g.

Colombian). Into the latter category falls packaging innovations as well as substantial investment in advertising and consumer promotions.

What is striking, however, about the brand is the consistency with which it has been managed. Advertising themes have been carefully researched and once decided upon, have been used over an extended period though with appropriate modifications and up-dating. The visual appearance of the brand has also been remarkably constant and the brand has remained firmly within the coffee sector.

All these factors mean that the consumer's faith in product quality, as well as consumer recognition and acceptance, have been maintained and reinforced over time such that a powerful 'bonding' has taken place between the consumer and the brand.

To many consumers Nescafé is instant coffee. The brand pioneered the sector and still dominates it internationally.

DEL MONTE ☆ □

Del Monte was founded in 1916 through the combination of several fruit canneries in California's Central Valley and is now the largest canner of fruits and vegetables in the US with huge businesses too in Europe, the Middle East, South America and the Far East. Del Monte is also a major brand of *fresh* fruit and until 1986 Del Monte also had a substantial beverage business, mainly under the Canada Dry brand. Particularly in the area of canned fruits, Del Monte has an unmatched reputation for quality, a reputation which the company is keen to exploit using the 'Man from Del Monte' advertising theme.

In certain respects, however, the Del Monte brand is not altogether what it seems. Del Monte was part of RJR Nabisco, the company taken over for $25.3 billion in November 1988 by KKR, the leveraged buyout specialists. In order to reduce debt KKR has been busy selling off parts of RJR Nabisco – a portfolio of European brands was, for example, sold to France's BSN for $2.5 billion in June 1989. Del Monte was also sold in 1989 – Britain's Polly Peck bought both Del Monte's fresh fruit operation and the rights to the Del Monte brand in respect of fresh fruit for $875 million. Meanwhile, Japan's Kikkoman, who had marketed Del Monte products in Japan since 1963, bought Del Monte's US processed food business and secured rights to Del Monte in Japan. Certain other parts of Del Monte were sold to the management.

The result is that an apparent single international brand with a worldwide reputation in the area of canned and fresh fruit is now, in fact, a series of separate brands controlled by totally unrelated companies.

The Heinz brand is applied to an enormous range of food products. Consistency in the use of graphics is essential to the maintenance of a coherent brand image.

Ownership of the Del Monte brand is now spread between a number of companies worldwide yet there is universal recognition that the brand represents high quality in juices and in fresh and preserved vegetables and fruits.

HEINZ ☆ ▢

Heinz is passionate about its brands – not just Heinz itself but also Weight Watchers, Star-Kist, and others. Heinz's President has repeatedly stated that 'our brands provide the profit base for our company in the 1990s and beyond'.

The Heinz company's most famous brand is, of course, the Heinz brand itself, an umbrella brand which embraces tomato ketchup, baked beans, soups, relishes, baby food and dozens of other products. Indeed the company's famous catch phrase '57 varieties' is no longer prominently featured as the Heinz range far exceeds 57 varieties.

Producers of food products for human beings often face a particular branding problem – that human beings are fickle, changeable, prone to boredom and thus demand constant variety. Under such circumstances almost all mainstream food brands are umbrella brands rather than single product brands and hence are often stretched quite widely and applied to a large and changing range of products as no producer could afford to brand each new product or variety separately. (By contrast, in such areas as animal foods, confectionery and soft drinks single product 'power branding' is altogether more feasible.)

Owners of such umbrella brands must be particularly careful to maintain the integrity of the brand. They must therefore only apply the brand to products which fit the brand proposition (would Heinz work equally well on breakfast cereals or flour?) and they must preserve the visual integrity of the brand. The Heinz brand does this well – though it is used widely it is always somehow appropriate; the distinctive shield device is also a highly effective linking motif.

It is difficult for even the finest brands to add value to commodity style products such as canned vegetables. Green Giant shows, however, that it can be done.

GREEN GIANT ☆ ▢

Green Giant, a brand of Pillsbury (now part of Grand Metropolitan) is the world's leading canned vegetable brand. It has been consistently and conservatively managed since 1907 and ensures a premium price in a relatively undifferentiated, commodity style market.

The brand has two interesting features:
● it is not the identical mark in each country. In France, for example, the name Green Giant is translated into French (Géant Vert), though the appearance and positioning of the brand is consistent across all markets.
● the brand benefits from having an extremely distinctive, associated device mark, the Jolly Green Giant himself, an image

created by the Leo Burnett advertisement agency. The reasons for this were not, however, primarily marketing reasons. What happened was that the company was unable at first to register the Green Giant trademark as it was held to be geographical – the Minnesota Valley had long been affectionately known as the Valley of the Jolly Green Giant – so a symbol was first registered in order to secure some form of statutory protection though, with evidence of use, the name was later registered in its own right. Thus the company came to possess two separate but related trademarks: one a name and the other a device, a strategy which has led to a particularly distinctive brand personality.

KELLOGG'S

Kellogg's ranks No. 2 among the world's great brands – all the products produced by the company are superb (Kellogg's produces no own label brands and retailers know from experience that their own label cereals products, produced for them by reputable and skilful suppliers, rarely match the taste, quality and consumer acceptance of Kellogg's branded products); they are massively supported (a higher proportion of total sales is ploughed back into advertising in the cereals sector than in virtually any other); and they are meticulously managed (Kellogg's has a very powerful and pervasive corporate culture which is intensely 'brand-centric').

Kellogg's Corn Flakes still leads the Kellogg's brand portfolio as it has done for generations and nothing seems to upset it – the introduction of mueslis, new healthy eating patterns, the growth of 'snacking', even the occasional World War.

MARS

The MARS Bar with its unique combination of milk, glucose, malt from barley and thick, thick chocolate has been a leading force in the confectionery market since its launch in 1932. In a market which was then almost exclusively block chocolate, the MARS Bar revolutionised the world of confectionery. The unique and satisfying ingredients coupled with an innovative and ambitious marketing strategy led to early brand recognition and tremendous growth of sales.

MARS was one of the first brands to use the new medium of television advertising and the successful and impactful advertising line 'A MARS A Day Helps You Work, Rest, and Play' maintained and strengthened the position of the MARS Bar as the most prominent filled bar.

As consumers enter the 1990s demanding an even wider range of high quality products the brand is believed to be increasingly relevant to modern living. It now boasts a

Kellogg's has made the world's breakfast cereals markets its own. Its products are unrivalled and the brand's reputation is exceptionally strong.

variety of portion sizes and new product developments outside the traditional confectionery product range already include MARS Milk and MARS Ice Cream. Consumer sensitive product development of this type is providing the brand with broader appeal and satisfactions across an even wider target market.

The MARS brand is also expanding rapidly in the international market. Sponsorship of major sports events such as the London Marathon, World Cup soccer and the Olympics has given the MARS brand an identity that crosses national and cultural boundaries.

The MARS Bar is one of the world's great bargains – a competitor recently admitted that it could not produce a rival product for even close to the MARS Bar's retail price.

LEA & PERRINS

Lea & Perrins Ltd call their sauce 'the world's most versatile sauce' – 'Americans throw it on their steaks, cowboys add it to their beans, Australians never barbecue without it, Spaniards sprinkle it on potato chips, Malaysians use it on their satay, Belgians beef up their steak tartare with it, Chinese dip their dim sum in it, Caribbeans creole with it and no bloody mary is complete without it'.

The sauce was reputedly first made in Worcester in 1855 for Marcus, Lord Sandys – he had just returned to Britain from India where he had been Governor of Bengal and took along his favourite recipe to his local pharmacists, John Lea and William Perrins, and asked them to make it up! They subsequently obtained Lord Sandys' permission to sell the sauce commercially and by 1859 Messrs Lea & Perrins were exporting their sauce to New York along with their branded surgical trusses.

The worldwide popularity of Lea & Perrins Worcestershire Sauce stems from its versatility and ease of use combined with a long shelf life and good keeping properties. The trend towards more ethnic tastes and creative cookery is resulting, paradoxically, in a traditional one hundred and fifty year old brand becoming even more relevant today than in the past.

Lea and Perrins is a still-thriving part of Britain's legacy from the Indian Raj, though it is now owned by France's BSN.

TABASCO

The Japanese are the largest users of Tabasco pepper sauce, a product first produced in Louisiana's fabled Cajun country in 1868. Tabasco pepper sauce is produced from Capsicum peppers and Avery Island salt which is made into a mash, mixed with vinegar to form a slurry and then matured in oak barrels. It is an essential ingredient in such traditional Southern recipes as gumbo and jambalaya, is at the heart of all bloody marys and is now served around the world as an accompaniment to steaks, chops, eggs and hamburgers.

Tabasco brand products are produced by the McIlhenny Company, controlled by the McIlhenny family, and the brand displays all the singlemindedness and idiosyncracy needed to produce a great brand, be it a champagne, an office consumable or a range of toys. The McIlhenny family are passionate about their brand, devote enormous efforts to quality control and seize every opportunity to market their brand and extend its reputation –

Specialist niche brands are rare and valuable assets. Tabasco's reputation extends back well over a century and is particularly powerful and well established.

Tabasco sauces have been consumed at the North and South Poles, on top of Everest, even in outer space. For well over a century the Tabasco product as well as its packaging and labelling has remained virtually unchanged, evidence of the enduring appeal of fine brands even in a rapidly changing world.

CAMPBELL'S

Not many brands have passed from commerce into art; Bass's Red Triangle is one (in 1882, Manet portrayed two bottles of Bass in his famous work 'Bar at the Folies Bergères'); another is Campbell's soup – Andy Warhol borrowed the pervasive imagery of the Campbell's soup can for his work.

Campbell's is something of a textbook example of a power brand – excellent high quality products; a reassuring, protected brand name; a distinctive, consistently applied red and white livery (borrowed, it is said, from the Cornell football team) and relevant supporting visual imagery including the gold medallion awarded at the 1900 Paris Exposition. These elements, combined with strong and consistent brand management and support and an international production and distribution network make up a powerful brand.

In recent years the profit performance of the Campbell Soup Company has trailed that of other major food companies and management is currently working hard to improve bottom line performance. It recognises that the Campbell's brand is the most potent weapon in achieving this.

Campbell's invented the concept of condensed canned soup at the end of the Nineteenth Century, one of the world's first major convenience foods.

The Tic-Tac mint is a small, tasty confection. But would it have achieved such international success without its unique flip-top container?

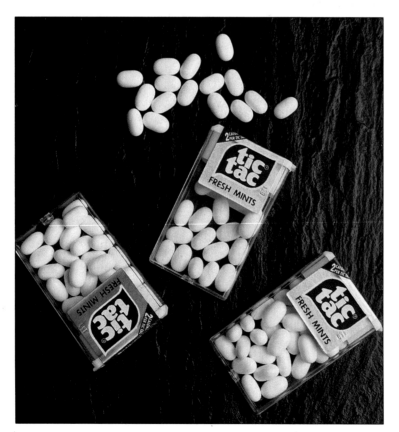

TIC-TAC

Tic-Tac is a brand owned by Ferrero, the major Italian manufacturer of confectionery and chocolate products based near Torino in Northern Italy. Other Ferrero brands include Rocher and Kinder Surprise.

Michele Ferrero, the owner of the company, aims to mass produce products for the whole world. His philosophy is to develop novel, strongly branded, high added value products and to use advanced engineering and packaging technology to place road blocks in the path of potential imitators.

Tic-Tac mints illustrate well how this philosophy is applied. Tic-Tac mints are small, tasty mints sold in a special clear-plastic injection moulded container. On any cost for weight basis the mints are astonishingly expensive yet their palatability, convenience and strong branding has led to their becoming a major international success. Moreover, the Tic-Tac brand, central to which is the special packaging, has muted competitive response because the cost of tooling-up to produce packaging to rival Tic-Tac would be daunting.

QUAKER ☆ ☐

The Quaker Oats Company is now a broadly based food company with annual sales approaching $6 billion, yet its original product, Quaker Oatmeal, is still its flagship brand.

Quaker aims for every one of its brands (and these include Quaker and its many sub-brands; Gatorade sports drinks; Aunt Jemima pancakes, syrups etc; Celeste pizza products; Rice-A-Roni and Noodle-Roni; Ken-L Ration and Fido pet foods; Cap 'N Crunch cereals; and scores of others), to be first or at worst second in its category and reckons currently that this is the case for brands representing about 77 per cent of its net worldwide sales. The reason for the focus on strong, dominant brands is that brand strength, Quaker believes, correlates closely with high profitability. Quaker calls its brands its 'Value

Portfolio' and sees these as the engines of growth and success. Currently, over 20 per cent of annual sales is spent on brand support (advertising, merchandising etc). This amounts to a whopping $1.3 billion, and no reduction is anticipated.

Quaker Oats sees its brands as central to its continuing success and profitability and the company is widely viewed as a nursery of the best new brand management practices.

WRIGLEY'S ☆ ☐

Wrigley's is a remarkably focused company whose housemark has become synonymous with chewing gum worldwide. The Wrigley's Spearmint, Doublemint and Juicy Fruit brand names, as well as others, are also well-known internationally.

The company has prospered as a result of its tight focus on a specific and resilient product area, strong promotion and ready availability at point of sale. Indeed, the company reckons that

probably no other product is available to the consumer in so many locations as chewing gum . . . its popularity makes it a desirable item for the retailer, its modest price means almost everybody can afford to buy it and, with only a small investment, the retailer can keep a good stock of brands on hand.

Few companies dominate their sectors as comprehensively as Wrigley's does in chewing gum.

WHISKAS

Make a list in any developed country of the top ten grocery brands and it is most likely that a cat-food brand and a dog-food brand will both appear on the list along with, in all probability, Persil, Coca-Cola and Nescafé. It is also likely that the cat food brand will be WHISKAS from the petfood division of Mars.

The size and importance of brands in the petfood sector is partly explained by the relative homogeneity of the market – animals know what they like and, unlike human beings, do not constantly seek new formulations, ethnic foods, convenience foods, etc. It is also explained in part by Mars' singlemindedness in developing the market. But fundamental changes in attitudes to pets have taken place, too, all over the world. In Germany, for example, only 33 per cent of German households in 1965 regarded cats as members of the family; now the figure is 60 per cent. In France the proportion of domestic pets fed on scraps has fallen from 37 per cent in 1975 to 12 per cent now. This change in attitudes towards animals has brought with it more concern for animals and animal nutrition.

WHISKAS cat food was launched in 1959 and now holds the position as the best selling pet food brand in the world.

In the UK, for example, the brand outsells its nearest competitor by 3 to 1 and the advertising slogan '8 out of 10 owners who expressed a preference said their cats preferred it', has undoubtedly become one of the most widely known advertising lines of all time.

The extensive WHISKAS range of different varieties and sizes has been key to the brand's success. There are now thirty different items in the WHISKAS range catering for everything from food specially made for kittens, through regular meals in three pack sizes, to Select Menus – a range of specially selected meals in plastic pots.

What makes him sit up?

Best Quality Ever...

Whiskas

A programme of on-going communication with the consumer through TV, press and media campaigns, extensive feeding tests and housewife research have kept the brand up-to-date and also encouraged the development of strong loyalty.

The on-going programme of development and improvement of WHISKAS, including a move into the area of pet care products and accessories, also ensures that interest levels remain high.

The major point of difference of WHISKAS is its high quality and its appeal to cats – a point which is entirely credible to cat owners as they see evidence for it every day.

SHEBA

The SHEBA brand of cat food is, by branding standards, a mere babe – it was first launched nationally in Germany in 1985 after a successful test market and has since been extended across Europe.

The SHEBA brand is owned by Mars and through it Mars demonstrate yet again their formidable skills in the branding area. SHEBA is a premium priced product of very high quality which cats find quite delicious and eat with obvious enjoyment. The brand is positioned in an intimate and caring way and competes mainly with fresh, home prepared cat food rather than with other brands of prepared cat food.

In 1989, the distinctive SHEBA packaging was improved and updated and the variety range was extended – most European markets now have ten to twelve varieties of SHEBA catfood. Mars' competitors have also responded to the enormous success of SHEBA by launching their own super-premium brands, though SHEBA has successfully resisted all such onslaughts.

The emotional bond between the cat owner and their cat is a powerful one. SHEBA fully recognises this and is developing rapidly into a powerful world brand.

PEDIGREE CHUM

Credible, endorsed advertising – for example 'Top breeders recommend it' – has helped establish the brand as a world leader in dog food.

Pedigree Petfoods, part of Mars, manufacture the best selling canned dog food in the world; known as PEDIGREE CHUM in the UK, the brand sells across the world under the PEDIGREE brand name.

In the UK, a typical market, PEDIGREE CHUM was launched in 1960, and 1964 saw the introduction of the now famous endorsed advertising campaigns: 'Top-breeders recommend it'. This expert endorsement for the product has reassured consumers as to quality and consistency and has affirmed their belief that it is the best food available for their dog.

PEDIGREE CHUM was the first canned dog-food brand to introduce the concept of 'varieties' – launching Chicken, Liver, and Rabbit & Heart in 1973 in addition to the popular Original variety.

A further major development was the launch of PEDIGREE CHUM Puppy Food in 1978 – the first canned dog food developed to cater for the specific nutritional requirements of a puppy. It also acts as an important introduction to the brand at the earliest stage for dog and owner.

On-going product development, launches of new varieties and range extensions including a move into dog snacks, treats and pet care accessories are all crucial in ensuring this established brand moves with the times and stays at No 1 in this competitive market.

PERSONAL CARE AND PHARMACEUTICALS

TOILETRIES AND PERSONAL CARE PRODUCTS (with the notable exception of prescription pharmaceuticals) share with drinks and cigarettes the very heartland of the branded goods sector. Within marketing and advertising circles the term *fmcg* (fast moving consumer goods) is applied to these sectors and many of the basic principles of branding have been derived from experience gained in these sectors. Companies such as Unilever, Procter & Gamble and Colgate-Palmolive, renowned for their marketing skills, are active in health and personal care areas and have proved adept at transferring *fmcg* skills from here into other areas.

Within many companies (but not, it must be said, in 'heavyweight' branded goods businesses such as Unilever and Procter & Gamble) the brand management function has traditionally been a training ground for high flyers whose main task has been that of maintaining a link between the company and its advertising and sales promotion agencies. The increased focus on, and interest in, brands seems certain to lead to a fundamental reappraisal of the role and status of brand management. Brand managers will be required to take a much more entrepreneurial view of their brands and will be held accountable for their profitability and for a proper return on brand assets,

tangible and intangible. Several major companies are already redefining the marketing function and overhauling the brand management system. Recently, one major brand owner, when appointing a new director to the board, showed recognition of this by changing the title from Director of Marketing to Director of Brands.

The redefinition of the role of brand management and the elevation of brand management's status result in a need for new disciplines and new tools to allow better brand management to take place. Foremost among these is brand accounting, a practice which is currently followed by only a handful of companies. As well as brand accounting, much better and more systematic brand planning will be required together with the formal tracking of all aspects of brand performance and not just market share.

But success in the highly competitive markets for health and personal care products already depends on such skills. Competition is fierce and every single percentage share point is hard won. It is a tribute to brands such as Gillette, Nivea, Kleenex and Colgate that in such a competitive environment they have led their sectors for generations. It is a demonstration, too, of the robustness of brand assets.

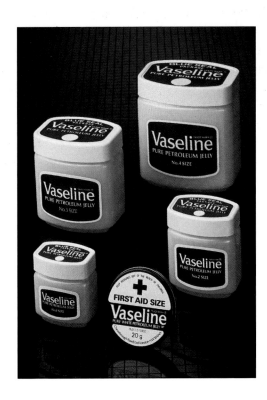

PERSONAL CARE & PHARMACEUTICALS

BRAND	LEADERSHIP	STABILITY	MARKET	INTERNATIONALITY	TREND	SUPPORT	PROTECTION	TOTAL
ALKA-SELTZER	□	●	●	□	□	●	●	□
BAND-AID	□	●	□	○	□	□	□	□
COLGATE ★	□	●	□	●	□	□	●	□
GILLETTE ★	□	□	□	●	□	□	●	□
JOHNSON & JOHNSON ★	□	●	□	●	○	●	●	□
KLEENEX	□	●	●	●	○	□	●	□
LUX	○	□	□	□	○	□	●	□
NIVEA	□	○	□	□	○	□	□	□
PAMPERS ★	●	●	●	●	○	□	●	□
TAMPAX ★	●	●	●	●	○	□	●	□
TIMOTEI	○	○	□	□	□	□	●	○
VASELINE	○	●	□	□	○	□	□	□
VIDAL SASSOON	○	□	□	□	□	○	●	○
ZANTAC	□	△	●	□	□	□	●	○

KEY ★★ Top Ten brand ★ Top Fifty brand ● exceptionally strong □ very strong ○ strong △ problem area

VASELINE □

Vaseline refined petroleum jelly dates from 1858 when Robert Chesebrough, a Pennsylvania chemist, first noticed oil workers treating cuts and burns with a residue from the oil pumps. It is now distributed worldwide and is perceived both as a medicinal product and as a product for the care of dry skin. It is viewed by consumers as utterly dependable and honest. More recently, the 'equity' in the Vaseline name has been used on line extension products. In 1970, for example, Vaseline Intensive Care Lotion was launched as an effective, caring, dependable moisturising lotion and in 1989 Vaseline Dermacare Ultra-Therapeutic Lotion and Vaseline Intensive Care Hand and Nail Formula Lotion both came to the market.

The Vaseline brand has shown that even when there is a close association with one particular product, opportunities exist to extend a well established brand.

Twenty years ago the Vaseline brand was starting to look a little tired and out-of-date. Since then, new introductions have transformed the brand's fortunes and appeals.

Lux

It would, today, be impossible to secure worldwide trademark rights to a three letter word such as Lux – with twenty-five million trademarks worldwide registers are simply too crowded now for such a name to have any chance of success.

LUX

Lux soap has been advertised by some of the most beautiful women in the world, including Sophia Loren, Raquel Welch, Ursula Andress, Marilyn Monroe and Elizabeth Taylor.

The brand was first launched in 1928 and its owners, Lever Brothers, claim it is the biggest selling soap of all time. Now, more than four million bars are sold worldwide every day.

Lux, like its major US rival Ivory, was launched as a luxurious toilet soap for women at a time when everyday household soaps were coarse, astringent and came in large, unwieldy bars – until the launch of brands such as Lux only the wealthy could afford speciality toilet soaps. The brand has, ever since its launch, been strongly supported by focused advertising – currently TV and other appropriate media.

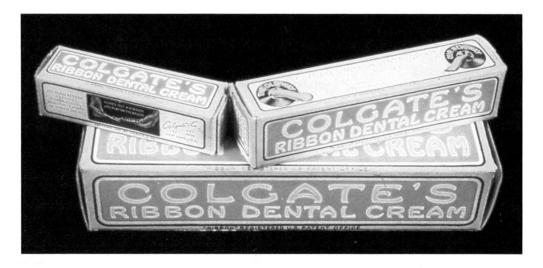

COLGATE ☆

In the toiletries and personal care markets powerful, long-established international brands such as Colgate predominate.

One of the problems which has been exercising the minds of accountants in recent years has been how to account for intangible assets such as brands, patents and copyrights. After all, tangible assets such as machinery, stock and investments appear on balance sheets, but intangible assets such as brands, which are often far more valuable, usually do not. And if brands are put on balance sheets, should you treat them like most tangible assets and amortise them?

Colgate belies the fallacy in the amortisation argument. The company was founded in 1806 by William Colgate as a starch, soap and candle business and, as early as 1873, produced aromatic toothpaste in jars. In 1896 Colgate Dental Cream was packaged in collapsible tubes similar to those in use today. Clearly, if the value of the Colgate brand were for any reason to appear on the company's balance sheet it would be ridiculous to write off the value over, say twenty years, as the brand is now almost 200 years old and healthier and stronger than ever.

 COLGATE-PALMOLIVE COMPANY

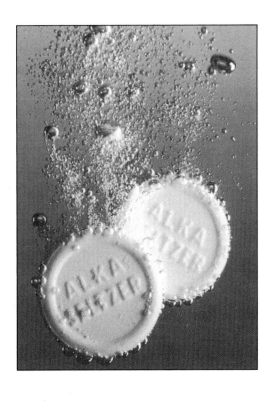

Alka-Seltzer is a curiously memorable and easy-to-pronounce name, even when one is suffering from a hangover.

ALKA-SELTZER

Alka-Seltzer is a trademark of Miles Laboratories, USA, part of the Bayer Group. The product itself is an effervescent tablet of bicarbonate of soda and aspirin used initially for treating colds and 'flu but now positioned mainly as an effervescent stomach upset remedy. It has the highest brand awareness of any product in its field – in Britain, for example, its brand awareness is 96 per cent and it has 35 per cent of an £11 million market. Its unique combination of aspirin (to cure headaches) and bicarbonate of soda (to calm upset stomachs) makes it an excellent cure for hangovers and brand awareness has gained mightily from its widespread use in movies and on television – the clink of an Alka-Seltzer tablet dropping into a glass and the fizz as it dissolves have been used by countless producers to bring home to viewers the misery of a hangover.

GILLETTE ☆

Gillette is almost a textbook example of branding: the company got there first (King Gillette invented his novel razor in 1885, though active marketing did not start until 1903); it used its early lead to gain a powerful position over competitors; it jealously protected its early lead through patent and trademark registrations; it quickly expanded its international base to head off overseas competition (the London branch was opened in 1906); the brand was vigorously promoted; and the brand has been the subject of massive support, continuous development and appropriate line extension ever since.

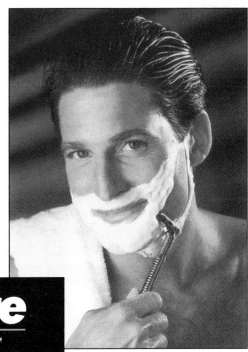

In the 1960s, Wilkinson Sword pulled off a rare coup – it stole a march on Gillette with the launch of its stainless steel blade. But not for long – Gillette's powerful marketing, technical and distribution capabilities and, in particular, its brand strength allowed it to respond quickly and powerfully.

Gillette
The Best a Man Can Get™

NIVEA

The Nivea brand is owned by Britain's Smith and Nephew plc in the UK, Eire, Australia, New Zealand, Canada and South Africa. Elsewhere it is owned by Beiersdorf, a major German toiletries and healthcare company based in Hamburg. Sensibly, there is much co-operation between the two companies, particularly in the area of new product development. (This phenomenon of dual ownership of brands is one which has particularly affected German companies as overseas rights to many famous German brands were expropriated as war reparations after the first and second world wars.)

Nivea, which means snow white in Greek, was originally launched as a soap but for decades has been most closely associated with a pure white creme with its highly distinctive blue and white packaging. Indeed, the core brand values, summed up in such words as 'good value, good quality, practical, trustworthy, pure, mild, gentle', are almost entirely based on Nivea Creme, the most widely known and used product, though in fact the Nivea range now covers sun-care products, lotions, talcum powders, shower gel, bath products, shampoo, conditioner, mousse and a facial skin-care range. The Nivea brand has proved to be particularly well suited to sun-care products where protection and gentle care are highly relevant values and the brand is growing by over 40 per cent per annum in this sector.

The distinctive blue and white packaging of Nivea Creme and the brand's qualities of purity, mildness and trustworthiness have served to create a powerful brand property.

PAMPERS ☆ ☐

Procter & Gamble created the disposable nappy (in the US *diaper*) market when it launched Pampers in 1961. At that time disposable products accounted for US retail sales of only $2.5 million; today they are some $3 billion and Procter & Gamble's brands, Luvs and, most importantly, Pampers have a 50 per cent market share.

Disposable nappies are now said to contribute over 20 per cent of Procter & Gamble's worldwide profits and the company claims that in virtually all markets in which it operates the Pampers brand outsells its nearest rival by at least 2:1, a tribute to product quality, constant investment in product development and product features, strong promotional support and skilled brand management.

The world's disposable nappy market has proved to be a massive prize, well worth competing for, and competition has been suitably fierce. Pampers however, has successfully dominated the market.

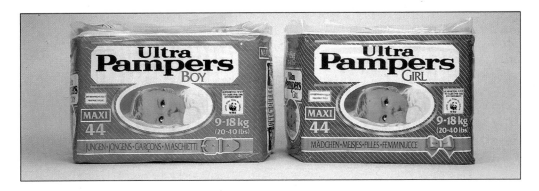

Johnson & Johnson has provided brand reassurance for generations – each new generation grows up with the brand and it fully delivers its promise of quality, reliability and performance.

JOHNSON & JOHNSON ☆ ☐

The most famous products from Johnson & Johnson (not to be confused with SC Johnson of wax fame) are its surgical dressings, first introduced in 1886, and Johnson's baby powder, first introduced in 1893.

No doubt the fact that the sight of the Johnson's baby powder container and the distinctive smell of the product are among the earliest stimuli that many future customers receive serves to create a particularly powerful and enduring bond. The brand owner has, however, been able successfully to extend the brand from dressings and baby products into a range of personal care products – lotions, creams, wipes and so forth – and has also used its branding experience to develop a number of equally powerful consumer brands including J-Cloths, Carefree, Vespre and Empathy.

KLEENEX

Kimberly-Clark's Kleenex brand, launched in 1924, was originally developed as a new outlet for Cellucotton, a cellulose-based cotton substitute which was used in the First World War for surgical dressings, gas-mask filters and sanitary products. It was first positioned as a 'Sanitary Cold Cream Remover' (hence the Kleenex name) and it was not until the early 1930s that its use as a handkerchief was first promoted. This, combined with the special 'Serv-a-Tissue' Pop-Up box with its unique interleaved packaging, introduced in 1929, led to a strong upturn in sales and the brand was established.

From the time the brand was introduced, Kimberly-Clark has worked hard to develop new applications for the brand, but only in recent years has the company needed to rethink the brand's visual identity – from the 1920s through to the 1970s blue and white packaging was used, most recently in the famous quartered design. In the 80s, however, in response to increasing competition, the packaging of the Kleenex brand was drastically changed to co-ordinate with modern bedrooms and bathrooms.

Kleenex was not originally envisaged as a disposable handkerchief brand – its originators saw it as a make-up removal aid. Consumers saw it otherwise to the enduring benefit of its owners.

Arguably, this development may have had an adverse effect on brand impact both at point of sale and in use as the very aim of the new packaging is to co-ordinate, not to stand out. The brand continues, however, as clear leader on a world basis.

Particular care has always been taken by the brand owners to maintain unequivocal proprietary rights in the trademark both through registration and at common law. Even during the civil war in Lebanon, for example, the company moved to enforce its trade mark rights against a local company.

Would Vidal Sassoon, born in London's East End, have prospered if his name had been Joe O'Reilly or Henry Smith? And even if it had, would Procter & Gamble still have purchased the brand name and developed it into an international brand property?

VIDAL SASSOON

Vidal Sassoon started life as a hairdressing salon in London. Vidal Sassoon himself gained a national, then an international reputation in the 1960s and 70s for fine hairstyling; he also proved to have a talent for publicity and became the preferred hairdresser to the stars.

The Vidal Sassoon range of products were originally own label products sold through the company's salons but the brand was subsequently sold to Procter & Gamble to whom the credit must go for developing Vidal Sassoon into a broadly based, international brand with a reputation for excellence in hair care.

TAMPAX ☆ □

Tampax tampons – 'sanitary protection worn internally' – were launched in 1936 at a time when feminine protection was considered such a confidential subject that few magazines would accept tampon advertising. Despite such difficulties, the brand prospered both in the US and abroad. It is now the world's leading brand of tampon and commands in many countries a dominant market share:

Spain	83%
Mexico	72%
Canada	64%
United Kingdom	62%
United States	60%
Belgium	53%
France	52%
New Zealand	43%

The brand has always been managed in a consistent, indeed conservative fashion so that the precise positioning and qualities of the Tampax brand have been perserved over time and not diluted. Most recently Tambrands Inc., owners of the Tampax brand, has disposed of its cosmetics and home diagnostics subsidiaries in order to focus exclusively on its tampons business and recent Tampax line extensions include the first deodorant Tampax tampon and the new compact Tampax tampon.

Tampax is near synonymous with tampons and still dominates the market worldwide despite determined attacks from well-resourced competitors.

Adhesive bandages are an altogether simple idea yet, in a small way, have added significantly to comfort and well-being. Credit for promoting the concept goes to Johnson & Johnson with the Band-Aid brand.

BAND-AID □

Johnson & Johnson's Band-Aid brand of adhesive bandages were invented by Earle E Dickson, a cotton buyer in the company's purchasing department, in 1920. He noted that contemporary surgical dressings were awkward and bulky for use around the home on small burns, cuts and grazes. He invented the adhesive bandage and his idea was taken up enthusiastically by the company's then president, James W Johnson. It is now a brand which is recognized and respected worldwide.

The selection of the name Band-Aid as the name for a charitable appeal to help alleviate famine in Africa has, no doubt, concerned the brand owners. The name is particularly apt for such an appeal (the appeal, run by Bob Geldof, is spearheaded by rock stars) but brand owners are normally concerned if their brand names are used in new areas remote from the brand without their permission or control. Chevrolet, for example, has taken action to stop the use of its name on public bars in Canada and the USA, even when those bars treat the brand in a friendly, nostalgic way.

ZANTAC

Very little true brand-building takes place in the pharmaceuticals industry. Instead, the product development process goes broadly like this: a research team develops a new chemical compound which shows some likelihood of a beneficial therapeutic effect; a patent is immediately applied for so that the drug company's rights are protected (competitors are most likely working on the same or a very similar compound). Patent rights normally do not exceed twenty years, and a dozen or so of these years will be taken up with laboratory testing, animal trials and human trials. Therefore, by the time the new drug is launched (if it is in fact launched: only a very small minority of new drugs will survive the testing and approval procedures) only a few years will be left on the patent. In these few years the company has to recover all its research and development costs, including those of all the unsuccessful drugs it has worked on, and make a profit because unbranded generic drugs will appear on the market the instant the patent expires and destroy the profits of the original drug.

In most countries of the world the largest purchasers of pharmaceuticals are governments through state-supported health and social programmes and most governments, in an attempt to reduce the cost of health care, now pursue a policy of 'generic substitution' – in other words, no matter if the doctor's prescription specifies a branded drug, a chemically identical generic will be substituted by the pharmacist, once patents expire and a generic becomes available. Indeed, governments will normally refuse to pay for anything but the cheapest generic.

In such circumstances drug companies put little effort into brand-building and rely instead upon making enough profit during the short-term patent monopoly to justify the costs and risks of new product development.

A few drug brands, however, are so innovative and so powerful in imagery terms that they gain a stature which, in part at least, transcends the short-term patent monopoly. Zantac is such a drug. Zantac (common name ranitidine) was launched in 1981 by Glaxo as a direct competitor to Tagamet (cimetidine), a breakthrough drug launched by SmithKline in 1976 for the treatment of peptic ulcers. Tagamet proved to be remarkably successful – prior to 1976 the only treatments for peptic ulcers were antacids, a bland diet and in severe cases, bedrest or surgery – but Zantac proved more efficacious even than Tagamet; it also had less interaction with other drugs, less side effects and a simpler dosage form.

Zantac has proven to be an astonishingly successful and profitable drug and one which commands enormous respect from both physicians and patients. The name itself is also powerful, memorable and incisive, as well as being suitable for use and protectable on an international basis.

Zantac is Glaxo's most successful and profitable drug.

Shampoo - Conditioner

TIMOTEI

Unilever, owners of the Timotei brand, reckon it is the best-selling shampoo in the world, outside the US. Annual sales currently run at almost £200 million and the brand claims around 8 per cent of the UK shampoo market, 12 per cent of the Swedish market, 10 per cent of the Japanese market . . . its success has been truly international.

Timotei was first lauched in Finland over fifteen years ago as a deodorant (its name is the Finnish for grass) and it flopped. It was then relaunched as a mild and natural shampoo suitable for daily use; it was a great success and the brand has grown from there.

It has not, however, all been plain sailing: Unilever has had to invest heavily and continuously in advertising and other forms of brand support and has had, too, to up-date and reposition the brand from time to time. The message of mildness and naturalness has however remained the same. Recent range extensions have included a facewash, a moisturiser and an anti-dandruff shampoo. Currently the brand is on test in California though a future US launch is by no means yet certain.

The increasing internationality of branding is demonstrated by Timotei. Developed and launched in Finland, the brand is now marketed widely.

COSMETICS

COSMETICS AND FRAGRANCE BRANDS overlap the fashion sector (indeed, brands such as Yves Saint Laurent and Chanel are both fashion and cosmetics brands) and the personal care sector (Estée Lauder for example produces fragrances, make-up and personal care products). They therefore share many of the characteristics of each sector and so the successful brand owner needs to combine creativity and flair with meticulous and conservative brand management. As these requirements are, to a large extent, diametrically opposed to each other it is no surprise that the successful branding of cosmetics and fragrances is notoriously difficult.

The industry is also enormously fragmented; in the French fragrance market, for example, the brand leader, Opium, has a market share of less than 10 per cent and some twenty brands have a market share in excess of one per cent. Within this fragmented market the performance of individual brands is constantly changing as a result of market shifts, changes in pricing and promotional policies by brand owners, and the appearance of new, aspirant brands, frequently with large launch and promotional budgets.

We have selected for inclusion in this section brands which we believe to be particularly strong and which also illustrate major trends in the market.

BRAND	LEADERSHIP	STABILITY	MARKET	INTERNATIONALITY	TREND	SUPPORT	PROTECTION	TOTAL
AVON	☐	○	☐	☐	☐	☐	●	☐
THE BODY SHOP	☐	☐	●	○	●	☐	○	○
CHARLIE	○	○	☐	☐	☐	△	●	☐
ESTÉE LAUDER ★	☐	○	☐	☐	☐	●	●	☐
OPIUM	☐	△	☐	☐	☐	●	●	☐

KEY ★★ Top Ten brand ★ Top Fifty brand ● exceptionally strong ☐ very strong ○ strong △ problem area

OPIUM
Jamais parfum n'a provoqué une telle émotion.

Parfums
Yves Saint Laurent

Fragrance markets lend themselves to dramatic attention-grabbing brands of which Opium, a huge success in the 1980s, is a prime example.

OPIUM

Brands need to be differentiated, to stand out from the pack, but in a way which is appealing and appropriate. The problem for many brand owners, when developing new brands, is to achieve the required degree of differentiation: market research often pushes in the direction of the 'bland brand' as consumers in research situations often specify that they require in the new brand all those features they know and like in existing brands. The result is that the new brand is often merely a *pastiche* of existing brands. On the other hand, if the new brand developer is too innovative, the new brand may be seen as merely bizarre.

But, as Yves Saint Laurent has shown with its Opium brand, the rewards of bold, innovative branding can be huge. Opium is now the world's leading fragrance. It has a powerful, distinctive scent and a dramatic name – so much so that when it was launched in the mid-1980s consumer groups and legislators tried to get it banned on the grounds that Opium is a narcotic and the name should not be allowed as a fragrance trademark.

Success of the Avon brand is due as much to its unique marketing and distribution system as to its high quality products.

AVON

Avon started life in the 1880s as The California Perfume Company, a business which specialised in inexpensive but good quality perfumes sold through canvassing agents. Its first product was The Little Dot Perfume Set with five different perfumes – heliotrope, violet, white rose, lily of the valley and hyacinth.

By 1928 the name California Perfume Company had become too restrictive for a business trading across the entire United States so the Avon name was introduced and the official corporate title was then changed to Avon Products Inc in 1939. Why Avon? After a visit to England the company's founder, David McConnell felt the land around his Suffern laboratory resembled that near William Shakespeare's birthplace, Stratford-upon-Avon.

The distribution system developed by Avon – the 'Avon Lady' who visits customers in their homes – has proved remarkably successful not just in the US but around the world and the company now claims that more women work with Avon than with any other company. Today, Avon has sales of well over $3 billion and is one of the world's largest and best known brands of fragrances, make-up and personal care products.

THE BODY SHOP.

Though a relative newcomer in international branding terms (The Body Shop began in 1976 in Brighton on Britain's South Coast), The Body Shop is now a major world brand in the cosmetics and personal care business. The Body Shop now retails its products from almost 500 shops in almost forty countries and, almost singlehandedly, has pioneered the concept of 'caring cosmetics'. The Body Shop operates on five basic principles:

- it sells cosmetics without hype and expensive packaging.
- it promotes health rather than glamour, reality rather than false promises.
- it uses natural ingredients whenever possible.
- it does not allow animal testing of its products.
- it respects the environment; for example, it offers a refill service, uses biodegradable materials, etc.

Though it is essentially a retailer, Body Shop manufactures 20 per cent of its own products and the company has also been active in Third World development projects and in community and educational projects.

The Body Shop is a remarkable example of a contemporary and innovative brand which anticipated and even shaped consumer needs and desires.

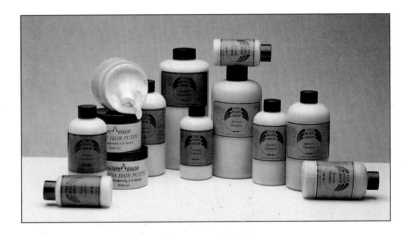

World consumer markets are dynamic and subject to constant change. The Body Shop has been uniquely successful in developing the concept of 'caring cosmetics'.

ESTÉE LAUDER ☆ ☐

Estée Lauder, based in New York, has been described as 'the high temple of up-market cosmetics'. The brand is positioned as exclusive, elegant and uniquely suited for use by confident, beautiful women.

Brand management and promotion has been consistent for decades – the world's most beautiful and elegant models have appeared in the company's advertisements and the brand offers certainty and confidence in a market which is often seen as fickle and unstable.

Recently the company has been criticised as having a '50s' feel and efforts are underway to up-date the brand but in a fashion which does not compromise existing values and loyalties.

Estée Lauder products enjoy an enviable reputation for quality, elegance and sophistication.

CHARLIE

The image of Charlie, the long-striding, confident but warm city girl is now a quarter of a century old but for many people the image is as fresh and memorable today as it was when the fragrance called Charlie was first launched by Revlon.

Branding has been described as 'thinking ahead of the consumer, anticipating and shaping his or her needs' and Charlie illustrates the process well. Consumers would never have conceived of a fragrance called Charlie – indeed the culture of branding when Charlie was first launched was one where most new fragrances carried feminine, elegant, French names and consumers at that time would have specified that any new brand must meet these parameters. Yet Charlie struck a chord with consumers around the world which was attractive and unique. The brand embodied a set of values and attributes which was appropriate, which stimulated consumer interest, which distinguished the brand from others and created a real piece of property for its owners. Charlie is a 'power brand', a uniquely successful blending together of qualities and attributes both tangible and intangible. The brand offers values and attributes which are appealing and which people are prepared to purchase. Furthermore, there is no doubt that Charlie represents for Revlon a valuable asset which has enduring and international appeal.

The positioning of Charlie, reinforced by powerful memorable advertising, struck a unique cord with consumers.

FASHION

ONE DEFINITION OF FASHION IS, according to the Oxford English Dictionary, 'The mode of dress, etiquette, style of speech etc. adopted in society for the time being'. The phrase 'for the time being' is a particularly telling one; it betrays the shifting, constantly changing nature of the fashion industry and hints at the problems involved in establishing powerful, robust, long-lasting brand properties in this sector.

A number of major brands have, however, succeeded in this difficult branding task; they have established a fashion which transcends short term shifts in consumer taste (e.g. Louis Vuitton) or they have shown an ability constantly to transform themselves, albeit within the framework of a coherent, recognisable brand proposition as, for example, Levi's and Hermès have done.

The paradox of branding in the fashion sector is that while branding is exceptionally difficult in this area and requires great skill, sensitivity to changing market conditions and a passion for brand values, the intangible elements of the brand are more important in this sector than in any other. Traditionally, fashion brands have started life as the passion of one single-minded person — the caricature of such a person is the histrionic, demanding French couturier but the same sorts of drives have guided the establishment of brands in all branches of the fashion industry. It is when that original 'brand manager' dies or quits that fashion brands often lose their way. The powerful, enduring brands are those which have established a more generalised, communicable set of values which do not rely solely on an individual.

Adidas, Dunhill and Scholl have quite clearly achieved this. In the case of Laura Ashley observers are still waiting to see whether, under Sir Bernard Ashley, the brand will retain its vigour following Laura Ashley's death.

Those involved in the more 'fashionable' end of the fashion business seem to get completely hooked on the verve and excitement of the industry, the need to sell the brand totally anew with each new collection. They are aware too that the fashion sector, more than any other, is a graveyard of hopes; those brands, therefore, that do survive command particular respect.

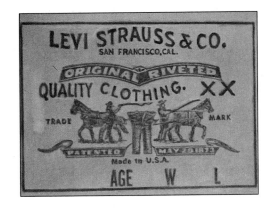

BRAND	LEADERSHIP	STABILITY	MARKET	INTERNATIONALITY	TREND	SUPPORT	PROTECTION	TOTAL
ADIDAS	○	□	□	□	○	□	●	□
AQUASCUTUM		○			○		●	
BATA	○	○	○	○	○		●	○
BENETTON	○	○	○	□	○	□	●	□
DUNHILL★	○	●	□	□	●	●	●	□
GUCCI	○	□	□	□	○	○	□	□
HERMÈS	○	□	□	○	□	○	●	○
LAURA ASHLEY		○	○	○	△		●	
LEVI'S★	○	□	□	□	○	●	●	□
LOUIS VUITTON	○	□	□	□	●	○	□	□
RAY-BAN	○	○	□	○	□	○	●	○
REEBOK	□		□	○	●		●	□
ROLEX★	○	●	□	□	□	○	●	□
SCHOLL	○	○	○	○	○		●	○
SWATCH	□	○	●	□	●	□	●	□
WRANGLER	○	○	□	○	○	□	●	○

KEY ★★ Top Ten brand ★ Top Fifty brand ● exceptionally strong □ very strong ○ strong △ problem area

The streets of the world's cities would now look very different if Levi Strauss had selected a red, green or gold dye for the work trousers he manufactured.

LEVI'S ☆ ☐

Denim (from *serge de Nîmes*, a type of heavy cotton cloth which originated in France) was selected in 1850 by Levi Strauss, a young entrepreneur, as a material from which to make hard wearing work trousers for miners working in the California gold fields. He also selected a special indigo blue dye and, in 1873, added patented copper rivets to the pockets as customers had complained about pockets ripping under the weight of mining tools. Levi's are largely unchanged since then.

The Levi's brand has a number of unique features – it was there first and hence has an unbeatable pedigree; it possesses certain proprietary design features including the copper rivets and the orange double arc design on the back pockets and it has received strong and consistent brand support, especially since the late 1940s when management decided it was in the fashion apparel business, not the work clothing business, and decided to focus its attention on the development of its brand image.

Levi Strauss & Co is now the world's largest apparel manufacturer.

BENETTON

New brands are extremely expensive to develop and launch. Several years of continued spending on the brand is needed before its success or failure can be ascertained. And in any case most brands fail. Clearly, new product development is not for the faint-hearted. Indeed, in recent years some observers have predicted the total demise of all new product development, arguing that it is a mug's game, that far and away enough brands already exist, and that no sane company would consider any form of brand development other than brand extension.

Benetton (along with Apple, Walkman and scores of others) proves such doom-laden predictions wrong. For young people worldwide Benetton provides the style they

require at a price they, or their parents, can afford. With design studios in Italy and franchised retail outlets around the world Benetton has, in less than twenty years, established a powerful brand reputation in a difficult and changing market sector.

Part of Benetton's success can be attributed, it is said, to the fruits of competition with its arch rival, Stefanel.

GRANT OF ARMS
TO AQUASCUTUM LTD

Aquascutum
OF LONDON

AQUASCUTUM

Aquascutum have been 'makers of fine clothes since 1851'. The original business was built upon a process for showerproofing wool coats – indeed, the name Aquascutum comes from the Latin for 'watershield' – and when Britain went to war with Russia in 1855 business boomed as it also did during the First and Second World Wars.

Aquascutum products are now sold in some fifty countries and 70 per cent of the company's turnover (a surprisingly modest £50 million in 1989) is from non-UK sales.

The brand is now positioned as a luxury fashion brand for men and women and products sold under the brand include raincoats and trenchcoats, suits, blazers and accessories, all with a classic, somewhat 'British' look. In Japan, Aquascutum is now one of the most successful imported brands and the continuing Japanese fascination with prestigious Western brands has ensured unbroken volume growth for thirty years.

Even today the Aquascutum brand conveys images of Edwardian England, Gentleman's Relish and Bath Oliver savoury biscuits. The brand is, however, thoroughly modern, as evidenced by its growing export success.

ADIDAS

adidas is the world's largest sporting goods manufacturer. The name is taken from that of its founder, Adi Dassler, who first made sport shoes in Herzogenaurach in Western Germany in 1920 and who founded the present company in 1948. The Three Stripes device was also specifically selected at that time as a simple, recognisable branding device and in 1967 the trefoil device consisting of three leaves with three stripes running across them was developed mainly for use on sportswear.

The adidas brand is now used in virtually every major sport except equestrianism and downhill skiing and is particularly strong in football, tennis, track and field athletics, and winter sports. The company devotes substantial resources to product development and to the sponsorship of leading athletes – in 1987, for example, 60 per cent of the participants in the European Track & Field competition and 53 per cent of the participants in the World Track & Field relied on adidas products.

Continental brand owners often seem to adopt branding rules to achieve distinctiveness which well-intentioned observers inadvertently transgress – adidas with its lower case 'a' is one example.

Does the Marlboro cowboy wear Levi's or Wrangler jeans? Levi's have the heritage but the Wrangler brand name, if not the positioning, seems most closely matched to his lifestyle.

WRANGLER

Wrangler, the world's No 2 jeans company, claims that, in 1947, it gave the world the first ever denim jean that was designed to fit the body rather than hang off it – until then, jeans tended to resemble foreshortened versions of bib overalls, a popular form of work apparel. It is now the major brand of VF Corporation, an enormous clothing conglomerate.

The Wrangler name is recognised worldwide and has powerful, and appropriate, all-American, Wild West associations, though the brand owner tends to have used these associations in a relatively low-key fashion and has not, for example, tried to develop a powerful cowboy theme along the same lines as Marlboro.

BATA

Bata is a leading international footwear company which sells over one million pairs of shoes every day and operates in over 80 countries. In many countries, the Bata name and logo are synonymous with shoes.

The Bata flagship brand stands for good value, good quality footwear for the family market but the company also has a number of supporting international brands for specialist markets such as fashion and sports. Likewise, in retail store development, the traditional Bata family store remains the cornerstone, catering to the large middle market but specialty stores have been added to the network to reach specialist markets. Today, Bata's 6300 retail stores are found in major cities such as Milan, Paris, Buenos Aires and Bangkok and in developing countries like India, Indonesia, Kenya and Peru. Indeed, in many Third World countries Bata is often a key employer, as well as an active participant in community development programmes. In the US Bata has over 600 stores although none of them carries the Bata name.

Thomas Bata founded the company in 1894 in Zlin, Czechoslovakia. His dream was to be

shoemaker to the world and when he died in a plane crash in 1932, his son Thomas J Bata took over. Today, Thomas G, grandson of the founder, carries on the tradition. The company relocated to Canada during the Second World War and the corporate head office has remained there ever since while worldwide manufacturing, retailing and distribution activities have flourished.

Bata, now based in Canada, started life in Czechoslovakia and is particularly strong in developing countries where the company's high quality, well priced products have great appeal.

SCHOLL

Dr William M Scholl, founder of a worldwide business whose products are sold in over 150,000 retail outlets, refused to believe the adage that 'feet just naturally hurt' and that foot ailments were 'a curse without a cure'. Dr Scholl invented hundreds of products to improve foot comfort and preached the message of foot comfort with unmatched zeal and single-mindedness. The current strength of the Scholl brand can be traced to four key factors: a tight brand focus, meticulous brand management and support, constant innovation and a global perspective.

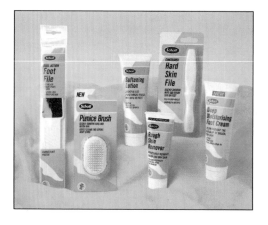

Foot care is not the most glamorous product sector and that perhaps helps explain Scholl's success. But the brand owner's tenacity and marketing skills deserve the lion's share of the credits.

DUNHILL ☆ □

Alfred Dunhill started his business in 1899 supplying products to make the then highly uncomfortable hobby of motoring more bearable. In 1907 as automobiles got more 'user friendly' he switched to selling pipes and smoking tobaccos and prospered so thoroughly that overseas stores were opened in New York in 1923 and Paris in 1924.

By the 1960s and early 1970s the company had become overdependent on the sale of gas lighters and, in 1975, a conscious decision was taken to transform the brand into a broadly based luxury brand for men starting with menswear and leathergoods. Now the Dunhill brand also includes jewellery, watches, writing instruments, fragrances, whisky and eyewear, all distinguished by their luxury and exclusivity.

The Dunhill brand is meticulously managed, though its owners claim that, over the years, it has developed such an unequivocal 'personality' that it almost manages itself –

what is right or wrong for the brand is so clearly determined by the brand's character that brand related decisions almost make themselves.

Less than twenty years ago, Dunhill was a niche brand focused mainly on pipes and gas lighters. Now, it is a major international luxury products brand and its success is a tribute to careful, skilled brand management.

LAURA ASHLEY

Laura Ashley is an exponent of *le style anglais*, a nostalgic, almost rural style of design which the company has translated into a range of female fashions and home furnishings and into a retail concept which now spans the globe.

The first Laura Ashley business was started in London in 1953 printing tablemats and scarves for sale to small shops and department stores. In 1963 production was moved to the unlikely location of rural mid-Wales and the company is now among the top twelve clothes manufacturers in the UK and accounts for 10 per cent of all UK clothes exports to the US. The company also produces dyed and finished fabrics as well as wallpaper and paint and operates more than 400 shops, almost half in North America.

A recent development has been the establishment of a Laura Ashley Brand Management Division responsible for design, promotion, product sourcing and the supply of goods to the retail businesses. The Division is also specifically charged with 'image protection', a measure of the importance which the company attaches to its brand.

Laura Ashley has a very particular positioning which appears well adapted to the environmentally concerned 1990s. Despite this, innovation and image development will, nonetheless, be required in the future.

LOUIS VUITTON

Louis Vuitton was born in 1821 in Moulin d'Anchay in the Jura mountains. In 1837 he walked to Paris to find work. Arriving penniless, his first job was that of a *layetier* (packer) visiting all the great households of Paris to pack the ladies' gowns, underwear and hats into the large travelling trunks used by all for the long *sojourns* around Europe and the world. Wherever the wealthy journeyed, they required great wardrobes of hand-tailored silks, wools, furs, laces, linens and stays which no one, not even a loyal servant, was entrusted to pack but the *layetier*. Louis Vuitton soon acquired a reputation as that of a specialist and in 1853 Napoleon III, Emperor of France appointed him *layetier* to his wife the Empress Eugenie.

In 1854, Louis Vuitton opened his first shop at rue Neuve des Capucines in Paris. With the reputation as the only man who understood packing, he started to combine his skills with trunk-making and invented the flat-topped trunk which easily fitted under the seats of trains and beds of ship's cabins. As each new mode of transport was developed so Louis Vuitton created the perfect item of luggage.

Since 1854, Louis Vuitton have continued to make unique luggage in their traditional ways. Every item is craftsman-made from the finest materials and components: matured poplar, solid brass pick-proof locks and canvas with the distinctive Louis Vuitton logo.

Old Louis Vuitton trunks and suitcases are now collector's items and Louis Vuitton products are highly desirable. So desirable, in fact, that counterfeiting has become a major problem for the brand owner. Indeed, in the mid 1980s it was estimated that 92 per cent of all so-called Louis Vuitton luggage sold was in fact counterfeit, much of it made in Korea. As nearby Japan is Louis Vuitton's major market the problem was serious and the company has gone to great lengths to safeguard its trademark rights and combat counterfeiting.

The distinctive Louis Vuitton logo is found on some of the world's most exclusive luggage, but the company is facing powerful problems from counterfeits.

REEBOK

Until the early 1980s the world sports shoe market was a relatively gentlemanly place, dominated by adidas. Over the last ten years, however, it has become bitterly competitive with constant changes in fashion and technology. In New York, for example, favoured brands, colours and styles change constantly and the *cognoscenti* can tell at a glance what district, even what street, a person comes from by the sports shoes they wear. Even whether or not the laces are tied imparts a wealth of information to the initiated. So, although the average price of a pair of sports shoes has risen substantially over a ten year period so too has the complexity of the market and the risks.

Reebok can trace its origins back to the 1880s when the original Reebok running shoe was made in Lancashire but it is only since 1979, when US rights were sold to Paul Fireman, that the brand has really taken off. In the early 1980s Jane Fonda started to introduce aerobics to the world and Reebok was the preferred shoe. Reebok, along with Nike, swiftly overtook the established brands adidas and Puma due to better styling and low-cost sourcing in the Far East. By 1988 Reebok had US sales of $1.8 billion, Nike of $1.2 billion and six year old LA Gear managed almost $250 million.

The collapse of the aerobics market in the late 1980s damaged Reebok and allowed Nike to make headway but Reebok has since repositioned itself more towards the active sports market and has doubled its research and development budget.

Reebok is a relatively recent phenomenon and its longer term brand direction is not yet clear. Meanwhile, its success in the 1980s has been phenomenal.

GUCCI

Gucci is perhaps the best known Italian brand of quality leather goods, fashionwear and accessories. Founded by Guccio Gucci in Florence in the early 1900s, the brand developed initially as a footwear brand before extending to the wider range seen today.

The Gucci trademark itself is extremely well known and is powerfully supported by a number of device marks – the Gucci shield (incorporating the luggage bearer), the interlocking Gs and the green-red-green stripe device. However, the company is now moving to a simpler visual identity both to add coherence to the brand and to reduce the major problem of counterfeiting – the aim of Gucci in the future is to develop such an unequivocal 'Gucci look' that any counterfeit product will be shown up unerringly for what it is. Therefore, merely applying the Gucci name without authority to a product will be insufficient to lead to success as the distinctive 'Gucci look' will be more difficult to counterfeit.

GUCCI

Well publicised family disputes appear to have done little to harm the power and appeal of the Gucci brand.

SWATCH

By the early 1980s it appeared that the Japanese had destroyed the lower price sector of the Swiss watch industry – the Japanese seemed to have the Swiss beaten in terms of technology, production and marketing. In 1983 Swatch was launched, an inexpensive quartz watch with half the moving parts of other quartz watches and made by entirely new technology. In 1984, 3.6 million Swatch watches were sold and the brand has grown in strength ever since.

The brand's cheeky, snappy name, relative low cost and, in particular, its brash trendy advertising have all contributed to its success as has clever exploitation of the product's colour and design possibilities.

The success of Swatch has largely restored Swiss confidence in the nation's mass-market watchmaking capabilities; the Swiss retain great respect for the Japanese but believe now that they can design products as good as any the Japanese can design and that their production capabilities and efficiencies can also match those of the Japanese.

swatch®✚

The low-cost, cleverly marketed Swatch brand has restored Swiss industry's confidence in its ability to produce high volume timepieces.

A Rolex watch, more than almost any other item of personal jewellery, is a 'must' for many people around the world.

ROLEX ☆

It was not until the early part of this century that it became normal to wear one's watch on one's wrist – until then the fob or pocket watch was the normal type of personal timepiece, worn on a chain to discourage thieves and prevent breakage.

The Rolex Watch Company, originally founded in London by Hans Wilsdorf, produced in 1910 a miniaturised watch to be worn on the wrist. It was embedded in a solid metal case to guard against shock and moisture and in 1914 a Rolex watch was awarded a Class A certificate by Britain's Kew Observatory – it was sufficiently accurate to be used as a marine chronometer.

The famous Oyster waterproof watch was introduced in 1926 but otherwise the appearance, qualities and performance of Rolex watches have remained largely unaltered for three quarters of a century. Rolex is a classic watch and the pleasures of owning such a beautiful piece of engineering appeal as strongly today as ever before, despite the advent of the quartz watch.

HERMÈS

Hermès is based, together with its leather manufacturing shop, on the corner of the Faubourg Saint-Honoré and Rue Boissy d'Anglais in the centre of Paris (a site which is soon to be redeveloped as a Hermès department store). The company is a family-owned luxury goods manufacturer with an international reputation. The business was founded in 1837 by Emile Hermès and more than 90 per cent of the business is still in the hands of his descendants. Sales are currently around £270 million, 37 per cent in France, 15 per cent in the rest of Europe, 14 per cent in the US and 11 per cent in Japan and pre-tax profits are thought to be at least 20 per cent of sales.

Hermès in the last ten years has unashamedly targeted itself at the young 'newly rich' and provides them with leathergoods, footwear, perfume, crystal, watches and of course silk scarves.

Unlike Cardin and Dior, Hermès refuses absolutely to license the brand to third parties; indeed, most of the products which bear the Hermès brand name are made by the company. Nor does the company plaster its initials or logo on all its products; it believes that the design and quality of a Hermès product speaks for itself.

Hermès, a family-controlled business, makes a range of high fashion items all with the distinctive 'Hermès look'.

RAY-BAN

Ray-Ban® sunglasses, developed by Bausch & Lomb for the US military to protect pilots from glare, still have powerful associations with Douglas MacArthur and the Second World War yet they are as much in demand now as they were half a century ago – the slopes above St Moritz are as thick with Ray-Ban sunglasses as once were the skies over Germany and the Pacific.

Ray-Ban sunglasses are discreet – unlike products from Gucci, Louis Vuitton or Yves Saint Laurent they do not sport a distinctive logo or design device. The brand satisfactions of owning a pair of Ray-Ban sunglasses are therefore 'private' satisfactions – a good product with a good 'feel' and the knowledge that in owning and using the brand one is, in a small way, owning and using a classic.

Ray-Ban®

Ray-Ban sunglasses are prized for their style and their performance. First developed for military use, they are now used by style-conscious consumers worldwide.

HOUSEHOLD PRODUCTS

ONE OF THE KEY INGREDIENTS for success in any business is being there first; if you are first into a market, go for it hard and hang on tight you have a good chance of leading your sector. The household products brands featured in this section demonstrate this point well; at least twelve of the featured brands — namely, Black & Decker, Yale, Duracell, Perspex, Formica, Thermos, Tupperware, Singer, Hoover, Tipp-Ex, Scotch and Biro-BiC — virtually invented the sectors in which they operate and which they still lead. And all of the other brands featured have played a leading rôle in forming and shaping the markets in which they operate.

Moreover, even though virtually all these brands enjoyed at the outset powerful patent rights which conferred on them a finite monopoly in the product sectors for which they are now best known, patents now play little part in the brands' success. Rather, brand reputation coupled with production, distribution and marketing skills account for continued sector leadership long after the expiration of the original patents and when the basic product and manufacturing technology is available to all.

Household products featured here cover four main areas: domestic appliances, glass and chinaware, household stationery and kitchenware. By far the most changeable of these sectors is domestic appliances. Technical developments and a constant need to refine and update product design and styling added to a

continuing demand from the housewife for new products to reduce the burden of housework has meant manufacturers have had to apply very effective brand management to their product range. Hoover, a name almost synonymous with the vacuum cleaner, has diversified its product range considerably to include washing machines, tumble dryers, irons and other electrical goods in its range. Electrolux, which has a similarly high profile, is fighting hard to maintain its position in the electrical goods market. With brands such as Moulinex growing in power and aiming to dominate its field, it is clear that no-one can afford to relax.

The battles being fought in the domestic appliances market cannot be related to brands like Waterford and Wedgwood. Maintaining their position in the glass and chinaware sector requires a very different set of brand management skills. These brands owe their success to their long history, a reputation for high quality and their appeal to purchasers in the luxury goods market. Exclusivity, craftsmanship and aesthetic beauty are the hallmarks of these brands.

Compare this to the high-profile advertising and marketing requirements needed to keep Persil on top of the detergent market and it will be seen that what may be required for one sector of the market may be very different for brands in another sector of the market.

HOUSEHOLD PRODUCTS

BRAND	LEADERSHIP	STABILITY	MARKET	INTERNATIONALITY	TREND	SUPPORT	PROTECTION	TOTAL
BIRO/BIC	□	●	●	●	○	□	●	□
BLACK & DECKER★	□	●	□	□	●	●	●	□
DURACELL★	□	□	●	●	□	□	●	□
ELECTROLUX	○	□	□	□	□	□	●	□
FORMICA	□	□	○	□	○	△	○	○
HALLMARK	□	●	□	□	□	○	●	□
HOOVER	○	□	□	●	□	○	●	□
MOULINEX	○	□	□	○	□	□	●	□
PERSIL	○	●	□		○	□	●	○
PERSPEX	□	□	○	○	○	△	○	○
SCOTCH	●	●	●	□	○	□	●	□
SINGER	○	○	○	○	○	○	●	○
TEFAL	○	○	□	○	□	□	●	○
THERMOS	○	○	○	□	□	○	△	○
TIPP-EX	□	●	□		○	△	□	○
TUPPERWARE	○	○	□	○	□	○	●	○
WATERFORD	○	□	□	●	○	○	●	□
WATERMAN	○	□	○	□	○		●	○
WEDGWOOD	○	□	□	●	○	○	●	□
YALE	□	●	□	□	□	○	●	□

KEY ★★ Top Ten brand ★ Top Fifty brand ● exceptionally strong □ very strong ○ strong △ problem area

Innovative products which help make our lives a little easier will always have appeal. Tipp-Ex correction fluid is one such product.

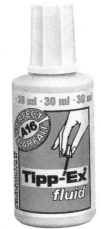

Tipp-Ex®
corrects the world over

TIPP-EX

The Tipp-Ex company was founded only some thirty years ago, in Frankfurt-am-Main, Germany. Its original product was coated correction strips for typing errors, but the Tipp-Ex trademark is now most closely associated with correction fluids.

The popularity of correction fluids is due in large part to the more widespread use of photocopiers, but use of Tipp-Ex correction products has now expanded from the office workplace into homes, schools etc.

The success of Tipp-Ex is based on an original product concept, the rapid establishment of a powerful, international distribution network and strong branding.

PERSIL

Fabric detergents are the largest packaged sector within the retail grocery trade. In 1989 in Britain, for example, packaged detergent sales at retail, according to Nielsen, were £639 million, ready-to-eat cereals £549 million, non-mixer soft drinks £536 million, coffee £530 million, tea £441 million and canned cat food £370 million. The British picture is repeated in most developed countries so clearly any leading fabric detergent brand is likely to be a very major brand indeed.

Persil is one such brand. It was developed in Germany at the beginning of the century and takes its name from the roots of two ingredients *perborate* and *silicate*. In 1909 UK and certain other rights were sold to a company which later became part of Unilever so one of the world's leading brands is now owned in different countries by two powerful competing groups, Henkel and Unilever.

Persil
automatic

The Financial Times recently described the detergents industry as a

'battle ground where the fighting is so intense, the pressures so precise, that the margin for error, or for failure of nerve, is virtually non-existent.'

Persil illustrates well the continuous effort which needs to be put behind a brand to ensure success. The brand has been continually adapted and developed and consistently supported.

In 1950s movies, portrayals of Madison Avenue ad. agencies always involved big-budget detergent brands with names like Sudz or Kleanoh. The Persil brand epitomises the international detergent brand and, in the 1990s, the stakes are as high as they were in 1950s Hollywood movies.

WATERMAN

More than one hundred years ago, French businessman Lewis Edson Waterman was writing an insurance policy when his pen leaked. Enraged, M Waterman vowed that he would invent a better pen and one year later, in 1884, the fountain pen was born.

Waterman Pens rapidly became a flourishing business with exports throughout Europe and the United States, until the arrival of ballpoints in the 1950s seriously damaged sales. Undaunted by this setback – and by a series of domestic crises that beset the company during this period – Waterman continued production of fountain pens and in the late 1960s the great-granddaughter of the founder, Madame Francine Gomez, took over as President. Madame Gomez revived the business and succeeded in rebuilding Waterman's US market where the luxury image of the brand has strong upmarket appeal.

Today, Waterman's products enjoy a worldwide reputation for their quality and craftsmanship. With Gillette's support (Waterman was acquired by them in 1986) it is expected that the brand will capitalise on the widespread trend towards high quality fountain pens that is a feature of western markets in general and the newly-affluent Asian markets in particular.

Waterman, which sounds archetypically English is, in fact, a French brand of writing instruments.

SCOTCH

Scotch is the major product trademark of 3M and the Scotch brand is currently used by twenty-one operating units within 3M on over 160 different product applications. These include adhesive tapes, masking tapes, audio and video products, surface treatments for carpets and fabrics, self-stick notes and reflective highway signs.

The philosophy of 3M is that certain Group assets, including the 3M and Scotch trademarks, should be available to all the operating units provided the products themselves meet certain performance standards and provided, too, that the intended new application does not conflict with the brand's existing values or positionings. Even 3M might baulk at allowing an operating unit to use the Scotch brand on a defoliant or an innovative toothpaste product.

By making established, respected trademarks available to its 'internal entrepreneurs' 3M ensures that all its new products reach the market not just with the benefit of 3M's financial, manufacturing and distribution muscle but also with the benefit of both the corporate endorsement and a strong product brand.

The problem of course is to ensure that the brands, Scotch in particular, are not stretched too far. Therefore an internal procedure exists to ensure that all proposed applications of the brand meet Group guidelines.

The best known application for the Scotch brand name is still of course on adhesive tapes, an application which grew out of 3M's experience with pressure sensitive masking tapes. Scotch brand cellulose adhesive tapes were first launched in 1930 and by the Second World War had become a ubiquitous part of American life. Scotch is now the world's leading brand of adhesive tape and is subject to constant development and improvement.

It has been suggested that 3M selected the brand name Scotch for its new adhesive tapes so as to emphasise their economical, frugal nature!

BIRO/BIC

The Hungarian inventor László Biró invented the ballpoint pen before the Second World War. He settled in Argentina to escape the Nazis and patented his invention in 1943 and the first commercially produced Biro pens appeared in the US and the UK in 1945.

BiC (the other component of the Biro-BiC name) is derived from the name of Marcel Bich, a Frenchman who ironed out many of the teething problems of early ballpoint pens and, in 1958, launched the first low-cost, throw away ballpoint pens on the French and British markets, a development which revolutionised the writing instrument market.

Today, the Biro name is used generically (but wrongly) by many people to describe any brand of ballpoint pen and BiC remains the leading brand of disposable ballpoint pen.

The Biro and BiC brands occupy a unique position in, particularly, the world market for disposable ballpoint pens.

HALLMARK

Hallmark Cards Inc, until 1954 known as Hall Brothers Inc, produces more than eleven million greetings cards a day in twenty languages for sale in over 100 countries. It also produces gift wrapping, party goods, Christmas ornaments, jigsaw puzzles, mugs, photo' frames, ribbon and writing paper. It has a creative staff of 700 people making more than 14,000 greeting card designs annually and is clear leader in the world greetings card industry. The brand name Hallmark and the Hallmark crown device are now recognized by 99 per cent of Americans and the corporate slogan – 'When You Care Enough to Send the Very Best' is rated by consumers as the most truthful in the nation.

The Hallmark brand is, for Americans and others, indelibly associated with greetings cards and special occasions.

WEDGWOOD

Until the second half of the Nineteenth Century virtually the only products which truly had the status of brands were luxury products for the very, very wealthy – Gobelins tapestries, Meissen china, Mr Chippendale's furniture.

Wedgwood was founded in 1759 and came to prominence through its famous Jasper ware, a position which was reinforced in the

Fine porcelain and tableware has been produced in Europe since the Eighteenth Century and Wedgwood has been one of the most desirable brands since that time.

Wedgwood

early Nineteenth Century when Josiah Wedgwood II, son of the founder, first produced strong lustrous bone china by including animal bone, mainly ox bone, in the clay – a British reinvention of a process which the Chinese had used for a millennia.

Fine tableware and the brands associated with it – Wedgwood, Spode, Meissen, Royal Doulton, Villeroy & Boch, Noritake and scores more – still command enormous respect internationally but brand owners have found it curiously difficult to translate brand recognition and respect into volume and profits. Part of the problem is that even in the affluent 1990s the market for such products is quite limited and a good part of that is institutional, for example hotels and airlines, who shop for the best price. The industry is also very fragmented, design led and craft based. Economies of scale are therefore limited and brand owners have often learned by hard experience that occupying a comfortable niche may be a better strategy than seeking to build a dominant, powerful, luxury products brand, possibly through line extension.

WATERFORD

Waterford crystal was first produced in Waterford in Southern Ireland in 1783 and the original business survived until 1851, long enough to establish a remarkable reputation for fine quality, hand cut crystal. In 1947, a small crystal business was re-established just outside Waterford City and this time it prospered – the current Waterford glass works is the largest handcrafted crystal manufacturing unit in the world.

Many of the current designs, which are particularly well appreciated in the United States, are based on the Eighteenth and Nineteenth Century designs and the craft-based production process is still remarkably similar to that employed 200 years ago – only in batch mixing, where pure raw materials are consistently blended for much greater accuracy than was previously possible, has a significant technological advance been made.

The craft-based manufacturing process gives the brand its individuality and appeal yet, at the same time, provides a barrier to wider brand exploitation. Glass blowing, cutting and engraving are all highly skilled processes involving years of training and Waterford's fine quality products leave little room for automation. In recent years Waterford has encountered both skill shortages and labour problems. In 1986 it acquired Josiah Wedgwood and Sons Limited to form Waterford Wedgwood plc.

A small country town in South-Eastern Ireland is, perhaps, an unlikely home for one of the world's leading brands of fine crystal.

PERSPEX

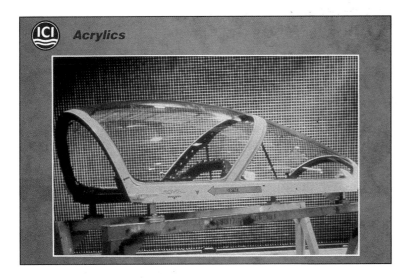

The Perspex brand is essentially an industrial brand yet it is widely familiar and has strong consumer appeal.

Perspex is a brand of acrylic sheet made by Britain's Imperial Chemical Industries (ICI). Though the name is frequently and wrongly used generically, it is in fact a registered trade mark and has been so since 1934.

Perspex was originally developed for use in the canopies of wartime fighter aircraft and is still used today in modern fighters. One of the major current applications for Perspex sheet is the manufacture of baths due to its glossy surface, ease of cleaning and range of colours; three in four baths sold in the UK are made from Perspex acrylic sheet.

BLACK & DECKER ☆ □

Black & Decker do-it-yourself power tools have a worldwide reputation and Black & Decker has maintained brand leadership by constant innovation and the careful monitoring and development of the brand image.

One particular problem which Black & Decker has encountered, along with other famous 'big ticket' brands, is the propensity of discount retailers to use the brand as a loss leader. The process goes like this: if you are a major discount retailer you take a well-known branded item such as a popular Black & Decker drill, discount it heavily and feature it prominently in advertising. You may, for example, take a drill which normally sells for £24.95 and, for the period of your special promotion, sell it for £19.95. Though this may afford you no profit at all it should draw customers into your store who may then buy paint, tools and other items. In addition, the value-for-money aura created by the heavy discount on one big brand item will create the impression that all the goods stocked by the retailer are equally keenly priced.

Black & Decker, originally known mainly for hand-held power tools, is extending the brand to cover a wide range of domestic appliances.

The problem with this practice for companies such as Black & Decker is that it can create mayhem with other major customers – they will suspect the brand owner of making a special deal for their competitor, they will stop selling the heavily discounted item, they will demand 'exclusive' models which competitors will be unable to discount heavily in this way and so on. In many countries it is illegal for manufacturers to control selling prices or establish exclusive networks of (it will be argued) acquiescent retailers under the control of the brand owner. Thus heavy discounting by retailers of famous brands in price led promotions has become almost routine. (Interestingly, Japanese brand owners who can control distribution and retail prices in their home markets, often find the unregulated nature of Western markets particularly perplexing.)

In 1984, Black & Decker acquired the household electrical appliances division of the US General Electric Company, though not the rights to continue the use of the General Electric name on these products, and took the decision to apply the Black & Decker name to its newly acquired hair dryers, irons, toasters, blenders, etc. Though the short term response in the US to this brand extension has, reportedly, been favourable, in Britain and elsewhere, where Black & Decker branded appliances are also now being sold, the initial reaction has been rather less positive – consumers seem to feel that the Black & Decker brand is manly and aggressive and does not sit comfortably on hair dryers, curlers or irons.

Yale

Yale invented the pin tumbler lock and thus helped dramatically improve domestic and commercial security.

YALE ☐

Yale Security Inc, based in Charlotte, North Carolina, is a world leader in commercial, consumer and electronic security. The company was founded in 1868 and its reputation was based upon Linus Yale's invention of the pin tumbler lock, a product which was exceptionally difficult to pick and where the key weighed only ounces or a fraction of an ounce rather than a pound or more, the norm at that time.

Yale now manufactures in six countries and sells its products worldwide and the name Yale has powerful international associations with locks and security products.

FORMICA ◯

Formica Corporation, the world's largest supplier of laminate used in building, was established in March, 1913, by Herbert A Faber and Daniel J O'Conor to manufacture insulation materials for the booming electrical industry. Until that time the mineral, mica, had been widely used as an insulation material in this industry. Faber and O'Conor discovered that by encasing layers of paper in a thermosetting resin, they achieved a product with mica's insulation qualities but greater versatility. This new discovery was called Formica.

Formica produced and sold laminated products for electrical insulation, radio parts, pulleys and timing gears and, in 1927, discovered that by adding a layer of decorative paper to laminated products made on a flat bed press appealing woodgrain and marbling effects could be achieved.

After the Second World War the huge demand for housing led to explosive growth for the company both in the US and abroad – production started in the UK in 1947 and, in later years, in over a dozen other countries from Argentina to India.

In 1978, the US Federal Trade Commission started a proceeding which contended that the Formica brand name had become generic – in other words had become a common descriptive term usable by anyone in connection with any laminate. Since the FTC's position was contrary to the very purpose and function of a well-established and properly used trademark, the company strenuously contested the case. After over two years of litigation, Congress stepped in and prohibited the FTC from spending any more of its funds on proceedings which attempted to cancel the registration of famous trademarks such as Formica. The FTC's case was dismissed thereafter and Formica Corporation maintains its registration of the Formica trademark and its right to exclusive use of the Formica brand name.

Formica is the dominant brand in laminates worldwide. Though the name is often used generically by consumers, it is in fact a carefully protected registered trademark.

83

DURACELL ☆ ▢

Up to the mid-1970s battery markets were dominated by the conventional zinc carbon battery and the world's major brands were Union Carbide's Eveready brand (in the US), the entirely unconnected Ever Ready brand in Britain, Varta in Germany, Mazda in France and so forth. Then the Duracell longlife battery was launched by Dart & Kraft in the US; in less than ten years long-life batteries, mainly Duracell, accounted for 50–60 per cent of unit sales in the US and over 70 per cent by value. Union Carbide complained that 'Duracell sneaked in on us' but the truth is that the market leader saw little to gain from obsoleting its production capacity and introducing a new product which lasted several times as long as existing products. It was a sitting duck.

Britain's Ever Ready was a sitting duck too; Duracell entered the British and European markets in 1979 when alkaline batteries were a tiny specialist sector. In 1978 Ever Ready had changed its name to Berec (**B**ritish **E**ver **R**eady **E**lectrical **C**ompany) in an attempt to impose uniformity and, too, because it was piqued at being constantly confused with its US competitor. Hanson Trust bought Berec in 1981 and promptly restored the Ever Ready name but Duracell had again caught the market leader napping and profited mightily from this.

DURACELL ®
Up to 6 times longer life

Duracell came from nowhere to challenge the world's major battery brands and, in the main, has won.

Duracell is now firmly established as the world's leading brand in the important and growing longlife sector of the market. Though 80 per cent of the world's battery market is still zinc carbon, in developed countries alkaline batteries predominate due to the increasing use of batteries in cameras, radios, toys, etc.

Duracell's success in batteries closely matches that of Michelin in tyres – both brands took on entrenched interests which, when faced with a superior, longer life product refused to take the threat seriously. As with tyres, the existing brands in time started to respond and their brand strength ensured that the newcomer did not just ride straight over them. But the battery market will never be the same again.

THERMOS

The name Thermos is famous worldwide for vacuum flasks and is a registered trademark in over eighty countries worldwide but not, unfortunately, in the US: in 1963 the trademark registration was successfully challenged in the US Courts on the grounds of 'genericisation' and the name then became a common or dictionary word in that country, available to all. The Thermos name was first registered in 1906 and the loss of the valuable rights in the name in the US (though not, it should be emphasised, elsewhere) serves as a cautionary tale for owners of famous brands around the world.

The basic concept of the Thermos vacuum flask has changed little for decades. Thermos has, however, greatly expanded the range and styling of its vacuum flasks to maintain the brand's market position.

THERMOS ®

TEFAL

Tefal is a subsidiary of the French SEB Group which has operations worldwide. It owes its origins to the ingenuity of a French scientist who found a way of bonding PTFE on to aluminium and so led to the founding of the original company in 1953.

PTFE – polytetrafluorethylene – is the technical name for a non-stick substance which was discovered in the nineteen-thirties and whose non-stick properties were originally used in industrial and medical applications. However, the new bonding process revolutionised cooking and led to Tefal producing the world's first non-stick frying pan in 1956. Tefal is now the world's largest producer of non-stick cookware. Following on their success in cookware, Tefal's reputation for innovation has driven the company to No 1 in the kitchen with electrical products such as the Supercool fryer range; the cordless kettle; Thick 'n' Thin toasters and the Ultraglide Elite tap water iron.

Tefal used a PTFE bonding process to produce the world's first non-stick frying pan.

TUPPERWARE

There has, of course, to have been a Mr (or Ms) Tupper and there was: Earl Silas Tupper, a chemist, who in 1945 recognised that moulded polyethylene would make an ideal container for food and who went on to develop the unique Tupperware airtight seal.

The brilliance of the Tupperware concept, however, extends beyond the product itself: frustrated at trying to sell its products through department stores (they did not demonstrate the products properly or adequately communicate their benefits), the newly formed Tupperware company laid the foundations of the company's famous party plan home sales method. Products were removed from all stores and home demonstrations were substituted, a policy which continues to this day.

The name Tupperware is, somehow, curiously well adapted to airtight plastic containers.

MOULINEX

Moulinex makes ovens and fryers, vacuum cleaners, food preparation equipment (mixers, blenders, electric knives etc), coffee grinders and makers, juice extractors, electric kettles and certain non-electrical appliances. The company is decentralised, pragmatic in a way which only French companies can be, fast to react to market needs and highly dynamic and aggressive. Brand awareness is exceptionally high and the company's clear objective is to lead its market on a world basis.

SINGER ○

The name Singer is inextricably linked with sewing machines but, paradoxically, in the early 1980s the manufacture of sewing machines almost brought the company down as competition from, in particular, Japan, South Korea and Taiwan led to huge losses. In a bid to meet this competition the company established low-cost manufacturing bases in South America and Asia – it even purchased Singer branded machines from its major competitors. All to no avail; eventually the company sold its sewing machine interests and now concentrates exclusively on high tech products for the aerospace and related industries.

Since then the Singer brand, as applied to sewing machines, has passed through various hands and each new owner has tried to find the secret of how to use profitably what is undoubtedly a massively well known and respected brand name. For example, they have examined various repositioning strategies – Singer brand home interest products; Singer retail outlets selling fabric, tapestries and wool; Singer brand domestic appliances; but with only mixed success. It seems that the Singer brand is so inextricably linked with home sewing, and that home sewing has become, in the developed countries at least, such a relatively rare activity, that the brand may not be capable of enjoying again the exposure and power which it did during its first century of existence.

Moulinex combines style and dependability in its range of kitchen appliances.

The Singer brand is the most powerful brand worldwide in respect of home sewing.

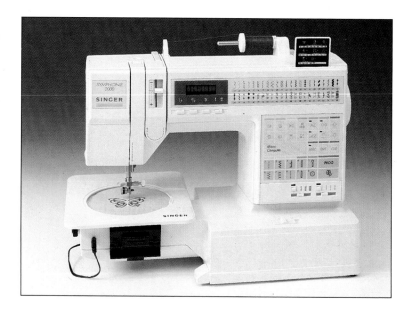

HOOVER

The Hoover vacuum cleaner 'beats as it sweeps, as it cleans' and the success of Hoover's vacuum cleaners has made Hoover a household name around the world.

Among the golden rules of proper trademark usage which are, supposedly, engraved on every brand manager's heart, is one which states that a trademark should never be used as a verb, always as an adjective, thus:

Improper use: 'Hoover your carpet'
Proper use: 'Clean your carpet with a Hoover vacuum cleaner'

Routinely, every brand manager objects to this rule as it can, at times, be a little clumsy and, it is argued, Hoover has been widely used as a verb for generations without any damage to the company's proprietary rights in the

Hoover invented the vacuum cleaner and is still the world's leading vacuum cleaner brand.

trademark.

This is true, except that Hoover themselves have never encouraged such use of their trademark, in fact, the reverse – they have, since 1908, been meticulous in their trademark management. And, having done so, they should not be, and have not been, penalised by having their valuable proprietary trademark rights taken away from them and turned into a generic available to all comers simply because consumers, without any encouragement from the brand owner, find that the word Hoover so perfectly sums up the qualities and attributes they seek that they prefer the trademark to the generic terms vacuum or vacuum cleaner.

Hoover have therefore fully retained all their trademark rights yet have seen the name become synonymous with, in particular, vacuum cleaners.

ELECTROLUX

Electrolux grew out of A B Lux, a Swedish company formed in 1901 to manufacture mantles for oil lamps. It is now one of the world's leading manufacturers of domestic appliances.

Perhaps somewhat fortunately for Western domestic appliance manufacturers, the European and US domestic appliance markets have thus far largely escaped massive competition from Japanese companies – Sony, Hitachi, National Panasonic, etc. However, the position of such companies is now so well established worldwide in such markets as televisions and hi-fis that strong competition from them in domestic appliance markets seems inevitable at some stage, particularly as all these brands have strong positions in Japanese and Far Eastern domestic appliance markets and have

The Electrolux brand of domestic appliances is well placed to resist any Japanese onslaught on its core markets.

therefore the necessary technical know-how and manufacturing base. Electrolux is determined that, in increasingly competitive world markets, it will come out on top. Massive effort has therefore been devoted in recent years to 'zero fault' design, to new manufacturing programmes, to the development of strategic alliances and to brand building.

HIGH-TECH

CONSIDER THE ROLE OF BRANDS in the market for office equipment. Until about ten years ago the average investment in equipment to support one office worker was only a few hundred pounds, a tiny fraction of the invested capital for the average industrial worker.

Although the situation has by no means been reversed, in the last decade massive investment has been made in office automation. This does not simply mean that the traditional typewriter has been replaced with a word processor, or that operations originally performed by the human brain have been 'replaced' by artificial intelligence in the form of computer systems.

While computerisation has been one of the single most fast developing areas of new technology, in the last decade other supporting areas such as monochrome and colour photocopiers (Xerox and Canon have been leaders in this field), laser printers, fax and telex machines have also benefited from huge investment in the creation of the modern office. Branding has played an enormous part in helping to shape consumer decisions and attitudes in these areas and will continue to do so as investment grows still further to keep pace with continuing developments.

Apple, in particular, has been highly successful in the area of word-processing, personal computing and desktop publishing. It entered the arena with a branding strategy that was approachable, no-nonsense and which demystified computing for many non-specialists. It was fresh, different and importantly, the products themselves were innovative and of high quality. It quickly wrong-footed virtually all other computer manufacturers by making them appear trapped in their arcane rituals and language.

Since Apple's introduction onto the computer scene, other major computer manufacturers such as Unisys and the massively successful IBM, have adapted their own equipment to be similarly user-friendly. The success of these companies has resulted from their ability to respond quickly, innovatively and boldly to market needs, providing high quality systems and after-sales training and care.

Of course it is not only in the area of office automation that branding has played a part in the exploitation of new technology and it is here that the Japanese have so successfully challenged the European and American brand owners. Nikon, Sony and Pioneer are leaders in the fields of photography and hi-fi, while Casio is the clear market leader in the area of calculators.

As technological innovation continues to explore new areas and further exploits existing areas branding will play an ever more crucial role, guiding the consumer and developing market share for brand owners in this multi-million dollar market.

HIGH TECH

BRAND	LEADERSHIP	STABILITY	MARKET	INTERNATIONALITY	TREND	SUPPORT	PROTECTION	TOTAL
APPLE ★	□	○	○	□	●	●	●	□
CANON	□	●	□	□	□	●	●	□
CASIO	○		○	□	○		●	○
DICTAPHONE	○	○	○	○	△		○	
IBM ★★	●	●	●	●	□	●	●	●
KODAK ★★	●	●	●	●	●	●	●	●
LOTUS 1-2-3 ★	○	△	●	□	□	○	●	□
NIKON		●	□	●	○	●	●	□
PIONEER	○	□	□		○	□	●	○
POLAROID	○	○	□	□	○	△	○	○
SONY ★★	□	●	□	●	□	□	●	●
3M	○	□	□	□	□	○	●	□
UNISYS		○	○	□	○	○	●	○
XEROX	○	□	□	□	○		●	○
WALKMAN	●	○	□	□	○	○	○	○

KEY ★★ Top Ten brand ★ Top Fifty brand ● exceptionally strong □ very strong ○ strong △ problem area

IBM ☆ ☆ ●

The mighty International Business Machines Corporation (IBM) has been making products to support business since 1911 and is now the largest computer manufacturer in the world with sales of over $60 billion and almost 400,000 employees in well over 100 countries. Its products are designed to record, process, communicate, store and retrieve information and impact in one way or another on the lives of all of us as they are used in manufacturing, banking, at grocery check outs, for forecasting weather, in the health services and in education.

IBM ('Big Blue' as it is often affectionately known because of its corporate colour) now possesses one of the world's most powerful trademarks and has succeeded in investing a set of three letters with a power and imagery that is unique – other manufacturers such as ICL who have followed the IBM branding route have found it altogether more difficult to invest a set of letters with imagery and appeal.

IBM has also supported its brand with a simple, attractive and consistently applied logo and visual identity system which works well in a wide number of applications from notepaper to corporate signs.

IBM has succeeded, almost uniquely, in investing a mere set of three letters with enormous power and differentiation.

DICTAPHONE

If you were testing, for the very first time, the world's first practical invention for recording and reproducing sound, what words would you use? 'Testing, testing, testing. One, two, three, four?' Charles Sumner Tainter, in October 1881 chose a quotation from Act 1, Scene V of Hamlet:

> There are more things in heaven and earth, Horatio, than are dreamt of in your philosophy.

Or so it is claimed . . .

Tainter was a researcher who worked with Alexander Graham Bell, the inventor of the telephone, and his cousin Chichester Bell on the development of a recording device for use with the newly-invented telephone. They were successful and formed the Columbia Graphophone Company to market their 'Commercial Graphophone', a name abandoned in 1906 for commercial applications in favour of the less clumsy trademark Dictaphone.

However, for many years the major application for sound recording was for entertainment purposes and stenographic and commercial applications took a back seat, so much so that in 1923 Columbia Graphophone sold all its rights in office dictating equipment and in the Dictaphone trademark to a group of investors. (Despite their relative lack of interest in business communication equipment, Columbia Graphophone still got the then

The name Dictaphone is the most famous brand in the area of commercial dictating machines though competition, mainly from Japan, has eroded, even eliminated, its technical edge.

huge sum of $1 millon from the sale.)

Up until the late 1960s Dictaphone prospered mightily – its products were popular with presidents, news correspondents, novelists, statesmen, academics and businessmen and were used to record parliaments, to provide evidence in court cases, for correspondence – even for quality control in wartime aircraft engine factories where trials of new engines were recorded.

The Dictaphone Company's pre-eminent position in sound recording, coupled with a memorable and widely protected trademark, led to Dictaphone becoming the dominant brand in its sector on a worldwide basis. Indeed, many dictionaries still list Dictaphone as (for example): 'a registered trademark for a phonograph instrument that records and reproduces dictation'. In the last two decades the technological lead enjoyed by Dictaphone has in many sectors been eliminated but the power of the brand remains.

The nomenclature strategy of Xerox whereby it registered the trademark Xerox yet coined the closely related generic term xerography to describe dry copying is particularly adept.

XEROX

The trademark Xerox is derived from the Greek χeros, 'dry' and the words xerography (to describe the dry copying process) and Xerox (to identify the products) were introduced simultaneously in 1948. Xerox Corporation is now a company with revenues approaching $20 billion and over 100,000 employees worldwide, of which 60 per cent are in the US.

Xerox has, over the years, faced the same problem of potential 'genericisation' of its trademark as is faced by owners of such famous marks as Hoover and Tipp-Ex. The Xerox trademark is, however, so highly distinctive and carefully managed that the company's rights have never been seriously challenged.

![PIONEER]

The Pioneer brand enjoys a worldwide reputation for quality and technical excellence.

PIONEER

Pioneer Electronic Corporation is a major manufacturer of radio, video and other electronic products including televisions, laser disc players, even home use karaoke systems.

In the car electronics area the company offers the Carrozzeria brand as well as the Pioneer brand though across the company most support is, in practice, put behind the Pioneer brand name.

Pioneer is a brand which, in Western markets, has never had the 'unequivocally Japanese' image of brands such as Hitachi, Akai and Sony, a factor due in large part to its adoption of a Western brand name rather than a Japanese name.

POLAROID

The Polaroid company came into existence in 1937 (polarised sunglasses were its original product and are still produced, and well respected, today) and the Polaroid 'instant' camera was invented in 1947. Its inventor was the company's founder, Dr Edwin Land, and hence was called the Polaroid Land Camera.

Over the last forty years the trademark Polaroid has almost become the generic term for instant photography – almost, but not quite, because the company has always jealously guarded its intellectual property rights and has fiercely resisted the genericisation of its trade mark.

In recent years, and despite its success in a massive legal battle with Kodak over patent rights to the instant photography process, Polaroid has found the going has become tougher. This has been attributed in part to a lessening of interest in the company's products due to the perceived lower picture quality of instant photographs as well as to the high price of instant pictures. These factors, combined with the availability of inexpensive, easy-to-use 'conventional' cameras as well as

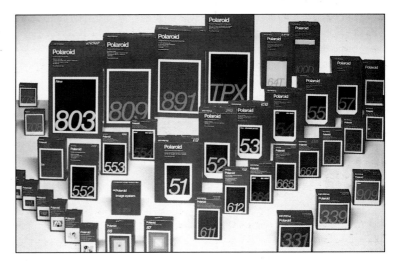

the proliferation of rapid film processing services have, it is believed, tended to 'marginalise' Polaroid and its instant photography process.

But the Polaroid brand retains enormous equity and the appeals of instant photography are as strong as ever. Moreover, the company has an exceptionally powerful technical base and has proved its ability to respond promptly and appropriately to changes in market demand.

The Polaroid brand is closely particularised to instant photography and the brand owner's task is to keep it relevant and contemporary in a changing world.

Polaroid.

3M

The name 3M started out as the popular nick-name of the Minnesota Mining & Manufacturing Company, a business formed at the turn of the century to mine ore in northern Minnesota but which found the ore deposits less rich than originally assayed and so turned instead to the manufacturing of abrasives and related products. Now 3M and the 3M corporate symbol denote one of the world's great manufacturing companies which is renowned, in particular, for its skills in exploiting materials innovations and in translating technical breakthroughs into industrial and consumer products which are both original and appealing.

3M is a world leader in adhesives, abrasives, reflective materials, certain specialist pharmaceutical sectors and in a score of other product fields. It has a powerful corporate culture central to which is a respect for innovation and technical excellence, a focus on relatively small working teams embracing manufacturing, marketing and development functions and a great respect and affection for 3M and what it stands for.

3M's brand image has undergone controlled development over almost a century.

APPLE ☆ ☐

If you had been sitting around in the 1970s trying to think of a name for the new computer company you were starting in your garage, would you have called it Apple or anything like it? Most probably not. At that time the culture of computing was remote and mysterious and the high priests initiated into the black art of computing – programmers and the like – talked a private language which they all seemed to understand, but which excluded all outsiders. Highly technical, industry-specific brand and corporate names were preferred at that time as these flattered the expert but were, conversely, daunting to the non-expert.

The fresh, easily recognised Apple logo fully matches the distinctive brand name.

In naming his new company Apple, Steve Jobs demystified computers and computing. He recognised that the future of his new business lay not with the fanatical, knowledgeable computer expert but with the man and woman in the street. He had to appeal to an audience which knew nothing about computers and did not wish to know anything: they would buy a computer to do a job of work but did not wish to join a type of religious sect.

The Apple brand name has worked brilliantly. It is fresh, memorable, iconoclastic and has wonderful visual imagery, a factor which the company has fully exploited.

UNISYS ○

Unisys was born of the merger in 1986 of Sperry and Burroughs, both multi-billion dollar companies, and the new merged company now has worldwide sales of $10 billion, second only in its field to the mighty IBM.

Choosing a name for a new merged company can be a nightmare as many boards of directors have discovered:

● if the name of one party to the merger is chosen it is assumed by all comers, including the employees, that the party whose name has not been chosen is the underdog.

● if a joint or composite name is chosen, this can be clumsy and, in any case, who comes first?

● if a new name is chosen, are you not discarding all the equity in the existing names? And, in any case, how do you

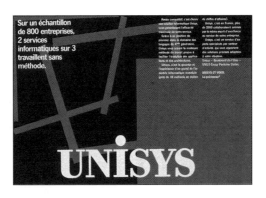

The Unisys name was not universally liked when it was first used in 1986, but it is now very well accepted.

develop a new name, complete all the legal clearances and design a new corporate identity, all perhaps in a matter of weeks when you have, in any case, 1,001 other things to do?

Unisys used an employee competition (normally a highly risky undertaking but, in this case, successful) and the winning name, submitted by a number of employees, means 'union of systems'.

In the last decade computers have become part of all our lives. Brand personalities must now appeal as much to the non-specialist as the specialist.

SONY ☆ ☆ ●

Akio Morita, one of the founders of Sony in 1946, entitled his recent autobiography 'Made in Japan'. Sony can claim with some justification to have been instrumental in turning the phrase Made in Japan from pejorative into praise.

The name Sony relates to sonus – Latin for sound – but also to Al Jolson's song 'Sonny Boy', a favourite of Mr Morita.

Over the last 40 years Sony has become one of the world's most powerful brands. The reasons for this include:

● a passion for the Sony brand above all else and a refusal to act as a sub-contract producer of other people's brands.

● a clear corporate image structure; any damage to one part of the corporate brand is seen as damaging the whole.

● a clear focus on a single product area, electronics.

● particular skills in bringing innovative new products quickly to market.

● a free-thinking unbureaucratic environment.

● an early focus on world markets.

Recently, a number of observers have contrasted the focus and precision of the Sony brand with the more generalised image of many of its Western competitors.

Sony, an abstract, short, internationally acceptable name has a precision and brand focus which is unrivalled.

SONY®

WALKMAN

Sony's Walkman portable tape player was launched in 1979 and sales currently run at over ten million units a year, 40 per cent of the world market. At the time of its launch most people in Sony's sales and marketing department were sceptical about the product – they felt that people would find the headphones annoying and would not wish to buy a unit which could not both record and play back. The decision to launch the Walkman was taken by Akio Morita, Sony's Chief Executive, who tried out one of the prototypes. His faith in the product was quickly vindicated – in 1980 Sony sold 600,000 units and in 1981 well over two million units.

Interestingly, competitors proved as sceptical about portable tape players as many of Sony's own staff and no competitive response was felt for over a year after launch, a delay which allowed Sony to improve its products, introduce new models and consolidate its market position.

To date Sony has sold over sixty million Walkman tape players and it dominates the world market for such products: no other manufacturer comes close and the brand name Walkman has become virtually synonymous internationally with the product.

Most of Sony's products do not carry a sub-brand. Walkman is an important exception.

The Casio brand has a reputation for innovation as evidenced by Casio's LCD colour television.

CASIO

The pace of change in the area of electronic technology is breakneck and companies who flourish in this area need to be creative, bold and decisive. Casio is one such company. Over the years it has expanded from electronic calculators into timepieces, electronic musical instruments, electronic office machinery and audiovisual equipment. It now has a turnover of more than $2 billion, a superb technical base, worldwide distribution and a brand name which, potentially, enhances the prospects and reputation of any electronic product on which it is used.

NIKON

Nikon has been synonymous with fine optics since the company was founded in 1917. During its seventy years of operation, Nikon has developed outstanding know-how in optics, precision manufacturing and electronics, placing its products at the leading edge.

Cameras and lenses, which have given the Nikon brand a powerful reputation, are just one area where the Company's technology has been brought to bear in serving customer needs. Steppers and mask wafer inspection equipment used in the manufacture of highly reliable integrated circuits, surveying instruments, magneto-optical disks, colour film scanners, colour printers, microscopes and binoculars are also important parts of the company's product portfolio.

Nikon's activities are guided by a passion for optical and precision excellence.

Nikon®
We take the world's
greatest pictures.®

Nikon is now one of the world's leading brands in the area of fine optics.

LOTUS 1-2-3 ☆ ☐

Lotus Development Corporation, owners of the Lotus 1–2–3 brand, started life in April 1982 as a $1 million venture capital start-up business; it had just eight employees. By the end of 1983 it could look back on a year in which it had revenues of $53 million and where employee numbers had grown to 300. By the end of 1989 the company had billings of some $550 million and 2,700 employees.

Lotus 1–2–3 is now the world's leading spreadsheet and Lotus Development Corporation has a strong reputation for service and support as well as for constant innovation and development. The Lotus portfolio of branded software products currently includes Agenda, Magellan, Prompt CD, Symphony, Manuscript and Freelance, among others.

Lotus 1-2-3 is the market leader in computer spreadsheet software packages.

Lotus 1-2-3

KODAK ☆ ☆ ●

In 1887, George Eastman patented the dry-plate process, an invention which obsoleted the need for cumbersome equipment and on-the-spot developing in photography. The dry-plate process brought photography to the masses and, having invented a camera which could take an incredible 100 pictures Eastman wanted a powerful brand name so that his product would achieve maximum marketing impact. The name Kodak was first registered on September 4th 1888 and Eastman later related how he came to create it.

> I knew a trade name must be short, vigorous, incapable of being misspelled to an extent that will destroy its identity and, in order to satisfy trademark laws, it must mean nothing. The letter K had been a favourite with me – it seemed a strong, incisive sort of letter. Therefore, the word I wanted had to start with K. Then it became a question of trying out a great number of combinations of letters that made words starting and ending with K. The word Kodak is the result.

Today the mighty Eastman-Kodak company of Rochester, New York is the undisputed world leader in photographic and related products and the Kodak brand name is among the most powerful brand names in the world.

Few companies are so bold as to take a totally abstract name and invest it with all the properties and association they require. Kodak shows, however, that the rewards can be enormous.

Canon amply demonstrates the 'bridging' at which Japanese companies are so adept. Originally formed as a camera manufacturer Canon has used its technological base to become a leading manufacturer of business machines.

CANON

Canon derives its name from Kwah-non, the Japanese name of the Chinese Goddess Kwan-jin who brings grace and fortune. Kwanon became Canon in 1947, fourteen years after the company was first formed as a camera manufacturer, and Canon Inc. is now a leading world manufacturer of business machines as well as of cameras and other optical products. In addition to the wide variety of copiers, laser beam printers, Bubble Jet printers, memory systems, facsimile equipment, electronic typewriters, Japanese-language word processors, DTP systems, calculators, cameras and other products marketed under the Canon brand name, Canon also markets both Apple and NeXT computers in Japan and the Far East. It also operates Imageland in the United States where customers can use colour laser copiers (CLCs) to produce original artwork.

Canon are now the major world competitors to Xerox in copiers and their technology is so advanced that the new Canon high fidelity colour copier is giving Governments around the world a major headache – it can produce colour photocopies of bank notes which are of such a high standard that a rush of forged banknotes is feared. Already the Bank of England is redesigning the currency with the Canon copier firmly in mind.

AUTOMOTIVE

AUTOMOTIVE BRANDS ARE AMONG the most ubiquitous brands in the world — the automobile industry is the biggest in the world and men, in particular, take a great interest in cars and car accessories, aeroplanes and virtually all other aspects of the industry. Thus even long-dead brands such as Riley (United Kingdom), Studebaker (USA) and Simca (France) still have enormous recall — out of all proportion to their historic market position or influence.

In selecting brands from the automotive and related sectors for inclusion in this book we have, therefore, tried to focus on brands with precision and personality, not just on those which merely have consumer awareness. This has inevitably meant that more generalised 'house brands' such as Ford, Chevrolet and Opel have not been included because such manufacturers produce a wide range of vehicles and much of their branding effort is focused on specific models, rather than on the house brand. Manufacturers of more specialist cars on the other hand, among them Mercedes-Benz, Volvo and Jaguar, have a more focused market positioning and are able,

therefore, to put the bulk of their branding effort behind the core brand using in the main alpha-numeric codes to denote individual models, e.g. 450 SE, XJS, 740, etc.

Even though the automotive industry is remarkably 'product-centric' (those working in the car industry are frequently motoring enthusiasts), in recent years there has been a growing appreciation of the important rôle of branding, not merely product specification, in influencing consumer choice and for this reason Ford paid a huge premium to secure the Jaguar brand and General Motors paid massively for the loss-making Saab brand. This process is taking place, not surprisingly, at a time when actual product characteristics and specifications are moving closer together and hence when intangible brand qualities are becoming more potent than ever in guiding consumer behaviour.

But our analysis of brands goes beyond just cars — we have also examined brands of aircraft, tyres, oil and construction equipment and all the brands we describe command international recognition.

AUTOMOTIVE

BRAND	LEADERSHIP	STABILITY	MARKET	INTERNATIONALITY	TREND	SUPPORT	PROTECTION	TOTAL
BMW ★	○	□	□	●	□	●	●	□
BOEING ★	□	□	○	●	○	○	●	□
CADILLAC	○	□	□			□	●	○
CASTROL	○	○	□	○	□	●	●	○
CATERPILLAR	○	○	○	□	□	○	●	○
CITROËN	○	○	□	○	○	○	●	○
CONCORDE	□		□	□	△		●	○
ESSO/EXXON ★	□	△	□	●		□	●	□
HARLEY-DAVIDSON	○	○	□	○	○	○	●	○
JAGUAR		○	□	□	△	□	●	○
JCB	○	○	○	○	○		●	○
JEEP	○	○	□	○	○	△		○
MASSEY-FERGUSON	○	○	○	□	□	○	●	○
MERCEDES-BENZ ★★	□	●	□	●	●	●	●	●
MICHELIN	○	□	○	□	○	○	●	□
NISSAN	○	●	□	●	●	□	●	□
PORSCHE ★	○	○	□	●	○	□	●	□
ROLLS-ROYCE ★	○	□	□	●	○	○	●	□
TOYOTA ★	○	●	□	●	●	□	●	□
VIRGIN ATLANTIC		△	□	○	●	○	●	○
VOLKSWAGEN	□	●	□	□	□	□	●	□
VOLVO		○	□	□	○	□	●	○
YAMAHA	○	●	□	□	□	●	●	□

KEY ★★ Top Ten brand ★ Top Fifty brand ● exceptionally strong □ very strong ○ strong △ problem area

CADILLAC

The name Cadillac, despite fierce and increasing competition from European and Japanese marques such as BMW, Volvo, Mercedes-Benz, Jaguar, Acura and Lexus, still represents to many Americans the epitome of automotive style and luxury. In volume terms, too, it is America's number one luxury car brand – in 1989 Cadillac sales in the US topped 267,000 vehicles, almost 27 per cent of the total luxury car market. (Total industry sales in the US are currently around ten million cars per annum of which the premium, luxury sector comprises some 10 per cent.)

Cadillac, which has been a division of General Motors for many years, can trace its origins back to the turn of the century and as early as 1908 Cadillac won the Royal Automobile Club Dewar Trophy for Automotive Excellence. Though the brand does not have the exclusivity of many imports, it has for a large proportion of American motorists aspirational qualities which are unique.

Cadillac, an attractive, lush name, epitomises for many American motorists attainable luxury.

ROLLS-ROYCE

Rolls-Royce make the most expensive and prestigious saloon cars in the world and the Rolls-Royce name, the RR logo, the distinctive grill and the Flying Lady (properly the 'Spirit of Ecstasy'), all of which are registered trademarks, are among the most potent, aspirational symbols in the world.

This, however, is not without its drawbacks. The owners of the Rolls-Royce trademark frequently have to contend with infringers around the world who seek, by using Rolls-Royce's trademarks on their own products or services, to have some of Rolls-Royce's goodwill accrue to them. Some of the infringements are relatively innocent and unintentional – a manufacturer, when describing his products as 'the Rolls-Royce of dental chairs', may think he is honouring the trademark, not misusing it – but others are not. Cheap clothing, watches, pens, fragrances or other 'luxury' items bearing the Rolls-Royce brand without authority and without adequate quality controls can have a seriously adverse effect on the brand. The company, therefore, jealously guards its brand and is exceptionally vigilant in patrolling its rights on a worldwide basis.

Rolls-Royce, more than any other brand stands, on a world basis, for luxury, style and prestige.

CITROËN

The first Citroën car, a Torpedo, came off the production line in May 1919 and ever since Citroën has enjoyed a reputation for style and innovative, even daring, engineering.

The company's style is well illustrated by its advertisements, its 'happenings' such as the use of the Eiffel Tower from 1925–34 as a large neon sign and its attractive showrooms. Its innovative engineering is demonstrated by its avant-garde technology (e.g. front-wheel drive from 1934 onwards, air-cushioned suspension, early use of steel-braced radial tyres etc.) and its wonderful, idiosyncratic designs as evidenced by the *Traction Avant*, DS, 2CV, CX, SM and XM.

Not all motorists appreciate Citroën cars but those who do love them with a passion. In the motor industry few brands have such a clear, differentiated image and personality.

Citroën's unequivocal brand personality is fully reflected in its highly original motor cars.

VOLVO

Volvo was founded in Sweden in the 1920s and the Volvo Group now has a worldwide turnover of some £10 billion. The word 'Volvo' means in Latin, 'I roll' and this distinctive trademark was originally given to the fledgling car company by SKF, the Swedish bearing manufacturer, who had registered the name some years before but no longer needed it.

Volvo reserves the brand name exclusively for its automotive products and has resolutely refused to allow third-party licensing even for gift and novelty items as it is concerned that any dilution or mis-use of the name may fundamentally damage its most valuable asset.

VOLVO

In the luxury passenger car sector of the automotive market Volvo has a highly distinctive brand positioning with particular qualities of fine engineering, reliability, family values and care for the environment, all in a relatively wholesome Scandinavian context.

Most recently Volvo has formed an alliance with Renault to create a firm foundation for technical co-operation. The Volvo and Renault marques will, however, be kept entirely separate and no dilution of the brand identities will be allowed.

Volvo ranks alongside Kodak and Exxon in terms of bold, abstract branding and, like them, has benefited from being able to build a clear differentiated image.

JAGUAR

Jaguar, now part of Ford (who paid an enormous premium over tangible net assets for the company, arguably to secure control of the brand), is a fine example of the robustness of brands and of their ability to retain consumer loyalties even when the going is tough; in the 1970s product quality and reliability at Jaguar plummeted and sales followed the quality spiral downwards; once, however, new management restored quality, consumer loyalty rapidly returned. Now, under Ford's direction, it is expected that the model range will be widened and that Jaguar will emerge as a more broadly based car manufacturer capable of challenging Mercedes-Benz on a world basis.

The name Jaguar and the feline sleekness of its cars are in clear harmony.

BMW ☆ ☐

Sets of initials are notoriously difficult to invest with personality and meaning. BMW – and IBM – are rare but important exceptions to the rule.

BMW, builders of fine cars and motorcycles, are based in Munich and have a worldwide reputation for advanced technology, excellent product quality and fine styling. The company started out in the First World War as an aircraft engine manufacturer and its beginnings are still evident in its white and blue symbol, conceived as a stylised rotating propeller.

In the world of corporate identity BMW is renowned for the attention it pays to its brand image, i.e. to its corporate brand. For example, if you visit a BMW show-room or service centre anywhere in the world, you will find that they all share the same distinctive BMW 'look' and that all carry a message of quality, efficiency and professionalism.

BMW's origins date back to the First World War but its reputation as a builder of exclusive high performance motor cars really started to be established in the 1960s.

PORSCHE ☆ ☐

Porsche (properly 'Dr Ing. h.c.F. Porsche AG) claims to be the world's largest specialist manufacturer of high performance road cars – over 30,000 were built in 1989. Porsche (pronounced Por-sche as a two-syllable word) has won Le Mans a record twelve times and owning a Porsche car represents for many motoring enthusiasts the pinnacle of their motoring ambitions. Porsche cars are built for drivers who see their car as a form of pleasure, not merely a means of transport and all Porsche sports cars seem to combine performance, handling and styling in a unique fashion. The latest Porsche road car, the 959, has been described as 'a masterpiece of automotive design' and is already a collector's item.

But the Porsche brand now stands for more than just cars. The company undertakes research work for other manufacturers as well

as for Governments and it also licenses the trademark for use on other products (e.g. sunglasses), provided they meet Porsche quality standards.

The Porsche brand name conveys images of high performance, beautifully engineered, somewhat ascetic sports cars.

MERCEDES-BENZ ☆ ☆ ⬤

Emil Jellinek was a successful German businessman who, at the turn of the century, lived in Nice and had a passion for motor cars and motor racing. He ordered his motor cars from Gottlieb Daimler and Wilhelm Maybach, proprietors of Daimler-Motoren-Gesellschaft, and proved to be both a knowledgeable and demanding customer constantly requiring increased engine power, reduced fuel consumption, lower traffic noise and greater reliability. He competed in car races against other enthusiasts such as Baron Rothschild under the pseudonym 'Monsieur Mercedes', the name of his eldest daughter and in 1900 he proposed to Daimler and his chief engineer Maybach the deal of a century: he would buy thirty-six of their new design of car, one quarter of their output, for 550,000 gold marks as long as he got sole agency rights for Austro-Hungary, France and America, a place on the Supervisory Board and as long, too, as the new car was named after his eleven year old daughter, Mercedes.

The three-pointed star was adopted in 1909 when it was decided that some sort of visual identity was required, for example on radiator grills, and in 1926 Daimler combined with competitors Benz to form Daimler-Benz AG. Thus one of the most valuable and powerful alignments of trademarks in the world was completed, Daimler, Benz, Mercedes and the three-pointed star. These trademarks are now central to a brand with worldwide respect, enormous power and outstanding associations with excellence, quality and reliability in automotive engineering.

A brand is not merely a label, it is a credible guarantee of origin, quality and product performance. Mercedes-Benz has been delivering unmatched motoring satisfaction since the turn of the century.

NISSAN

Nissan is the world's fifth largest car manufacturer. It was founded in 1911 by Masujiro Hashimoto and its earliest car was named 'Dat' from the first letters of the names of the three financial backers, Den, Aoyama and Takeuchi. In 1931, after a merger, the company was named Datson (literally 'son of Dat') and this was changed to Datsun in 1932 after a tidal wave destroyed the Ayokawa factory: 'sun' was considered to have more favourable associations in Japanese than 'son'.

Datsun was merged into the Nissan Jidosha Kogyo in 1934 and the Datsun and Nissan names were both used until 1982 when it was decided to phase out the Datsun name in favour of Nissan. Today Nissan is a ¥5,000 billion ($30 billion) company manufacturing cars, trucks, aerospace equipment, textile machinery, and industrial and marine equipment.

Twenty-five years ago the Nissan and Datsun brand names were little known outside Japan. Now, Nissan is one of the world's leading automotive brands.

TOYOTA ☆ □

The Toyota brand is so respected in Japan that the company enjoys a more than 42 per cent share of the domestic new car market (excluding mini cars) and a growing number of sales outlets. To have such a commanding market share in one of the world's toughest and most knowledgeable car markets speaks volumes for the company's products, quality, service and overall brand reputation.

Toyota's products cover a wide variety of user categories and lifestyles, from compact cars to luxury vehicles. Newer lines include the Lexus line of luxury saloon cars, while such traditional winners as the Crown, the sporty Celica, and the Mark II (known as the Cressida outside Japan) continue to enjoy strong support and marketing acceptance.

Toyota's origins are in the manufacture of looms, complex pieces of equipment which operate under arduous conditions. The move into motor car manufacture capitalised on these skills.

TOYOTA

YAMAHA □

Yamaha, whose corporate symbol is based on a visualisation of a tuning fork, is a major manufacturer of musical instruments as well as of motorcycles, home electronics products, home furnishings and sporting goods.

The company's mission is to 'support the maximum enjoyment of life, at home or at leisure'.

As with many major Japanese brands, the Yamaha brand is quite generalised, rather than being specific to one product or one

Yamaha make products as diverse as organs, motorbikes and small boats. All, however, are characterised by high quality and an attention to detail.

range of products, a branding culture which can be traced back to the powerful influence of the mighty *zaibatsu* industrial combines (e.g. Mitsui, Mitsubishi and Sumitomo) on Japanese economic and industrial life. Under such a system where productive capacity is concentrated into a relative few hands the brands of major corporations tend to be applied to a wide range of diverse products all made by that corporation, a situation which is also echoed in Korea.

YAMAHA
YAMAHA MOTOR CO.,LTD.

Harley-Davidson is more than just a brand, it is a lifestyle.

HARLEY-DAVIDSON

Harley-Davidson is an archetypal US brand with international appeal which has maintained a strong cult following despite massive competition from Japanese motorbikes.

Harley-Davidson's main appeal lies in its brand image and the brand's owners have been increasingly concerned in recent years to develop and exploit this image. Brand extension, for example, has proved lucrative and the Harley-Davidson catalogue now contains such items as jewellery, male fragrances, leather clothing and gift items.

VOLKSWAGEN

Many of the strongest and most distinctive brands in the automobile industry are 'niche' brands with a narrow positioning and a *cachet* resulting, in part at least, from rarity. Examples of such brands are Ferrari, Rolls-Royce, Porsche and Jeep. Volkswagen is unusual because it has the distinctive brand identity of a specialist manufacturer yet is one of the world's leading car manufacturers.

The reason for this can be traced back in large part to the Beetle, a car which was first conceived of by the pre-war German Reich Government, designed by Porsche Design, resurrected in 1945 by the British Military Government and of which, by the end of 1988, over 20 million had been produced.

Interestingly, at the end of the Second World War both the British and the Americans were offered the Beetle. Lord Rootes headed the British Motor Industry Commission to Wolfsburg, home of Volkswagen, and reported,

The vehicle does not meet the fundamental requirements of a motor car. To build the car commercially would be a completely uneconomic enterprise.

The Americans were even more direct: a director reported to Henry Ford II

Mr Ford, I don't think what we are being offered here is worth a damn!

The Beetle established for Volkswagen a reputation for reliability, value and sound engineering which is still its hallmark today and which is continued in existing Volkswagen models. Volkswagen's 260,000 employees now build some three million vehicles a year and both Audi (Germany) and SEAT (Spain) are part of the Group.

Volkswagen has succeeded in transferring its brand image, originally developed around the 'Beetle' onto a complete range of 'mainstream' motor cars.

JEEP ○

The name Jeep is a trademark, not a generic term, and was first registered in the US in November 1940. Its origins are obscure (one claim is that it derives from the initials GP for general purpose, another that it was based on a comic strip character who could do anything and went 'jeep, jeep'). In any event, by the time Willys Corporation had turned out almost 600,000 of their famed four-wheel-drive quarter-ton trucks during the Second World War the name was known to a world audience and was indelibly associated with this type of versatile, go anywhere vehicle.

Jeep Corporation is now part of Chrysler Motors and the Jeep brand continues to be used on Cherokee, Wagoneer, Comanche and Wrangler models though for many people, especially those outside the US, the name is still most closely associated with the rugged vehicle of the Second World War.

Jeep®

The rugged, go-anywhere imagery of Jeep is now applied to a range of recreational vehicles.

MASSEY-FERGUSON ○

Mention tractors and farm machinery anywhere in the world and the brand name most likely to spring to mind is Massey-Ferguson, the world-wide market leader in tractor sales for almost three decades. The Massey part of the company, however, dates way back to 1847 (David Massey's first workshop was in Ontario, Canada and Massey's successor company, Massey-Harris developed the world's first successful self-propelled combine harvester in 1938). The Ferguson part of the company was founded in Britain by Harry Ferguson, a brilliant engineer who in 1933 invented a light, inexpensive tractor which gave enormous benefits in terms of cost, speed, safety and manoeuvrability. In 1953 Massey-Harris and Ferguson merged to form Massey-Ferguson.

The rugged, reliable products of Massey-Ferguson are particularly well suited to the

MASSEY-FERGUSON

needs of developing countries and the company has associated and licensee operations in seventeen countries around the world. One commentator recently observed that Massey-Ferguson has probably done more to help feed the earth's growing numbers than any other single organisation.

Massey-Ferguson build more tractors than anyone else in the world and are particularly strong in the developing countries where reliability is especially prized.

CATERPILLAR

Caterpillar Inc., headquartered in Illinois, is the world's largest manufacturer of earthmoving, construction and materials handling equipment, and a major manufacturer of diesel and natural gas engines and gas turbines. Sales in 1989 were almost $11 billion, $5 billion in the US and the rest throughout the world.

The company's success is based upon its invention, in 1904, of a tracked vehicle which, in effect, could lay its own roadbed and solved the problem of traction in muddy fields, a problem which particularly afflicted the large, heavy harvesters of the day. The Caterpillar trademark, first registered in 1910, shows the word written in the form of a caterpillar, quite clearly alluding to crawler tracks and their ability to make good progress over difficult surfaces.

The Caterpillar name is now largely synonymous with large, powerful earthmoving and construction machinery. Even though 'hard' factors such as price, specification, reliability, delivery, after sales service, financing etc. are the key factors which influence purchasing decisions in this area, nonetheless the Caterpillar brand name is enormously reassuring to customers and, in today's highly competitive business environment, is a powerful and valuable business asset, which often helps tip the balance in favour of its owner when customers are faced with a choice between competitive brands.

Caterpillar has an unmatched reputation for ruggedness and the ability to tackle daunting tasks efficiently and without fuss.

JCB

JCB, named from the initials of its founder Joseph Cyril Bamford, produced one of the world's first hydraulically operated tipping trailers in 1948, followed by a series of hydraulic lifting devices and then, in 1953, the JCB Excavator Mark I.

The company now has a worldwide reputation for excavators and backhoe loaders and a reputation, too, for constant improvement and innovation, substantial re-investment and close attention to research and engineering.

The term JCB has become almost the generic term for backhoe loaders and now appears in the Collins English Dictionary. The JCB logo (the curious tapered shape is derived from the fact that it was designed originally for use on the tapered cutter of a tractor-borne grass cutter) is similarly well-known worldwide.

In Britain, where the manufacturing industry suffers periodic crises of confidence, JCB is widely regarded as an exemplary story of efficient, dedicated management.

CASTROL

Castrol, and its GTX multipurpose motor oil, launched in 1968, is the world's leading specialist brand in the area of lubricants and allied products. The brand has a truly world-wide presence and Castrol lubricants are used in a wide range of industrial, marine, electrical, aeronautical and automotive applications.

The brand has benefited considerably from its tight focus and its unequivocal associations with lubrication – while major oil companies have much more broadly based brands covering a host of products besides lubricants, Castrol has maintained the position of a specialist. This has not, however, been easy as the major oil companies would prefer to sell their own branded lubricants through their fuel outlets rather than the Castrol brand. The brand owners have necessarily needed therefore to invest heavily in product development and in marketing including advertising, motorsport and other forms of sponsorship and promotions. In this they have been outstandingly successful and it is the power of the brand and its high consumer esteem and awareness which will ensure future success.

A major investment journal recently remarked that 'so much of the price of any of the Castrol products is in the brand name . . . not in the raw materials'.

ESSO/EXXON

The name Esso derives from the initials of the Standard Oil company of New Jersey (**SO**), the chief company of the Rockefeller Oil Trust set up in 1888. When however the Trust was split up in 1911 the new Standard Oil of New Jersey did not retain the Esso name in all parts of the United States and was therefore obliged to trade under different names in certain states, for example Sinclair Oil.

In 1973 the company decided to tackle this unsatisfactory situation head on and, in the United States and certain other countries, it abandoned the Esso name in favour of the newly coined name Exxon. At the time the name change cost the company the then incredible sum of $100 million, most of which was spent on new signage for retail outlets, repainting trucks, etc.

The name Exxon was selected mainly for its distinctiveness and legal availability (the only language in the world with a double X is, it seems, Maltese) though a clean 'baton change' from the old name to the new was also helped by the fact that both names are of approximately the same length and both have the same first letter. Care was taken to use broadly the same colour combinations for both the old and the new identities.

The legal clearance of the new name on a world basis and in a large number of trademark classes (the range of products was vast) proved a major task which had to be conducted in great secrecy.

PUT A TIGER IN YOUR TANK!

MAKES EVEN '23's SKIDDOO!

If your car is feeling its age, give it a 3-way power boost with High-energy Esso Extra. It's the gasoline that: (1) cleans up fouled carburetors to restore lost power and mileage; (2) neutralizes harmful engine deposits to renew full firing power; (3) gives you the high octane for youthful performance. To bring power back alive, hunt for the Tiger . . . at the sign of *Happy Motoring!*

HUMBLE OIL & REFINING COMPANY · AMERICA'S LEADING ENERGY COMPANY . . . MAKERS OF ESSO PRODUCTS · Esso

In 1973, Esso largely abandoned the Esso name in favour of Exxon, a move which cost, at the time, $100 million.

MICHELIN

For most of the last thirty years Michelin have dominated the world tyre market and have displayed an obsession with product quality, a passion for production efficiency and an attachment to brand values which have left competitors reeling. The Michelin name and the distinctive device mark of Bibendum (the little man made out of tyres) have assumed a position of enormous authority in relation to tyres worldwide.

Michelin was founded in 1890 but its success in recent decades can be directly related to its pioneering work in steel braced radial tyres from the 1930s onwards. It was recognised by tyre technologists as early as the last century that a steel braced radial tyre represented the 'ultimate' tyre – radial construction would ensure that a solid slab of rubber was presented to the road to maximise grip, supple sidewalls would ensure a good ride and steel bracing would stop the tyre squirming and deforming and would therefore minimise wear.

Most tyre manufacturers, however, chose to give only faint recognition to the steel braced radial tyre and this attitude persisted well into the 1960s. After all, they argued, steel bracing might result in a harsher ride and it was known that manufacturing tolerances on radial tyres were far higher than on cross-ply tyres. They were none too keen, either, to promote tyres which lasted three or four times as long as existing tyres or to junk all their existing tyre making equipment.

Michelin cared nothing for such arguments – they knew how the best tyres should be made and they focused all their efforts in one direction. By the mid-1960s both consumers and car manufacturers recognised that Michelin had got it right and competitors found themselves with the daunting task of catching up with a highly efficient competitor who was setting high performance, price and quality standards.

Much of the restructuring of the world's tyre industry in the 1970s and '80s – for example the demise of Dunlop and the sale of its European tyre interests to Sumitomo of Japan – is attributable to the success of Michelin. In recent years as tyre technology has become more ubiquitous Michelin's product lead has been closed but the brand's reputation for performance, quality and value remains.

The Michelin brand name and the famous Bidendum character constitute an outstandingly powerful brand in respect of all types of tyres.

MICHELIN UNIVERSAL CORD

Sure footed on all roads and in all kinds of weather

A sturdy, oversize cord tire that establishes a new standard for durability and freedom from skidding.

MICHELIN TIRE COMPANY · MILLTOWN, NEW JERSEY

Other factories: Clermont-Ferrand, France; London, England; Turin, Italy. — Dealers in all parts of the world.

VIRGIN ATLANTIC

The Virgin brand, so closely identified with the Group's founder, Richard Branson, is now used in a number of quite distinct product areas – music, retailing, television, publishing, travel and an airline. The name was first used in 1970 and the current logo, with its flamboyant 'V' shown as a tick, was adopted in 1978. In 1990 over £700 million worth of goods and services were sold under the brand name and Virgin ranked as the third largest private company in Britain.

When Virgin first entered the airline business it was widely predicted that it would go the same way as an earlier transatlantic independent operator, Laker – into liquidation – but the Virgin Atlantic airline has proved remarkably popular, not least because of its strongly branded 'Upper Class' business class service. The Virgin brand is now established as a broadly based entertainment and travel brand with a dependable but nonetheless somewhat 'fun' and irreverent image.

Virgin Atlantic is a newcomer in airline terms, yet is has established a powerful and clearly differentiated brand personality.

BOEING ☆ ▢

Boeing, a major wartime builder of military aircraft, first manufactured jet transports and tankers for the USAF after World War II and, having produced fifty-six propeller driven Stratocruisers for civilian use, saw the need for a new passenger jet. The predecessor of the Boeing 707 flew in July 1954 and in October 1955 Pan American placed an order for twenty of the new aircraft; the first 707 entered service on 26th October 1958.

In 1952 when Boeing first seriously considered building a passenger jet transport they needed to allocate to it a development code number. Numbers up to 499 had already been assigned and 500 to 699 had been reserved for industrial products and gas turbines. The project was therefore coded as project 707, a felicitous choice which has

already led to a family of aircraft embracing the 727, 737, 747, 757 and 767 models.

Boeing is the world's leading manufacturer of military and commercial transport aircraft and has only two serious competitors in the non-communist world – McDonnell Douglas and the increasingly important Airbus Industrie. Boeing is now able to claim that one of its aircraft takes off or lands somewhere in the world every two and a half seconds.

Boeing's new 747-400 flies non-stop for up to fourteen hours with a passenger load of up to 400 people – the company's contribution to international travel is quite unmatched.

CONCORDE

It is somewhat ironic that a venture which proved to be for its sponsors (the British and French Governments) one of the most costly commercial failures of all time should have led to the development of an aircraft which, a quarter of a century after it first flew, is still by far the fastest and most elegant passenger aircraft in the world and still, by a huge margin, the means of international transport which carries most prestige. Concorde, as a means of transportation, carries a *cachet* that no other aircraft can match. But even within the rarified world of the frequent Concorde traveller there are little nuances which are

When the French and British Governments first discussed co-operation on the building of a supersonic passenger aircraft the question of the name was one of the thorniest issues which had to be resolved.

considered important. The front cabin, for example, is the place to be, not the rear cabin.

When the British and French Governments first decided to co-operate in the development of a supersonic passenger aircraft one early decision which needed to be made was what to call it. Resolving the issue almost led to the collapse of the project: the name Concord/Concorde was agreed on at an early stage, but the British wanted the English spelling, the French the French. Resolving this delicate issue, it is reputed, required diplomatic skills of the highest order.

LEISURE AND CULTURAL

IN 'THE GRADUATE', THE ADVICE given to Benjamin Braddock, the character played by Dustin Hoffman, about his career was to 'get into plastics'. For much of the last three decades a popular piece of advice for companies has been to get into the leisure industry, wherever and however they can. The conventional wisdom is that new office and manufacturing technology, combined with higher and higher wages will find people with more spare time on their hands and more money in their pockets to buy goods and services to fill that time.

To a certain extent, at least, this view of the prospects for the leisure industry has been borne out but companies have found it extremely difficult to build major brands in this wide and highly fragmented sector.

Hotels are a case in point; merger and takeover activity in this sector has been frantic and the groupings and re-groupings which have taken place resemble, quite uncannily, a game of Monopoly. In the middle of all this change a few trusted brands continue on and are mainly made up of individual hotels rather than large chains: the Okura in Tokyo, Claridges in London, the Ritz in Paris and The Pierre in New York.

In the publishing industry, however, the power and value of brands has been fully realised. In 1984, News Group, the Australian flagship company of Rupert Murdoch's worldwide publishing empire, included a valuation for 'publishing titles' in its balance sheet. Murdoch did this because the 'goodwill' element of publishing acquisitions — the difference between the value of the net assets and the price paid — can be enormous and, being an acquisitive company, the goodwill write-offs which his company was being forced to take were ravaging his balance sheet. He

knew well that much of the 'goodwill' he was buying comprised the publishing titles; he therefore placed a value on these and included this valuation in the balance sheet. This simple procedure restored his balance sheet, solved many of the problems of goodwill write-offs and dramatically reduced gearing.

Murdoch's example in valuing his 'mastheads' has been widely followed by other publishers around the world and, too, has served to pave the way for brand valuations in other industries ('mastheads' or 'publishing titles' are after all, merely brands by a different name). It has also provided the basis for an unprecedented round of merger and acquisition activity as publishing titles quickly came to be recognised as potential assets of considerable worth due to the promise they hold for consumer loyalty and hence for future cash flows and profits.

The toy industry has also seen enormous changes over the last three decades. There cannot be many parents who do not believe that their children have several times as many toys as they did when they were children. The variety of toys is also changing along with the quantities consumed. Sophisticated electronic and video games now account for a large proportion of expenditure on toys yet, despite this rapid change, popular trusted brands such as LEGO bricks, Barbie, Matchbox and Fisher-Price continue unchecked, as the pleasures and satisfactions they deliver are relatively timeless and are not subject to constant shifts in fashion.

The brands we cover in this book, however, are not just those in the hotels, publishing and toy sectors. We also feature brands of pianos, films and those concerned with learning and scholarship — clearly the sector is a broad one!

LEISURE & CULTURAL

BRAND	LEADERSHIP	STABILITY	MARKET	INTERNATIONALITY	TREND	SUPPORT	PROTECTION	TOTAL
BARBIE	○	○	□	□	□	□	●	□
BERLITZ		○	□	○	□		●	○
CLUB MED	○	□	□	□	□	○	●	□
FINANCIAL TIMES	○	●	□		□	□	●	○
FISHER-PRICE	□	○	□	□	□	□	●	□
HARVARD		●	●	□	□	○	●	○
HILTON		○	□	●	□	○	□	○
HOLIDAY INN	○	□	□	●	□	○	●	□
LEGO	□	□	□	●	□	●	●	□
MATCHBOX	○	□	□	□	□	○	●	□
MONOPOLY	○	□	○	○	○		△	○
PLAYBOY	○	○	□	□	○		●	○
READER'S DIGEST	□	●	□	●	□		●	□
SCRABBLE	○	○	○	○	□		□	○
STEINWAY	□	●	□	○	○		●	○
TRIVIAL PURSUIT	○	○	□		○	○	●	○
VOGUE	○	□	□	○	□	○	●	□
WALT DISNEY ★	□	●	□	●	●	□	●	□

KEY ★★ Top Ten brand ★ Top Fifty brand ● exceptionally strong □ very strong ○ strong △ problem area

CLUB MED

Club Med (properly Club Méditerranée) is a unique holiday business built around a unique concept – the fully equipped but carefree holiday village. The moving force in Club Med (at least as far as its one million guests are concerned) is the GO or *Gentil Organisateur*. The GO, loosely translated into English as the Gentle Organiser, is the life and soul of the village and is expected to be available, creative and enthusiastic in making the visit of all guests – or GMs, Gentle Members – a happy and relaxed one. The concept of the GO has given Club Med a unique spirit and this, combined with an all-inclusive price package, unmatched locations and excellent facilities gives Club Méditerranée its unique character.

Club Med now owns or manages 100 villages worldwide as well as timeshares, apartments, a City Club and other facilities and its revenues exceed $1 billion.

Club Med has successfully introduced to a world audience an entirely new concept in holidays and leisure.

HILTON

Hilton is a brand which is synonymous internationally with good hotelkeeping. Hilton was founded by Conrad Hilton and in 1964 was split into two quite separate companies, the domestic US operation and Hilton International. Hilton International became part of United Airlines and in 1987 was sold to Britain's Ladbroke Group for £645 million. The US Hilton Hotels, with 280 hotels and the famous Waldorf-Astoria in New York, continued as a separate, publicly quoted company, though throughout 1989 and 1990 speculation about a takeover sent the share price up from $50 to $115.50 in eight months

valuing the company at almost $6 billion. Much of the justification for the company's value is the esteem in which the company's brand name is held.

Some observers have claimed however that the separation of the US and International businesses has inevitably led to a discontinuity in the brand's image as between the US and the rest of the world. In the US the brand is not positioned as being quite as exclusive as it is in, for example, Europe.

Hilton International and Hilton US are now unconnected businesses under quite separate control, a situation which can be hazardous to a brand unless care is taken.

HOLIDAY INN

Holiday Inn hotels was founded in the US in 1951 as a value-for-money motel chain. The rapid expansion of the inter-state highway system provided a major opportunity for the new company and, mainly through the use of franchising, Holiday Inn became the largest hotel chain in the world, over three times the size of its nearest rival.

As with Hilton, Holiday Inn was split into separate operating companies and in 1987 Britain's Bass acquired the Holiday Inn chain outside North America and Mexico; in 1989 they paid $2 billion for the rest of Holiday Inn.

Holiday Inn's origins are firmly rooted in no-frills, good value hotel accommodation but, over the years, the company has developed into restaurants and casinos and into suite hotels. It has also set up a chain of 'four star plus' hotels under the Holiday Inn Crowne Plaza brand in an attempt to add value and continue the repositioning of Holiday Inn as a broadly based hotel brand offering a wide range of services.

Holiday Inn has successfully repositioned itself as a broadly based hotel chain from the no-frills, budget end of the market.

HARVARD

The name Harvard and the 'VE-RI-TAS' shield have been used commercially on sportswear (e.g. T-Shirts, sweatshirts, sports caps etc.) since the 1950s but they have denoted educational excellence since Harvard University was founded in 1636.

Harvard's brand licensing programme is particularly interesting. The items which the University will license include sportswear (excluding protective headgear), scarves, desk accessories, watches, jewellery, school supplies etc. Those they will not license include ashtrays, shot glasses, butane lighters, weapons of any kind, food and beverages.

The terms of a US license agreement with Harvard include a $300 up-front one-time license fee, a 7·5 per cent royalty on sales, a $1,000 minimum annual royalty, a mandate to submit samples and designs before production of any products begins, assignment of copyrightable material to Harvard, and a $1 million comprehensive

The Harvard name and shield do not just denote academic excellence but are also a source of licensing income.

general liability insurance policy.

Harvard has also operated a trademark licensing program in Japan for some years; however, an exclusive licensing agent is used there, and sub-licenses have been granted to Japanese companies for appropriate products to be distributed and sold in Japan only. Harvard University has also begun trademark licensing in Australia and in Canada (on non-exclusive bases) and is expanding its operations to include Europe.

The income generated by the Trademark Program, after paying the nominal expenses of the Program, is used for student aid at Harvard University. In order to maintain a diverse student body, Harvard's policy is to accept students on academic merit regardless of financial ability. The Trademark Program contributes between $300,000 – $500,000 per year to support students' attendance at Harvard University.

STEINWAY

Steinway, a US piano company founded by a German immigrant, is synonymous with fine pianos. The brand imagery is supported in large part by the fact that Steinway pianos are the pianos of choice of many, if not most, of the world's leading pianists. Indeed, for selected 'Steinway Artists', Steinway & Sons makes a Steinway piano available wherever they perform publicly in exchange for the out-of-pocket expenses of delivery and in-hall tuning charges. Steinway now has 350 pianos stationed with authorised dealers around the US. But Steinway pianos are also excellent investments. The company claims that its concert grands have, over a ten year period, appreciated more than gold, wine and many vintage cars!

STEINWAY & SONS

The world famous Steinway piano brand is chosen by many leading pianists.

BERLITZ

Berlitz is the world's leading brand in foreign language instruction. It has 260 language centres in twenty-five countries and annual revenues of some $250 million.

Like many great brands it was founded in the United States and its strong worldwide recognition stems at least in part from the powerful cultural influence of Hollywood and US popular entertainment on world taste due to the fact that Berlitz language courses frequently featured in movies, songs and musicals.

If you are considering learning a foreign language or improving your language skills the chances are in favour of you considering using Berlitz.

Like many international brands the name Berlitz is strong, distinctive, fairly short and has a letter formation which is memorable and unusual. Berlitz became in 1988 part of Maxwell Communication Corporation as a result of MCC's purchase of Macmillan (US) and in 1989 MCC also acquired Linguarama. On distinctiveness and memorability alone one would rate Berlitz above Linguarama, a name which is somewhat complicated, difficult to pronounce and which has none of the visual impact of Berlitz.

WALT DISNEY

The Walt Disney company virtually invented the business of 'character merchandising' – licensing others to use your brand (usually a literary, television or movie character such as Mickey Mouse, Kojak or Thomas the Tank Engine) on products not related to the business activity for which the character was originally developed. Thus, Mickey Mouse and his friends are now used not just in films, TV, records, video, comics, books and magazines, but also on clothing, watches, toys, jewellery, lunch boxes, children's furniture and even on food. Recently, for example, Disney signed an eleven year licensing agreement with Nestlé, the world's biggest food company, and from 1991 until 2002 Nestlé will have the exclusive right to Disney characters on branded foods in Europe and certain other countries. Disney will earn $176 million in license fees and Nestlé knows it has a winner – it successfully pioneered the concept in West Germany with Mickey Mousse, a chocolate-flavoured dessert.

Disney and Mickey Mouse became household names in 1928 with Steamboat Willie. Now the company has huge publishing interests, theme parks (in California, Florida,

Disney

Japan and France, the latter under construction), movie studios, record labels, stores, a mail order business, hotels and resorts and even a television station (KCAT in Los Angeles). Disney's philosophy is to build 'an integrated system in which each Disney property enhances and reinforces the whole'. As such, the company is an extraordinary example of the power which can flow from well managed brand properties.

Walt Disney's portfolio of world famous trademarks is probably unmatched and its brand properties are assets of enormous value.

THE FINANCIAL TIMES

The *Financial Times*, when launched in 1888 had on its mast-head 'Without Fear and Without Favour' and described itself as the friend of 'The Honest Financier' and of 'The Respectable Broker', the enemy of 'The Unprincipled Promoter' and of 'The Gambling Operator'. It is clear that Stock Market hype, unscrupulous promoters and gullible investors are not just phenomena of the late Twentieth Century.

The *Financial Times* is now established as one of the world's leading English language newspapers. It is accurate and authoritative and its daily world-wide circulation is now almost 300,000. In addition to the London edition international editions are printed in Frankfurt, New York, Roubaix (France) and

FINANCIAL TIMES
EUROPE'S BUSINESS NEWSPAPER

Tokyo and the familiar 'FT pink' newsprint is now recognised by businessmen around the world.

Indeed, the decision to print the FT on pink paper, taken in 1893 by Douglas MacRae, is a stroke of marketing genius and is the one single factor which gives the brand such distinctiveness. As a simple but effective branding device it stands in a league of its own. Its only drawback is that of protectability – establishing any proprietary rights in a colour is very difficult.

The *Financial Times* pink paper differentiates it in a simple but striking fashion and contributes to a brand of great power and authority.

VOGUE

Vogue is a publishing title of the mighty Condé Nast publishing empire based in the US. Though it is a coherent and powerful world brand with the same positioning and general appearance in all markets it does in fact appear as a series of national editions (UK, US, France, etc), each with its own local orientation and appeal.

On an international basis, *Vogue* has become synonymous with sophistication and high fashion. In the US and Europe scores of glossy new magazines for women have been launched in recent years with large promotional budgets and high expectations, but none has come close to challenging *Vogue*.

Vogue has an image of style and sophistication which allows it to prosper in an increasingly crowded publishing market.

MONOPOLY

Monopoly, one of the world's great board games, is the registered trademark of Parker Brothers, part of Tonka Corporation of the US, and is produced in Britain under license by Waddingtons Games and by other licensees in other markets.

Though in essence the game remains unchanged in whatever market it is sold, 'local' versions use local street names, spellings and so forth so as to reflect local tastes and conditions, a classic example of 'think global, act local', a key lesson in international branding. The US Boardwalk, for example, becomes Mayfair in the UK version, Rue de la Paix in French and Paseo del Prado in Spanish. 'Monopoly money' is also always in the local currency. Indeed, seeing a Monopoly game in a foreign country with 'funny' street names and 'funny money' has been identified as one of the main cultural shocks experienced by the novice traveller.

The licensors of Monopoly are fiercely protective of their trademarks, copyrights and registered designs, and rightly so. As with all such powerful brand names, it is tempting for

MONOPOLY

REGISTERED TRADE MARK

third parties to attempt to 'borrow' some of the brand's goodwill and apply it to their own products. The brand owners have been involved over the years in some well-documented infringement cases and know that, in protecting their brand, they cannot be too vigilant.

The Monopoly brand is so familiar that terms such as 'do not pass GO' are now recognised around the world.

MATCHBOX

Matchbox toys, and in particular Matchbox cars, have been an integral part of childhood since they were launched in the UK in 1947 though today the products are manufactured mainly in Thailand and mainland China. Matchbox toys are now available in over 120 countries and an astonishing three billion toy Matchbox vehicles have been sold over the years, more than the combined output of General Motors, Ford, Chrysler and Toyota.

Matchbox is the clear number one toy vehicle brand throughout Europe and this leadership position has been achieved largely through better design, better assembly and a greater attention to detail than its rivals.

Matchbox diecast toy cars have been loved by boys for generations and well-preserved, early models which have their original packaging, are collectors' items.

Indeed, it is the authenticity of Matchbox models that makes the brand a must for all young boys and for some not so young boys – Matchbox collector's clubs flourish in many countries and many of the more collectible models are way beyond the pocket money of even the most affluent boy.

TRIVIAL PURSUIT

Trivial Pursuit was invented in 1981 by three Canadians, Chris Haney, John Haney, and Scott Abbott and worldwide sales of the game are now well in excess of fifty million sets. Though the game itself is, obviously, of critical importance to its success, the decision to commercialise the game worldwide through a series of licensing arrangements has been the key to its swift acceptance on an international basis.

Horn Abbot Ltd, based in Barbados, hold all copyright, trademark, patent and other 'intellectual property' rights relating to the game and authorise licensees around the world to market the game. Each country has its own questions and special editions of the game have been developed for young players and other age categories as well as for special interest groups (e.g. film, music, sport).

Many people have good ideas but only a few have the astuteness to commercialise them successfully and retain in full the intellectual property in their ideas. Trivial Pursuit is an example of how it can be done.

FISHER-PRICE

In 1930 Herman G Fisher and Irving L Price founded their toy business on the precept that each toy should have 'intrinsic' play value, ingenuity, strong construction, value for the money and action. 'Children', they wrote, 'love best the gay, cheerful, friendly toys with amusing action, toys that do something new and surprising and funny'. These ideas were immediately translated into action – their first line of products included Granny Doodle and Doctor Doodle, gaily decorated toys made from wood which, when they were pulled, moved their beaks and quacked merrily. Such lighthearted elements are now key distinguishing traits of the Fisher-Price line of toys.

Fisher-Price now is a company of 10,000 employees which enjoys a worldwide reputation for robust, enjoyable, good quality, good value for money toys. The company also enjoys a reputation for customer care and

While other toys break or lose their appeal, Fisher-Price toys, it seems, go on for ever. They are, therefore, highly popular with both parents and children.

service – its Consumer Affairs Department deals with 250,000 letters and 'phone calls a year. Some 84 per cent of all infant and pre-school children in the developed world now own a Fisher-Price toy.

PLAYBOY

Hugh Hefner's Playboy brand was considered in the 1960s and 1970s to be both outrageous and exciting. Playboy started life as a glossy soft-porn magazine. It was a clever mixture of titillating sex and man-about-town sophistication. It reassured its readers that all red-blooded, sensible, successful males liked to look at wholesome, pretty, unclad girls and its confidence and quality meant that it escaped any association with the poorly produced men's magazines which had previously been the staple soft-porn products.

Playboy expanded into Playboy Clubs (famous for their 'bunnies') and also into licensing, for example of fragrances, clothing, etc. Hugh Hefner's extravagant lifestyle (e.g. a private black DC9 jet complete with sunken bath and the famous bunny logo on the tail) and his flair for publicity meant that Playboy became virtually a symbol of the emancipated, post-pill male.

Things started to go wrong, however, in the early 1980s. Playboy sold its highly lucrative

In recent years Playboy has returned mainly to its publishing roots, an area where the brand has retained its awareness and appeal.

London casinos in 1982 after a licence renewal was refused and later pulled out of Atlantic City. Playboy Enterprises Inc. is now run by Christie Hefner, daughter of Hugh, an altogether less flamboyant character. The company's focus now is on the magazine, on brand licensing and on videos. Though awareness of the Playboy brand is still very high, it has little of the celebrity and excitement today which it once had.

BARBIE

The Barbie fashion doll is now over thirty years old yet has retained its appeal for young girls throughout this period and has survived competition from Japan, Hong Kong and Taiwan without any apparent difficulties. Indeed, in an industry which is remarkably fickle and changeable and where a company's futures are based entirely on its latest collection Barbie has proved to have extraordinary staying power.

Barbie is owned by Mattel, the world's biggest independent toy manufacturer and is the most visible brand within its portfolio. Tomy, Japan's major toy company, unlike Mattel has no such single powerful and appealing brand and is unable therefore to benefit from the stability and certainty which a major brand can bring to an unstable and uncertain business.

In the helter-skelter, ever-changing toy industry, the Barbie fashion doll is a phenomenon.

READER'S DIGEST

Reader's Digest is reckoned to be 'the world's most widely read magazine'. Founded in a New York basement in 1922 by DeWitt and Lila Wallace the magazine has become the personification of conservative middle of the road opinion not just in the US by around the world. Now *Reader's Digest* is based in Pleasantville, a small town forty miles up the Hudson from New York and each monthly issue, published in thirty-nine editions and in fifteen languages, sells twenty-eight million copies and attracts some 100 million readers. In *Reader's Digest*'s own in-house language its home town of Pleasantville is known as P-Ville and staff members are known as Digesters and the clubby atmosphere of the Company's headquarters is carried through into the magazine and is shared by readers. Subscribers to *Reader's Digest*, an exceptionally loyal customer base, share *Reader's Digest*'s vision of the world and

enjoy the idiosyncrasy, even quirkiness of the magazine. *Reader's Digest* is therefore an exceptionally powerful brand property. The company now makes most of its profits, however, not from the magazine but from books, records, videos and other home entertainment products. It is also starting to market magazines for other publishers as well as insurance – the company's database is huge (more than half the households in the US, for example) and the confidence inspired by the *Reader's Digest* brand name is such that it can be applied successfully to all types of broadly related goods and services.

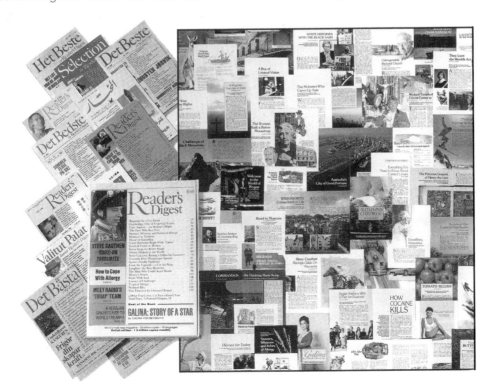

Even though the *Reader's Digest* brand is adapted to suit the needs of different audiences the overall cohesion of the brand is fully retained.

LEGO

The LEGO brand name is virtually synonymous with interlocking toy building bricks; indeed, it is so synonymous that its owners, LEGO System of Billund in Denmark, maintain a very active trademark policing programme in all countries where the mark is used – 125 in all – to ensure that any misuse of the name, inadvertent or otherwise, is quickly stopped.

The name LEGO is derived from the Danish words 'leg godt', 'play well' in English, and was adopted in 1934 by the company's founder Ole Kirk Christiansen. The plastic LEGO brick was not, however, introduced until 1949 – the company's early products were mainly sturdy wooden toys such as ducks, prams and cars.

LEGO products are now sold throughout the world – the company manufactures in five countries and has owned sales companies in over twenty and the company takes enormous care to ensure that it fully complies with all safety legislation and other statutory requirements. It also works closely with educationalists, research institutes and other professional advisers to ensure that the LEGO name stands for the highest product and ethical standards.

The LEGO Group are keen supporters of Marques, a European association of trademark owners, evidence of the importance and value which the company attaches to its brand name.

SCRABBLE

Though some good ideas catch on instantly others have a much harder job to reach the limelight. Scrabble falls into the latter category. It was developed in the 1930s by Alfred Butts, a New York architect and he tried a series of names for his new game including 'It', 'Alph' (a play on his name), 'Lexiko' and 'Criss-Crosswords'. After the Second World War Butts teamed up with James Brunot, a government social worker and eventually in 1949 the game was launched as Scrabble, a name selected from a list of words submitted by a trademark attorney. It finally took off in 1952 with the help of Macy's Department Store in New York whose Chairman, Jack Strauss, had played the game with friends and placed a large order.

SCRABBLE®

Today, worldwide rights outside USA, Canada and Australia are held by J W Spear & Sons PLC and Scrabble is one of the most popular board games in the world; in the UK alone there are well over 200 Scrabble clubs as well as a national championship.

The Scrabble game is considered highly enjoyable and the Scrabble name itself is curiously satisfying – it 'echoes' the nature of the game and has a strong element of fun.

Trademark attorneys do not normally also aspire to be 'wordsmiths'. The Scrabble brand name was, however, invented by a trademark attorney and is a classic 'associative' trademark.

RETAIL, AGENCY AND CREDIT

BRANDING IS FREQUENTLY SEEN as the exclusive preserve of the manufacturer and the retailer is seen as the conduit through which manufacturers' brands pass in order to reach the consumer. This view is, however, becoming increasingly outdated and is frequently not shared by the retailer, a development which has potent implications for many brand owners.

The adoption of branding techniques by retailers such as IKEA, Tesco, Marks & Spencer and Sainsbury's is having a powerful influence on brand owners, not just in grocery sectors but across the board and this influence seems quite certain to grow. Generally retailers are neutral towards brand owners; they have no wish to destroy manufacturers' brands and are by no means antagonistic towards such brands. Nonetheless, they will not support manufacturers' brands unless there is some benefit to themselves in doing so. Many major retailers now adopt a 'mixed' branding policy: they stock those manufacturers' brands which are liked and respected by consumers and which are well-priced and supported by their owners. They also ensure that they have well-priced, well-packaged own label products in all key product sectors.

Brand owners need to become much more active if they are to meet the 'threat' from own label. Product range and quality will need to be improved and in many areas new product development activity will need to be stepped up. Most importantly, the responsiveness of manufacturers to the needs of the consumer requires improvement.

Achieving greater responsiveness will not be easy. One of the strengths of the retailer is that his brand inevitably has a broadly based personality and positioning. Harrods, for example, has powerful attributes of quality and sophistication, all in a relatively generalised 'British' context. The Harrods brand is not particularised to toys, food or clothing, and the brand can, therefore, be applied with more-or-less equal ease to a bottle of Scotch whisky as to an expensive coat. As long as certain qualities and values are preserved it is fairly unlikely that the brand will suffer.

This situation is not normally true for manufacturers' brands. Generally such brands have a much more targeted positioning and part of the reason that manufacturers frequently appear much more leaden-footed than retailers in brand development activities is that much more care needs to be taken with manufacturers' brands to ensure that any development enhances the brand's appeal.

Retailing is also extending into totally new service areas — car rentals, florist services, restaurants — and branding is playing an important rôle in providing consumers with confidence and structure in what could be a bewildering shopping environment. Catering, for example, has become increasingly branded over the last twenty to thirty years.

There now exists in the US, UK and elsewhere a large number of branded food chains including McDonald's, Pizza Hut, Kentucky Fried Chicken and scores of others. It is estimated that, in the United States, more meals are consumed out of the home than in, and that the majority of these are eaten in 'branded' food outlets.

Retailing has undergone a revolution in recent decades and this revolution is by no means completed. Manufacturers face increased competition from the retailers and the concept of retail branding is being extended into entirely new areas.

RETAIL, AGENCY & CREDIT

BRAND	LEADERSHIP	STABILITY	MARKET	INTERNATIONALITY	TREND	SUPPORT	PROTECTION	TOTAL
AMERICAN EXPRESS ★★	●	■	●	●	■	●	●	●
HARRODS	■	■	■	■	○		●	■
HERTZ ★	■	■	■	●	■	■	●	■
IKEA	○	○	■	○	■	○	●	○
INTERFLORA	■	●	■	●	■		●	■
McDONALD'S ★★	●	●	■	●	●	●	●	●
THOMAS COOK	■	●	■	●	○	■	●	■
VISA ★	■	■	●	●	■	■	●	■

KEY ★★ Top Ten brand ★ Top Fifty brand ● exceptionally strong ■ very strong ○ strong △ problem area

HARRODS ☐

It is perhaps curious to list as an international brand a retail store which, in effect, has only one main outlet – in Knightsbridge in Central London. Harrods, however, is recognised worldwide and has a powerful reputation for quality and excellence, all in a somewhat 'British' context. Harrods is, potentially, one of the most licensable brands in the world because, being a luxury retail brand, it could be applied equally successfully to almost any up-market product.

Though Harrods is essentially a single outlet retailer, the brand is known and respected around the world.

AMERICAN EXPRESS ☆ ☆ ●

A key function of banking has always been to provide facilities for travellers – after all any traveller carrying large sums of money has always been at considerable risk. Thus the Medici family, based in Florence, provided facilities to travellers in the Middle Ages and in the Eighteenth Century correspondent banks across Europe provided similar arrangements for wealthy travellers taking the Grand Tour.

By the late Nineteenth Century American Express had become one of the best known financial services brands in the US and its brand awareness was based mainly on the travellers cheque, a product which retains a remarkable appeal even today. But it is the American Express card which is now the most visible and potent manifestation of the brand. Indeed, though American Express is a broadly based financial services group, to many people around the world the brand is the card and nothing more.

The card was invented in 1958 and proved to be an instant success. It conferred an immediate status on users in situations where people most feel a need for such status – settling a restaurant bill after a client lunch, for example – and the American Express brand has maintained its status and exclusivity

despite powerful competition from more widely available products such as Visa and MasterCard.

Interestingly, an early competitor, Diners Club, has not fared as well as American Express due in part, it is believed, to the choice of name. The Diners Club name was a suitable choice provided the card was used only in restaurants; once, however, charge cards came to be used in a much wider range of situations the positioning conferred by the name became increasingly inappropriate.

American Express, a company with a long tradition, is now most closely associated with a very contemporary phenomenon – the charge card.

HERTZ ☆ ☐

Would Hertz have fared as well if it had been called U-Rent or Instacar? Throughout the world the brand name Hertz is immediately identified with car rental services and is proof of the fact that branding can apply highly successfully to services as well as to 'things'. It is also proof of the fact that powerful brand names by no means need to be descriptive.

Hertz is No. 1 in car hire and intends to remain so. The brand is distinctive, well managed and strongly supported.

THOMAS COOK

The Thomas Cook Group was started in the mid-Nineteenth Century providing travel services for the wealthy Victorian gentry, newly emancipated by the invention of railways and steam-driven ships. It was the brainchild of a young Englishman, Thomas Cook himself, who pioneered the concept of pre-arranged low-cost travel. His first tour lasted less than a day and cost only a shilling, but its success marked the beginning of what would become the largest, most respected organisation in the travel industry.

Today, the Thomas Cook Group is a major world company, a subsidiary of Midland Bank plc and an employer of almost 7,000 people. Its main activities include the provision of business and leisure travel services, travellers cheques and foreign exchange – all on a worldwide basis. Central to the success of these services however is the Thomas Cook name and the unequivocal associations this has with travel.

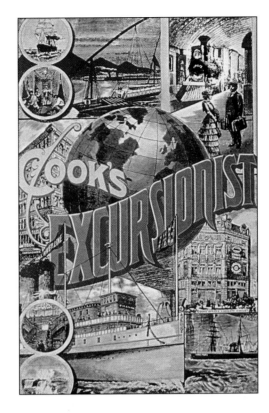

In the rapidly developing travel market, Thomas Cook is one of the world's best known and most respected brand names.

INTERFLORA

Commercial floristry is a business where, as in catering, the product has to be prepared on the premises. It is a business which, therefore, lends itself to small proprietor-managed businesses. Interflora is a member-owned association of independent florists – 55,000 worldwide – who co-operate in the provision of a high speed, personal, international delivery service. A private currency, called by members the Fleurin, and based on the Swiss franc, is used to settle internal accounts and the association also assists with training and the maintenance of trading standards.

The core *raison-d'être* of Interflora is, however, the provision of a worldwide flower delivery service under a single brand name. In this it has been remarkably successful – Interflora's annual business is currently well in

excess of £50 million, the brand name inspires confidence and reassurance and is almost synonymous with the service offered. Interflora, at the same time, offer an added dimension and authority to the businesses of its members.

The Interflora brand name and the winged messenger allow independent florists to work together in the provision of a highly sophisticated international service.

McDONALD'S ☆ ☆ ●

McDonald's, founded as recently as 1955, is now the largest and fastest growing restaurant chain in the world. Today it operates some 11,500 restaurants in fifty-two countries and it continues to expand.

Its formula is simple – it offers quality, service, cleanliness and value (in McDonald's terminology – QSC & V), its products are considered tasty and appetising and what it delivers is predictable – you know what you are going to get.

Many of the great branding success stories of the last thirty years have been in the area of retailing and services. In the late Nineteenth and early Twentieth Century most branding was concerned with things – Kodak film, Schweppes mixers, Ivory soap – and the extension of the concept of branding to services is, except in a few instances, a modern phenomenon.

Services are altogether more difficult to brand than products. Whereas Procter and Gamble can control the quality of Ivory soap in its own factories and can be confident that, at point of sale, an unpleasant or uncaring shop assistant will have no effect on how the consumer perceives its brand, this is not true of services. The product itself is prepared and provided at point of sale and so a scruffy, indifferent or unpleasant sales assistant can, at point of sale and way distant from the brand owner, seriously damage the brand in the eyes of the consumer.

McDonald's genius has been to provide a high quality food product and to control the process at every step in the operation – raw material, preparation, delivery, advertising, retail presentation etc.

The success of McDonald's, and its unique franchising skills, have been widely copied but McDonald's is still the acknowledged master of fast food retailing.

The concept behind the McDonald's brand, and its implementation, is widely considered to be quite brilliant, not least by competitors.

IKEA

IKEA is Sweden's – and Europe's – largest furniture retailing group and is widely tipped to be the clear Number One worldwide by the turn of the century. IKEA's formula is simple:

- huge out-of-town retail units with ample parking and enormous choice, plus home accessories, decorating hints, a restaurant, a crêche, clean toilets etc. – in fact, an environment which is designed to make furniture buying a pleasant activity and provide a day out for all the family.
- excellent value
- good quality
- instant availability from stock.

IKEA's furniture has a distinct 'Scandinavian' feel to it but, in Europe and beyond, the IKEA promise of choice, price, quality and availability has proved irresistible.

Levitz in the US, Queensway in Britain and others around the world, have all striven to make out-of-town furniture retailing profitable and successful. But IKEA has done the best job and seems likely to emerge as the world's leading brand in this sector.

VISA

Visa International is a credit and debit card payment system operator. Its major rival is the MasterCard network and the two brands are now in fierce competition for global leadership of the plastic card payment system market. The market is, however, a complex and rapidly changing one – success depends not just upon product and brand qualities but upon widespread distribution through participating banks and financial service organisations and upon availability of the service at point of sale. Rapid development and fierce international competition in the 'payment by plastic' market, the increase of electronic banking, changing alliances between banks and payment system operators, the launch of value added services (e.g. gold cards and debit cards), the entry of retailers into the fray and the development of EftPos systems are all tending to create in this area a kind of 'brand soup' which experts understand but which is often confusing to the consumer. In such a situation the reassurance provided by powerful brands such as Visa will be of increasing value.

The Visa brand name is well chosen – it has desirable connotations on an international basis with freedom, movement and the breaking down of boundaries.

WEAPONS

WEAPONS AND FIREARMS have always held an intense fascination and, most recently under the euphemism 'defence', have been a major area of public expenditure. Guns have been with us from the Fourteenth Century 'hand gonne' to, more recently, the Gatling gun, Hiram Maxim's machine gun, the Sten gun and the Kalashnikov rifle. Larger scale branded weapons include the Exocet missile and the Polaris submarine. Weapons are an unfortunate but, it seems, inevitably part of our lives. Inevitably, too, they have developed a mystique and an emotional charge which confers upon them powerful imagery and associations. The weapons industry relies on international trade and the importance of good brand management is vital if manufacturers are to succeed in this specialist market.

WEAPONS								
BRAND	LEADERSHIP	STABILITY	MARKET	INTERNATIONALITY	TREND	SUPPORT	PROTECTION	TOTAL
COLT	☐	●	☐	●	☐	☐	●	☐
EXOCET	○	△	☐	☐	☐		●	
KALASHNIKOV	☐	☐	☐	☐	○		●	○

KEY ★★ Top Ten brand ★ Top Fifty brand ● exceptionally strong ☐ very strong ○ strong △ problem area

KALASHNIKOV

The Kalashnikov AK-47 assault rifle with its characteristic curved magazine is arguably the most successful rifle of the Twentieth Century and ranks therefore alongside Colt, Remington and Lee Enfield in the rifle and hand gun hall of fame.

It was designed by Mikhail Kalashnikov of the Soviet Union and though not the most accurate of weapons, is prized for its simple, rugged construction and its reliability. Almost twenty million have now been built in a dozen countries. It is the standard rifle of the Soviet army and much prized by guerilla groups around the world.

The name itself, with its strong letter construction and alliteration, is curiously well suited to the product – it sounds powerful and destructive. When you say the name Kalashnikov you can almost hear the sound of rifle shots.

Observers of branding are waiting for Soviet brand owners to enter the brand licensing market. It is difficult to see, however, how the Kalashnikov name could be extended outside the weapons market.

COLT

SYMBOL OF QUALITY SINCE 1836

Sam Colt started his original firearms business in Paterson, New Jersey in 1836 but moved to Hartford, Connecticut in 1845. Since then the names Colt and Hartford have always been closely connected, particularly since the latter part of the Nineteenth Century when the Colt revolver became enormously popular in both North America and Europe.

Colt's revolver made obsolete the one and two barrel flintlock pistols previously available and more than thirty million revolvers, pistols and rifles have since been manufactured bearing the Colt name. The most famous of these is the Single Action Army Model 1873, 'the gun that won the West'.

The name Colt now has powerful asociations with masculinity, the outdoor life, the Wild West and with 'all American' values. In early 1990 Colt Firearms was purchased from its parent company and re-named Colt's Manufacturing Company. The company continues to manufacture a wide range of revolvers, pistols and rifles but in addition, it is rumoured, it plans an active brand licensing programme in areas such as male fragrances, sports equipment and sportswear in order to utilize more fully the outstanding power and appeal of the Colt brand name.

A Heritage of
Fine Craftsmanship

Hartford, CT 06101

The concept of the personal firearm is particularly well established in the US yet the Colt brand is familiar around the world.

EXOCET

Few except the military had ever heard of the French Exocet guided missile built by Aérospatiale until the 1983 Falklands War. Almost overnight the successful use by the Argentine Air Force of Exocet air to surface missiles to sink British ships, notably HMS Sheffield, made the brand a household name. (In fact the missile which hit HMS Sheffield did not explode but the ship was destroyed by a fire started by the still-burning rocket engine).

Interestingly, it appears that in subsequent years the brand name Exocet came to be seen by some governments to be such a potent symbol of national pride and virility that countries came to buy the missile in large part due to the appeal of the brand.

Aérospatiale chose the name Exocet because of its classical allusions; the weapon is, however, thoroughly contemporary in its performance and capabilities.

NATIONAL SECTION

US

IN BRANDING TERMS the US is something of a paradox: seven out of the world's top ten brands are American in origin, and thirty-two out of the top fifty, yet in many respects American branding is quite 'local' in nature. American companies often seem to work on the basis that if the brand works in the US it is likely to work outside, and if it does not, who cares? After all, with 250 million increasingly wealthy consumers the US market frequently represents half or more of the world potential for a new branded product.

American practice in the branding area, particularly as evidenced by brands such as Coca-Cola, McDonald's and Kodak, has inspired branded goods businesses worldwide and the practice of branding is largely an American phenomenon, though outside the US it is frequently adapted to suit local conditions. American branding is, by world standards, remarkably robust and direct. Brand advertising has none of the coyness, and little of the subtlety of, say, European advertising – it gets to the point quickly and style and gentle persuasion often take a back seat to getting the message across with maximum impact, speed and efficiency. In the selection of brand names, too, American practice is direct and to the point such that descriptive and semi-descriptive brand names are frequently favoured by brand owners, a practice which is encouraged by US trademark law which allows companies to secure proprietary rights in names which in other jurisdictions would be considered insufficiently distinctive to merit statutory protection except after extensive use.

Interestingly, in recent years the intense focus on, primarily, the domestic market which has typified much of American branding has tended to break down. American brand owners have been much impressed with the 1992 Single Market initiative of the European Economic Community and recognise from their own experience the opportunities afforded by a huge single market of 350 million consumers. In the past the attitude has often been to develop new brands for the US market and let colleagues outside the US take them up for international exploitation should they so wish; if the brand name proves unavailable or unsuitable outside the US, or if the product formulation does not appeal, too bad. Now, American companies are proving much more sensitive to international market opportunities and US branding is adding a truly international perspective which, in most instances, it did not previously have.

Many of the US brands featured in this book are in fact international to a greater or lesser extent: Grand Metropolitan, the new owners of Pillsbury, plan to take Häagen-Dazs around the world; currently it is market leader in Japan and certain other countries but is little known in Europe. Mars, owners of M&Ms, have recently introduced the brand to Britain (where it has replaced Treets) and to certain other European countries; Birds Eye is already a major brand in some countries outside the US but as part of Unilever's portfolio, not General Foods'.

This process of brand migration and internationalisation seems certain to continue; US markets are being increasingly invaded by Japanese, European and Australasian brands and many leading US brands, previously largely domestic in scope, are entering world markets.

BRAND	LEADERSHIP	STABILITY	MARKET	INTERNATIONALITY	TREND	SUPPORT	PROTECTION	TOTAL
AMTRAK	○					○	●	
AT & T	●	○	□		●	●	●	○
BETTY CROCKER	○	●	□		□	●	●	
BIRDS EYE	□	●	□	○	□	●	●	□
BUDWEISER	●	●	□	○	□	●	○	○
CLOROX	●	●			○		●	
COPPERTONE	○	□	□		□	●	●	
CORVETTE	○	●	□		□	□	●	
DR PEPPER	○	○	□				●	
DRANO	●	□	○		○	□	●	
FRISBEE	●	○	○		○	○	△	
FRUIT OF THE LOOM	○	●	□		○	□	●	
GOODYEAR	○	○	○	□	○	□	●	○
HÄAGEN DAZS	○	○	●		●	□	●	○
HERSHEY'S	□	●	●		□	□	●	○
IVORY	●	●	□		□	●	●	○
JACK DANIEL'S	○	○	□		□		●	
JELL-O	●	●	○		□	○	●	□
KRAFT	□	●	●		□	□	●	○
L'EGGS	□	○	□		●	○	●	
LIFE SAVERS	□	□	○		●	○	●	
LOUISVILLE SLUGGER	□	□	□		○	○	●	
M & M's	□	●	□	○	□	□	●	○
MAYFLOWER	□	●	□		○	□	●	
MERRILL LYNCH	●	●	●		□	○	●	□
MUSTANG	○	○	□			○	●	
NEW YORK YANKEES	○	●	●			○	●	
OREO	●	●	□		□	●	●	○
PLANTERS	□	●	●		□	□	●	○
PRUDENTIAL	□	●	□		□	○	○	
RAID	□	□	□		□	○	●	
RALPH LAUREN	○	□		○	□	●	●	○
SANKA	○	□	□		△	□	○	
SARA LEE	○	●	●		□	□	●	
WEIGHT WATCHERS	○	○	●		○	□	●	
WELLS FARGO		○	○		○		●	
WINDEX	○	○	○			○	○	
ZIPPO	○	○	○		△		●	

KEY ★★ Top Ten brand ★ Top Fifty brand ● exceptionally strong □ very strong ○ strong △ problem area

MUSTANG

The Ford Mustang, affectionately known to Americans as the ponycar, was introduced in April 1964 and since then more than six million have been sold. In the mid-60s the Mustang was a phenomenon – the original Mustang cost a very reasonable $2,368, had a 170 cubic inch (2.8 litre) six cylinder engine, floor-mounted three speed manual transmission, bucket seats and an attractive sports car styling. Buyers could order Mustangs in three models – convertible, hardtop or fastback. The car proved to be enormously appealing to Second World War baby boomers who wanted a different car from that of their parents.

The first year sales estimates were exceeded in just four months and more than 417,000 Mustangs were sold in the first year. Surprisingly, 16 per cent of these were sold to people in the 44–55 age bracket, 50 per cent of buyers already owned another car and most buyers specified optional high performance V8 engines, power steering and automatic transmission.

In the 1960s Mustang captured the mood of the moment; it was young, exciting and optimistic and, for many Americans, is still inextricably linked with the Beatles era, college days and early adulthood.

Over the years the Mustang has changed along with its early customers. By 1971, for example, the Mustang was a foot longer than it had been in 1966 and, today, although it is still sales leader in its segment, the Mustang is quite different from its predecessor of twenty-five years before. The Mustang brand name, however, still has a special spot in the hearts of American motorists.

Mustang caused a sensation when it was launched by Ford in 1964. Though the current Mustang is, arguably, a little more prosaic the brand's appeal is still strong.

NEW YORK YANKEES

The New York Yankees baseball team is the greatest team in the history of American sport. Since it was founded in 1903, the Yankees have dominated the Great American Pastime by winning an unprecedented number of pennants and World Championships.

The Yankees brand exudes many of the qualities most commonly associated with leading consumer products. Due to their longstanding winning tradition, the Yankees have developed a consumer expectation of quality, as well as outstanding name recognition and consumer esteem.

The Yankees logo and 'pin-stripes' uniform represent perhaps the most recognizable sports trademark in America, and would easily

match other leading brand identities in terms of symbol recognition. The 'NY' emblem first appeared on a New York Yankee uniform in 1910, while the other commonly associated logo – the Yankee Top Hat – made its debut in 1947.

US baseball and football teams have, in the last ten years, registered their names and logos widely around the world, a boon to many trademark lawyers. The New York Yankees is the best-known US baseball team and benefits greatly from brand licensing.

LIFE SAVERS

Life Savers candies were introduced in 1912 by Clarence Crane – a Cleveland, Ohio chocolate manufacturer – as an alternative to chocolate which often melted in the hot summer weather.

In order to differentiate the new product from other mint products, most of which were European imports, Crane hired a pill maker to press his new mints into a circle and put a hole in the middle. Since the product looked much like a miniature life preserver, he called it Life Savers and registered the name as a trademark.

Yes, they are called Life Savers because their shape resembles a life preserver.

The Life Savers brand, created in the early years of this century, still thrives in today's hard-roll candy market, worth some $550 million at retail, by keeping pace with consumer preferences. During the product's history numerous new flavours have been tried – while many have been discontinued due to lack of consumer interest. But though the preferences of the marketplace are subject to constant change, the brand continues to explore new or revived flavour options and thus remains relevant and contemporary in spite of changing tastes.

JELL-O

There are not many brands in the US which can claim to be a real American institution but ninety-two year old JELL-O gelatin is one of these.

It started with the famous inventor Peter Cooper of Tom Thumb Locomotive fame. He was granted the first patent for gelatin dessert in 1845 but did little to further its development. The idea sat on the shelf for fifty years until a cough medicine manufacturer named Pearl B Wait produced an adaptation of Cooper's idea and his wife coined the name JELL-O. Two years later Wait sold the business for $450 to the founder of the Genesee Pure Food Company, Orator Francis Woodward, who quickly ran into the same difficulties that plagued Wait. At one point he offered to sell the entire business for $34 and was rejected!

It was fortunate for Mr Woodward that his offer was turned down, because as the nation grew, so did JELL-O. In 1925, the JELL-O company and the Postum Cereal Company joined forces to form the nucleus of General Foods Corporation. Since that time JELL-O has evolved into a massively successful brand with a 92 per cent name recognition among all Americans.

US law affords quite strong protection to brand names which in other jurisdictions would be considered too descriptive to enjoy powerful legal rights. Even so, the owners of JELL-O take no chances in safeguarding this valuable brand name.

Like many of the world's leading brands, JELL-O has succeeded by being a truly differentiated product and by denying its competition any opportunity to catch it up. Even with an easily-copied recipe, JELL-O still today has no real challenger in the gelatin market and is truly a heavyweight among American brands.

Oreo cookies are America's best-loved cookie brand and every detail of the brand, down to the intricate patterning on the product, is important to the consumer.

OREO

Nabisco's Oreo cookies are claimed to be the best-selling cookies in the world. A delicious product, they consist of a rich cream sandwich in either plain or (a recent line extension) chocolate coated form.

In the US Oreo cookies command almost a national cult status – American children are weaned on them and remain devotees all their lives. In the recent 'cookie wars' Oreo was one of Nabisco's chief strategic weapons in its (successful) bid to retain leadership of the US cookie market.

KRAFT

From its humble beginnings to what is today a big part of America's largest food company, the KRAFT brand has symbolised the essence of a superstar brand – high quality, a scrupulously looked-after and well-managed brand identity, a sense of dependability and trust, and the ability to adapt to changing consumer needs.

Although products bearing the KRAFT name are sold in stores around the world, the brand has a strong American heritage going back to 1903, when J L Kraft started a wholesale cheese business in Chicago. In 1914, he started to manufacture his own cheese, and in 1916 he patented a method for producing processed cheese.

J L Kraft's company built on his early success by innovative sales, marketing and advertising techniques. The company was an early radio sponsor, most notably with the 'Kraft Music Hall' radio programme and sponsored the first network programme on television, 'Kraft Televison Theatre', from 1947 through to 1958. With these programmes Kraft established a high standard of advertising quality which still remains strong today. Kraft has also developed a notable reputation for innovative premium offers, eye-catching sales displays and ingenious packaging developments.

Through the years, numerous KRAFT products have been added to the company's product lines.

Today the brand is one of many well-known brands marketed by Kraft General Foods, the multinational food business of Philip Morris Companies Inc.

Kraft is best known for its process cheese yet is now a broadly based foods brand, albeit with strong dairy associations.

HÄAGEN-DAZS

The Mattus family registered the Häagen-Dazs ice-cream brand as a trademark in 1961 and since then a considerable reputation has been built on the promise of supplying the finest ice-cream in the world. Besides being quite delicious, one of the brand's main claims to fame is its extraordinary, perhaps even eccentric brand name. Despite a strategically placed *umlaut* and some creative spelling the name is not in fact a surname or even of authentic foreign derivation: the brand owners simply invented it to be distinctive, unusual, memorable and exotic.

In an enormous, but highly fragmented, ice-cream market Häagen-Dazs has created a strong niche which it has continually defended against competitors. In particular it has succeeded in maintaining its premium position across the entire US; previously such specialist brands had been purely regional.

Who could ignore the Häagen-Dazs brand name? It is intrusive, distinctive and quite unmistakable.

In 1983, the brand was purchased by The Pillsbury Company which in turn was acquired by Grand Metropolitan plc in 1989. Grand Met. now plans to transform Häagen-Dazs into a world brand.

ZIPPO

The uncomplicated, rugged Zippo lighter is an icon of the American way of life, or at least of the American way of life of the 40s, 50s and 60s as portrayed by Hollywood.

A Zippo lighter is a simple machine: a petrol soaked wick with a flint ignition system. It is robust, reliable and remarkably satisfying to use – the lighter is pleasant to hold, fits snugly in the pocket and using it can become an art form – you throw back the cover and spin the wheel with your thumb in one fluent movement.

The brand strength of Zippo comes from its unique design. However, the fact that the brand is so closely particularised to one product and one particular design is a major disadvantage in a world where smoking is contracting – it would be difficult to conceive of a pair of Zippo shoes or a Zippo camera, for how could the essential elements of Zippo be truly present in anything other than a lighter?

However, the owners of Zippo are attempting to extend the brand into new areas such as pens, a task which observers are viewing with interest.

Zippo is powerful proof that good design sells products – the simple, rugged Zippo lighter is a classic.

The successive visualisations of Betty Crocker, painted by famous artists, powerfully illustrate changing attitudes to women.

BETTY CROCKER

The Betty Crocker brand name and signature is used by General Mills as an indication of quality and reliability on over 130 of its convenience foods.

Betty was, however, not a real person: in 1921, a promotion for Gold Medal flour offered consumers a pincushion resembling a flour sack if they correctly completed a jig-saw puzzle of a milling scene. With the thousands of responses, a flood of questions about baking problems arrived at the Washburn Crosby Company, a flour milling concern and forerunner of General Mills. Advertising Manager, Sam Gale, believed that a woman would be an appropriate spokesperson and so he created Betty Crocker as a signature for responses to enquiries.

Over the years Betty Crocker's portrait has been painted for General Mills by a series of well known artists, including Norman Rockwell, the latest being in 1986 by Harriet Pertchik for the sixth edition of *Betty Crocker's Cookbook*. The new Betty Crocker portrays a professional woman, approachable and friendly but also competent, a reflection of constantly changing attitudes towards women and their rôle in society.

FRUIT OF THE LOOM

Today's Fruit of the Loom brand originated in a weaving mill in Providence, Rhode Island in 1851. There 'The Fruit of the Loom' name was applied to the quality muslin cloth used for home sewing. In 1871, the Fruit of the Loom trademark was registered with the US Patent office.

Fruit of the Loom is however best known for its underwear, a product introduced in 1938 and which is now the largest brand of basic and fashion underwear in the United States. It has secured its leading position primarily due to its mass merchandise appeal.

For reasons best known to sociologists and psychologists certain trademarks suddenly become popular on T-shirts and thus encounter severe counterfeiting problems. The Fruit of the Loom brand and logo is a case in point.

TRADEMARK USED WITH PERMISSION OF FRUIT OF THE LOOM.

WELLS FARGO

The famous Wells Fargo stagecoach is still used by Wells Fargo & Co, now a major banking group in the western United States, as a symbol of dependability and drive and of service to communities throughout the West.

Wells Fargo's history extends back to Gold Rush California – the company provided banking services, transportation of bullion and passengers, even a shipping service for agricultural produce – as early as 1856 Wells Fargo shipped cabbages, onions, vegetables and potted plants down to Sacramento to be distributed by the newly opened railroad and, by 1893, 5000 tons of produce a year was being carried by Wells Fargo to the Southern Pacific Railroad for shipment to Arizona, New Mexico and Texas.

Wells Fargo still benefits from its romantic past and from a brand image which is both exciting and differentiated. Now, however, Wells Fargo's world is not that of stagecoaches, cowboys and settlers but of loan portfolios, leveraged transactions, liquidity management and capital adequacy ratios. Based in San Francisco, the bank has 450 branches across the West as well as in key banking centres worldwide and it employs some 20,000 people.

The romance of the Wild West lives on in Marlboro, Colt, American Express, Wrangler and, of course, Wells Fargo though Wells Fargo is now a thoroughly up-to-the-minute banking group.

DR PEPPER

Dr Pepper is the oldest of the major soft drinks brands in America and ranks fourth in share of the US market.

Like its flavour, the origins of the Dr Pepper brand are somewhat out of the ordinary. The product was first made and sold at Morrison's Drug Store in Waco, Texas in 1855. The originator, Charles Alderton, jokingly named his new drink after a Virginia doctor who, as the story goes, discouraged the romantic affair of his daughter with Wade Morrison, the drug store's owner.

Over the years, Dr Pepper has built its reputation on its unique fruit-based flavour and has broadened its nationwide appeal by using such memorable advertising campaigns as the 'most misunderstood soft drink' and 'the most original soft drink'. In America consumers are weaned on Dr Pepper from an early age and come to appreciate its unique, even idiosyncratic taste. In other countries Dr Pepper does not have the same high profile; in the UK, for example, an attempt was made to launch Dr Pepper in the mid-80s but British consumers did not like the taste and the launch was unsuccessful.

To many consumers Dr Pepper tastes like a traditional herbal remedy, another explanation perhaps for the choice of brand name.

SARA LEE

The Sara Lee brand name is one of the best known consumer brands in the US and is recognized by 99 per cent of all Americans. Kitchens of Sara Lee was founded in 1949 by Charles W Lubin, a Chicago baker, who built a business based on high quality premium priced products – cream cheesecake, all butter pecan coffee cake, all butter pound cake and many more – and he named his new company after his young daughter because 'Sara Lee sounds wholesome and American'. Today, Sara Lee Bakery is one of the world's largest baking companies.

Charlie Lubin sold his business in 1956 to Consolidated Foods Corporation and in 1985 Consolidated Foods changed its name to Sara Lee as the old corporate title was somewhat anonymous and, in any case, non-food products accounted for some 30 per cent of sales making the original company name slightly inappropriate.

Now the Sara Lee name, besides being one of America's best known and loved product brand names, is also the corporate name of a $10 billion corporation which owns hundreds of famous brands around the world including Douwe Egberts, Hanes, L'Eggs, Dim, Kiwi, Radox and Aspro.

The controversial adoption in 1985 of the Sara Lee bakery products brand name as the corporate name for an entire $10 billion branded goods business has given the brand an exposure and recognition which would surprise its originator.

US

CLOROX

In 1913, five California businessmen invested $100 apiece to attempt the nation's first commercial production of liquid chlorine bleach, a corrosive and difficult product to manufacture. Using an electrolytic process, they successfully produced a powerful bleach solution and began marketing this new product – under the brand name Clorox – at the end of 1914.

In the following decades the Clorox brand became one of America's most familiar brands and by 1957 had attracted a buyer, the Procter & Gamble Company, who found Clorox to be a natural complement to its

Clorox is a classic household products brand name – strong, memorable and entirely 'no nonsense'.

existing laundry brands. Within three months of the purchase, however, the Federal Trade Commission challenged the acquisition on the basis of a monopoly, and after a ten-year legal battle P & G was forced to divest the company.

Due to the extremely close relationship of the Clorox name to bleach products it has been difficult for the Clorox brand to endorse major brand extensions outside of its core business. Instead, the Company has preferred to use Clorox as a 'identifier' to a host of sub-brands in order to trade off the Clorox reputation for quality and reliability.

SANKA

After Dr Ludwig Roselius inherited his father's flourishing European coffee business in 1901, he became more and more aware that some people refrained from drinking coffee because of its perceived stimulant effect. The German-born scientist searched for a way to remove caffeine from coffee without harming either its flavour or aroma.

Finally, in 1903 fate stepped in. A shipload of his coffee beans was deluged with sea water during a storm. Dr Roselius turned the brine-soaked beans over to his researchers whose early experiments led the way to a process which removed 97 per cent of the caffeine without injuring the coffee quality.

Dr Roselius called the product Sanka and introduced it into the United States in 1923. Nine years later General Foods bought the brand and the patents which went with it.

Today, Sanka is America's leading decaffeinated coffee and the Sanka brand is frequently misused by consumers to denote all types of decaffeinated coffees: 'What would you like, sir, coffee or Sanka?'

You can't beat the original.

Sanka brand decaffeinated coffee is frequently genericised by consumers in the US, a source of both pride and anxiety to its owners and something which they do not encourage.

147

HERSHEY'S

Milton Hershey produced the first Hershey's chocolate bar in 1894 and his name quickly became America's symbol for quality chocolate.

Hershey's reputation was built on individually wrapped bars of milk chocolate which were originally sold for a nickel a time. The company also pioneered the concept of mass availability, not just in every store but actually in specially selected high visibility locations within every store. The famous Hershey's Chocolate Kiss was added to the range in 1907 and the company now produces a wide range of strongly branded chocolate products.

Though many Americans perceive European chocolate to be of higher quality than domestic brands, the Hershey's brand has proved a formidable obstacle to the scores of foreign chocolate and confectionery brands to have hit US shores. Much of the success of Hershey's staying power lies in the high degree of consumer satisfaction delivered by

Families such as Rowntree, Cadbury, Mars, Fry . . . and Hershey have been distinguished by their sense of mission and singlemindedness. The Hershey's brand is a US national institution.

the brand and the careful steps taken by Hershey's to limit unwieldy brand extensions other than those which enhance the brand's core selling proposition.

It is interesting to note that for the first sixty-eight years it was in business Hershey's did not advertise.

WEIGHT WATCHERS

Weight Watchers was founded in 1963 by Jean Nidetch, originator of the Weight Watchers concept, and Albert Lippert, the commercial brains behind the organization. The company was publicly traded in 1968 and ten years later was acquired by the H J Heinz Company.

The Weight Watchers brand acts as a service trademark for the Weight Watchers weight-loss programme, as well as a product trademark on best-selling cookbooks, exercise tapes, a broad line of food products and a national magazine. Currently, Weight Watchers is the world's largest company in the field of personal weight control.

The brand's move into food products has been particularly successful and has

Like many American brands Weight Watchers gets to the point quickly, directly and with no equivocation – it tells it for what it is.

demonstrated the 'leveragability' of the Weight Watchers name. As the health consciousness of the United States consumer continues to grow, the brand is poised to continue its growth in food and food-related products.

WINDEX

The Windex brand was developed in the early 1930s by the Drackett Company as a new, convenient and economical means to wash windows. The product was first sold in regional markets but soon expanded to the entire United States.

Advertised heavily by the company, Windex gained a strong following and still enjoys clear leadership status and near total name recognition among American consumers.

Ironically the strength of the Windex name, which is closely associated with the concept of 'washing windows', leaves the brand owner in a quandry as to potential brand extensions. It is hard to imagine, for example, that the Windex name would be easily extended to other forms of cleaning agents. And yet, as technology continues to develop 'all purpose' cleaners for multiple surfaces, this is an area that the brand must ultimately consider.

Windex is a closely targeted brand which dominates the US market for window and glass cleaning products.

BUDWEISER

Budweiser, affectionately known as Bud to generations of American beer drinkers, is the best-selling beer in the US – it is easy to drink, heavily promoted and has strong, distinctive packaging.

Somewhat embarrassingly for its owners, Anheuser-Busch, the company has recently been involved in a new trademark dispute with the owners of another, unconnected, Budweiser brand. What happened was that Budweiser (US) was recently in negotiations with a UK brewer to allow the UK brewer to produce the US product under licence in Britain. A Czechoslovak brewery, Budvar, then pointed out that the Budweiser name dates from 1265, and that agreements were concluded between the two companies in 1911 and 1939 whereby the US Budweiser brand would be marketed only in the US and therefore that Anheuser-Busch must cease

Budweiser's powerful, incisive name and attractive, intricate graphics are important elements in the brand's appeal.

and desist in its plans for the UK. In the event, both the US and Czech Budweiser brands are now sold in Britain but Anheuser-Busch is precluded from selling its Budweiser beer in most of Europe, a market of 350 million people, at least until the current dispute is resolved.

MAYFLOWER

Founded in 1927, the Mayflower brand is now one of America's leading moving and transport companies specializing in the transportation by truck of household goods, trade shows and general commodities.

The company's massive moving trucks with their famous Mayflower ship logo are seen across America and the brand has come to be a part of the American landscape. It has also through time, built enormous brand awareness among American consumers as a leading moving company and has maintained a strong presence through careful management of its identity.

As the personal and commercial transport industry becomes more and more international, the Mayflower brand will need

to continue its overseas expansion in order to compete in this growing and lucrative sector of the industry. To achieve this, the Company has already established ventures in the Soviet Union, parts of Europe and in the Far East.

Mayflower removal trucks are a familiar sight on the highways of America.

GOODYEAR

Goodyear is the leading US brand of automotive tyres and rubber products (as well as a major international brand) and has benefited greatly from America's continuing love affair with the automobile. The company was founded in Akron, Ohio in 1898 by Frank A Seiberling and took its name from that of Charles Goodyear who, in 1839, discovered a process for the vulcanisation of rubber.

The company suffered, along with other American and European manufacturers, from powerful competition from Michelin, particularly in the 1970s and 80s but had the financial muscle, technical know-how and brand strength to cope with Michelin's challenge better than many of its competitors. More recently, new competition has developed, this time from Japan as Japanese tyre manufacturers have benefited from the increasing success of the Japanese car

industry in international markets. Again, Goodyear is fighting back – the Goodyear Eagle GA Touring Radial, for example, was developed by Goodyear for the Toyota Lexus luxury car and is now being shipped to Japan for fitment as original equipment on the Lexus LS 400.

The Goodyear brand has maintained its strong international position when other US brands have faltered.

COPPERTONE

Coppertone suntan lotion is another product for which we must thank war – it was developed for airmen shot down over the Pacific. Now it is the best selling suntan lotion in the world (and is especially strong in the US market) due to a combination of product performance, a highly distinctive fragrance, a strong brand name, distinctive packaging and powerful and consistent advertising.

Increasing concern about the effects of the sun's rays on unprotected skin seems certain to benefit the Coppertone brand.

AMTRAK

It was the railroads which led to the opening up of America and American folk history abounds with references to them, as many of Johnny Cash's most famous songs bear witness. In post-war years however the passenger railroad system virtually collapsed (except for short distance commuter travel in a few urban areas) due to competition from air travel.

Congress reacted sharply to this – it felt that a national railroad passenger system was essential to national interests so it formed the National Railroad Passenger Corporation, a quasi-public agency which initially operated 184 passenger trains serving 114 major cities. On 1 May 1971 the Corporation was renamed Amtrak in order to have an attractive and vigorous name and identify with which to attract customers and win back business from the airlines. Amtrak is now one of the most widely recognised brand names in America and the lucidity and appeal of the brand has played a major part in the renaissance of American passenger rail transport.

In the 1950s and '60s the new national airline companies put the long-distance passenger railroads out of business. Amtrak was formed in the early 1970s and fought back vigorously.

Louisville Slugger is a rich, evocative brand name. What baseball enthusiast could resist its appeals?

LOUISVILLE SLUGGER

One million Louisville Slugger baseball bats are produced each year, not in Louisville, Kentucky but in Jefferson, Indiana. These bats are highly prized by baseball *aficianados* for their high quality and fine balance and sell well in both the US and Japan, the two major baseball countries in the world. The brand owners, Hillerich and Bradsby, have also discovered 'collateral exploitation', the art of using a powerful trademark in appropriate, but not directly related product areas.
The name is now being successfully licensed for use in the US on children's wear.

IVORY

Ivory Soap is one of the longest established and best known brands in the US – it was launched by Procter & Gamble in 1879 – and has therefore had ample time to acquire a stock of well-loved legends, foremost of which is that Harley Procter, son of the founder, was moved to name the soap Ivory when listening in church to Psalm 45:8.

Ivory Soap was heavily promoted on the platform of quality and purity ('99–44/100% pure – it floats') and it fully supports the adage that 'brands drive out commodities' – when Ivory was launched hundreds of unbranded castile soaps existed yet the credible guarantee of the branded product led consumers to choose Ivory over the uncertainties of selecting an unbranded commodity product.

The foundations of Procter & Gamble, one of the world's leading branded goods companies, rest on Ivory soap.

PRUDENTIAL

The Prudential Insurance Company of America (not to be confused with the major British company of the same name) is a massive financial services brand. Under the flagship of The Prudential, the Company markets a host of insurance, financial and real-estate services both in North America, and increasingly, the rest of the world.

The Prudential logo is the well-known 'rock' symbol, originally derived from the Rock of Gibraltar. This symbol has undergone a number of evolutionary changes, yet today is still one of the most identifiable corporate symbols in America.

Like other financial institutions, the Prudential has responded to the uncertainties of financial markets in the 80s and 90s by diversifying the brand into other, less volatile areas and by stressing personal service.

Prudential is one of the most famous – and ubiquitous – financial services brands in the US.

MERRILL LYNCH

Founded in 1915 by Charles Merrill and his partner Edmund Lynch, the Merrill Lynch company is today one of the leading financial investment firms in America.

The Merrill Lynch brand has however witnessed a number of changes over the years, primarily as a result of mergers and acquisitions by the Company. In the past fifty years for example the Company has used four different corporate names, each, however, incorporating Merrill Lynch into the name. By so doing, the Company has maintained the key equities of the brand and suffered little ill effect from these changes.

The Merrill Lynch brand is characterised in advertising by the famous 'bull' logo which is used to represent a feeling of future confidence in financial opportunities. Use of this symbol helps position the brand as forward thinking and opportunistic.

Most recently, in order to ensure the brand's continued leadership in the near-saturated financial services market, Merrill Lynch has progressively moved toward a client-centred rather than a product-centred structure.

The Merrill Lynch 'bull' logo works effectively alongside the corporate name to present a powerful cohesive brand.

DRANO

The introduction of the Drano brand in 1923 was a timely response to a fundamental change in the lifestyle of the American consumer – the introduction of indoor plumbing.

Developed by the Drackett Company in Cincinnati, Ohio, Drano was positioned initially as the answer to clogged and unhealthy drains. Using hard sales efforts combined with the ingrained fear of consumers about the danger of germs from indoor plumbing, Drano quickly rose to prominence as the leading brand of its type in America.

Drano prospers from an outstanding brand name which is both suggestive and unique. The brand has been successful in building upon its name to maintain its leadership position in the face of increasing competition.

To American consumers Drano is an entirely familiar and trustworthy part of the domestic environment.

Bob Birdseye picked up the idea of quick-frozen food from native trappers in Northern Canada. In order to exploit the idea a retail distribution system and the widespread availability of domestic freezers were required.

BIRDS EYE

Birds Eye is a General Foods brand in the US but, in many other countries, it is owned by Unilever. Clearly, however, the two owners co-operate in the management of the brand as the product range, positioning and 'get-up' (i.e. the logo, packaging, etc.) are all very similar internationally.

Birds Eye is yet another brand which owes its origin to a passionate inventor and innovator, in this case one Clarence 'Bob' Birdseye of Gloucester, Massachusetts, who had observed, while trading and trapping in Labrador, that fresh-caught, quick-frozen food tasted particularly good.

Bob Birdseye's problems in promoting his ideas were, however, immense – in particular, no retail distribution system existed for frozen foods. The Birds Eye brand was initially successful, therefore, as an institutional catering brand but not before the inventor had been forced to sell out to General Foods.

CORVETTE

If there has been one car that has been lighting the passions of American car enthusiasts longer than any other, it is probably the Chevrolet Corvette. A high-performance sports car since 1953, this fiberglass two-seater has always been synonymous with driving fun.

Corvette has always had a brash, American character with a distinctive styling and a gutsy performance. The car has a colourful racing history and has one of the most loyal followings of any car, with hundreds of Corvette clubs and organizations worldwide. In 1990, Corvette also joined the world elite of high-performance sports cars with the new ZR–1. Its 32-valve, four-cam, aluminium-block engine produces 375 hp which will propel the ZR–1 to a top speed of approximately 180 mph.

Though it is not widely known outside the US, to American sports car enthusiasts the Chevrolet Corvette brand is a classic.

M & M's

Mars is one of the world's leading exponents of the art of branding. The company believes passionately in its brands and promotes them with skill and aggression. The company also provides consumers with outstanding products at remarkably keen prices.

In recent years observers of Mars – of whom there are many, not least their competitors – have noticed two new trends: globalisation of brands, not just of products; and a willingness

'M & M's', a Mars brand, is a good example of the company's belief in global branding.

to experiment with brand extension.

'M & M's' is an example of the former trend. Until quite recently 'M & M's' was largely a US brand but the company is now establishing it globally, often at the expense of the company's own equivalent local brands. (TREETS, for example, was a very successful, long established brand in the UK but was rebranded 'M & M's' to achieve the company's objectives of brand globalisation).

L'EGGS

The L'eggs name and packaging combine to produce a unique and differentiated brand personality.

One of the great marketing successes of recent times, the L'eggs brand of hosiery, was introduced in 1970 as the first major branded hosiery product sold through food and drug outlets in the US. Its rapid rise to the top has been remarkable and today L'eggs is the largest selling brand of pantyhose in the US, and in the world.

Originally developed by the Hanes Corporation, L'eggs is a virtual blueprint for new brand success. Among its strengths are a quality product coupled with a powerful and

differentiated brand identity. This includes a unique and exciting name, novel, egg-shaped packaging, powerful point-of-sale display and strong advertising.

The L'eggs packaging and merchandising programme represent a dramatic departure from the traditional methods used to package and merchandise hosiery. The brand owner used a 'packaged goods' marketing programme to sell hosiery to the consumer and in doing so has changed the way hosiery is bought and sold in America.

Jack Daniel's is a familiar, reassuring, dependable brand and is positioned and promoted as such.

JACK DANIEL'S

Brown-Forman, owners of the Jack Daniel Distillery, claim that in the US Jack Daniel's ranks clear number one in terms of awareness among all liquor brands. Jack Daniel's is a smooth, premium whiskey. It is technically a 'Tennessee Whiskey', a product which starts life as a bourbon but which, having been mellowed through maple charcoal, loses the characteristic bourbon aroma and becomes a Tennessee sour mash whiskey.

Jack Daniel's has always promoted itself with restraint: low-key advertising using black and white photography and real people, not actors; and copy which is conversational and tells about the charcoal mellowing process, provides historical information, and gives family-album glances into the life and times of the Jack Daniel Company. Theme consistency has been effective over the years in building an image of honesty and credibility and this, coupled with a fine product and distinctive packaging has served to create an emotional involvement with Jack Daniel's for the consumer, resulting in awareness and brand loyalty which is unique in the distilled spirits industry.

PLANTERS

Peanuts were not established as a popular American food until after 1906, when the Planters brand of peanuts first hit the market. The brand was the brainchild of two Italian immigrants who started the Planters Nut & Chocolate Company; they chose Planters as the company name because they felt it sounded 'important and dignified'.

The idea of selling branded salted nuts in penny and nickel bags was very daring at that time. The only commonly available peanuts sold for 10¢ a pound in bulk, while Planters sold in two-ounce bags for the equivalent of 40¢ a pound. The partners believed, however, that a branded product, easily identifiable for repeat purchases, even though higher priced, would succeed based on the perceived satisfactions delivered by the brand. They were true pioneers of branding!

Since that time Planters has gone on to become the largest peanut producer in

America and the brand has succeeded by offering a quality product combined with steady brand support. Today the brand is a part of PlantersLifesavers Company, a subsidiary of RJR Nabisco, which was itself acquired in 1989 by KKR Industries.

Until Planters came along, peanuts were sold loose by weight – quality was inconsistent and the customer ran a risk that his (or her) purchase would prove unsatisfactory.

Raid dominates the US market for domestic insecticides – the product is powerfully branded, strongly promoted, effective and well priced.

RAID

The Raid brand was created in 1957 by Samuel C Johnson (the fourth generation descendant of company founder S C Johnson) as the first convenient insecticide for the house and garden. At that time Mr Johnson, who is now company chairman, was the Company's new product director.

In a relatively short period of time Raid became an American megabrand and today it has over 45 per cent of the US market in its category. It is a brand which has maintained a consistent marketing strategy based upon product efficacy and consumer trust; the brand has also been successfully extended to embrace a broad range of related insecticide products. In so doing, the brand owner has maintained key consumer values and kept the Raid identity fresh and contemporary.

RALPH LAUREN

Ralph Lauren is the definitive statement of North American dress – classical and stylish yet casual; as such the brand is a true lifestyle statement. The brand was originally developed for menswear but more recently has been extended to cover ladies wear, accessories and fragrances. The polo player device and the Polo sub-brand all act powerfully to reinforce the Ralph Lauren brand proposition.

The Ralph Lauren style is also reflected in the company's stores which now adorn the fashionable streets of the world's major cities. The elegant country house image and the ability to be casually smart are the essence of the brand which looks set to maintain its strong position in a notoriously difficult and fickle business.

Branding in the fashion industry involves the development of a consistent, attractive, believable 'fantasy'. Ralph Lauren has developed a unique 'look' which is classical and stylish but, at the same time, casual. Through the name 'Polo', Ralph Lauren also endorses a range of men's luxury toiletries.

FRISBEE

One of the dangers of owning a famous trademark is that it will become generic – i.e. that it has been used so widely as a generic by the consumer, and its owner has done so little to discourage this, that the trademark owner

Playing with a Frisbee disc is 'the basic American game of catch'. (Brian Moore, *The Great Victorian Collection*, 1975).

loses his proprietary rights and the name becomes available to all comers. This has happened to such former trademarks as cellophane, aspirin, escalator, thermos (in the US) and many others.

In order to maintain rights in a trademark, owners must always use it correctly (e.g. always as an adjective – Hoover vacuum cleaners – never as a verb: Hoovering etc.) and they must also protect their name carefully at law. By carefully patrolling their marks, owners of trademarks such as Xerox, Formica, Sellotape, Band-Aid, Windsurfer, Technicolor . . . and Frisbee have successfully maintained full ownership of their trademarks.

But for Frisbee it has proved a tough battle and the brand owners are still fighting their corner more than thirty years after Walter F Morrison first invented the Frisbee (sorry, the Frisbee flying disc) in 1957.

AT&T

The American Telephone and Telegraph Company (AT&T) traces its origins back to Alexander Graham Bell and his invention of the telephone in 1876. The company was incorporated in 1885 and, as the parent company of the Bell System for almost 100 years, AT&T's primary mission was to provide telephone services to the US market. AT&T was also involved in the manufacture of telephone equipment during this time and the company enjoyed a virtual, though regulated, monopoly.

Through a government-initiated divestiture on 1 January, 1984, AT&T gave up the Bell Operating Companies in return for the freedom to enter new businesses, such as computers. In one day, AT&T saw its $150 billion of assets reduced by 75 per cent and its familiar logo (the bell symbol) taken away. Today AT&T is prohibited from using 'Bell' in its name.

Since divestiture, AT&T has faced a host of challenges. In particular it has had to make the transition from being a regulated monopoly to being a participant in highly competitive industries. In the long-distance telephone sector, AT&T has faced the added challenge of having to compete against rivals who are essentially unregulated, while AT&T remains subject to many of the regulatory burdens of its monopoly past. Also, AT&T has had to adjust to a market-place that is becoming increasingly global in nature.

The Company has been generally successful in meeting these challenges and the brand is still the long-distance choice for millions of Americans.

No country has, or uses, a telephone system like America. AT&T has been responsible for, and benefited from, America's love affair with the telephone.

1889

1900

1921

1939

FRANCE

FRANCE IS RENOWNED for its high quality food brands and for its elegant, luxury brands in sectors such as fashion and fragrances. Increasingly, however, France is establishing a world reputation in sectors outside these traditional areas, for example aerospace and electronics, and French brand owners have shown that French 'style' provides a desirable differentiation to all sorts of branded products.

Though any distinction between 'international brands' and 'local brands' is necessarily somewhat artificial, those brands in any country which are, predominantly, local in nature fall into two main categories:

1 Brands which are similar to other brands in other countries in terms of formulation, function and appearance but which for a number of reasons — for example, tariff barriers, established competition in overseas markets, trademark problems or lack of interest on the part of their owners — are not sold outside their home markets.

2 Brands which are so idiosyncratically adapted to their home markets that they are unlikely to have immediate appeal in foreign markets.

One point which French branding has demonstrated powerfully over the years is that no brand should be considered irredeemably local in nature and incapable of ever becoming international. Who would have imagined that aerated mineral water, bottled in Southern France, would find markets as far apart as Australia, Hong Kong and the United States? Who would have thought that cigarettes made from dark French tobacco, or aniseed flavoured spirits, would ever be much consumed outside France? Who would have believed that idiosyncratically French holiday villages would have any appeal to young people in the United States?

Yet Perrier, Gitanes, Pernod, Ricard and Club Mediterranée have all, to a greater or lesser extent, established overseas markets. Even the TGV high speed rail system will, it is suggested, provide important overseas markets for the French.

FRANCE

BRAND	LEADERSHIP	STABILITY	MARKET	INTERNATIONALITY	TREND	SUPPORT	PROTECTION	TOTAL
AIRBUS INDUSTRIE	○		□		●		○	
AIR FRANCE	○	○	□		□		○	
BACCARAT	□	□	□		□	○	●	○
CHANEL NO. 5 ★	●	●	□	●	□	□	●	□
COINTREAU	○	□	●	□	□	□	●	□
DIM	□	●	●		○	□	●	○
GITANES	●	△	□		△	□	●	
HACHETTE	○		□		□		●	
LACOSTE	○	○	○		□	○	●	○
LE CREUSET	○	○	○		○		●	
MOËT & CHANDON	□	○	□	□	□	○	●	□
NOUVELLES FRONTIÈRES	○				○		○	
PEAUDOUCE	○	□	□		○	□	●	○
PERNOD	○	●	●		○	□	●	○
RENAULT	○	●	□	○	□	●	●	□
RICARD	□	●	●		○	□	●	○
SPONTEX		○	○		○		●	
TGV	●		□		□		△	
YVES SAINT LAURENT	□	●	□	●	○	□	●	□
ZODIAC	○		○		○		●	

KEY   ★★ Top Ten brand   ★ Top Fifty brand   ● exceptionally strong   □ very strong   ○ strong   △ problem area

HACHETTE

Hachette is France's most famous publishing brand though in fact it now operates in some thirty-nine countries worldwide and makes half of its £2.5 billion annual sales outside France. Within France it is market leader in virtually every sector it occupies, including book, magazine and audiovisual publishing.

Hachette dominates publishing in France and has been quick to respond to changes in both consumer tastes and technology.

TGV

The TGV (*train à grande vitesse,* or high speed train) is the world's fastest train in regular revenue-earning service. It was introduced in 1981 at which time it provided a service between Paris and Southeast France at speeds up to 270 km/hr (almost 170 mph) and since then the network has been extended to the Atlantic Coast and to the south-west and operating speeds have increased to a maximum of 300 km/hr (almost 190 mph). In 1993, a new service will open at the same time as the Channel Tunnel bringing the TGV to Northern France and through to London, Brussels, Cologne and Amsterdam.

TGVs are highly sophisticated, comfortable trains which perform best on specially designed and designated track. As Europe's airspace and airports become increasingly crowded and as, too, the problems involved in journeying to airports, checking in and clearing security become more acute, it seems certain that high speed rail travel will

The French display particular courage and flair when it comes to 'grand' projects – Charles de Gaulle airport, Concorde, Airbus Industrie, Musée d'Orsay, Channel Tunnel . . . and TGV.

grow steadily in popularity and will become increasingly important in solving long distance travel needs. The TGV gives France a major lead in this area.

ZODIAC

Zodiac make products for the aerospace industry (arresting systems, escape slides, parachutes and floats) but are best known by consumers for their marine and leisure products (inflatable boats and rafts, beach products and pools). Over half of brand sales are made in France where the Zodiac name is

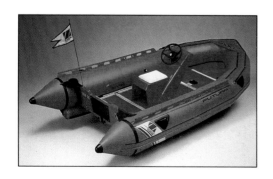

extremely well-established and respected but Zodiac, a £200 million company, is rapidly increasing its penetration of international markets using its brand strength and its technological skills in the area of textile structures.

The phrase 'textile structures' almost seems to be a contradiction in terms yet Zodiac have built a major business – and a powerful brand – in this area.

RENAULT

Renault is the twelfth largest company, and the fourth largest vehicle manufacturer, in Europe producing almost two million vehicles a year. Like many European and American car companies it can trace its lineage back to the turn of the century; indeed, the marque's reputation was such that in 1905 King Edward VII ordered a 14/20 hp Landaulette.

Renault is the national motor car brand of France just as Fiat is of Italy, Volkswagen of Germany and Rover of Britain. In France, Renault is highly visible and utterly familiar; its brand values are service, reliability, quality and value for money.

1900

1919

1906

1923

1959

1925

1972

Europe's motor industry is currently seeking strategic alliances in order to contain the cost of new product development. Renault now has an alliance with Volvo but both brands will be kept entirely separate.

THERE'S MORE TO LIFE WITH **RENAULT**

AIRBUS INDUSTRIE

Airbus Industrie is a partnership created by a number of major European aerospace companies (Aérospatiale, Deutsche Airbus, British Aerospace and CASA plus two associates). It was finally constituted in December 1970 and its first aircraft, the A300, entered service in 1974. The A300 was the world's first wide-body twin and the original A300 B2 carried a mixed-class load of 250 passengers 1500 nautical miles with previously unequalled economy. Since then, Airbus Industrie has gone on to develop a number of successor aircraft such as the A310, A320 and A330 and twenty years on has 500 aircraft in service with seventy operators and a further 1400 firm sales.

Much of the credit for the success of Airbus Industrie lies with French business and political interests who showed boldness and resource at a time when the position of companies such as Boeing and McDonnell-Douglas seemed virtually impregnable and the Airbus name now inspires particular pride within France.

The name Airbus almost seems too prosaic for the sophisticated, exciting aircraft designed and built by Airbus Industrie.

AIR FRANCE

Airline brands are some of the most visible brands in the world and airlines have learned to take enormous care with their corporate brands – i.e. their corporate identities – as an attractive and cohesive identity can influence customers, staff and suppliers in a positive way and conversely, a confused or unattractive identity can lower morale and esteem and can suggest that the lack of cohesiveness in the airline's identity merely echoes a lack of cohesiveness in the airline itself, a factor which will manifest itself in poor service and poor punctuality, even in poor safety.

Air France's careful use of its name and visual identity fully matches the 'best practices' followed by all the leading international airlines. Air France's current visual identity was adopted in 1976 (though the Air France name dates from the inter-war period) and a

The wide range of applications demands that airlines exercise particular care in the use of their names and visual identities.

detailed manual ensures consistent application – on planes, buses, cars, aircraft, staff uniforms, check-in desks, advertisements, tickets, lounges, cabin decor, menus, travel agencies, air cargo etc. Indeed, the range of applications is truly enormous.

LE CREUSET

It is not perhaps surprising that France, a country noted for its gastronomy, should also have developed excellent products for the preparation and presentation of fine food. Le Creuset is one such company; founded in 1925 it is the world leader in heavy enamelled, cast iron cookware. Le Creuset dishes, pans and casseroles are attractively designed by leading designers and come in a range of colours. They are therefore at home both on the stove and on the dining table and the brand enjoys an important niche positioning on an international basis.

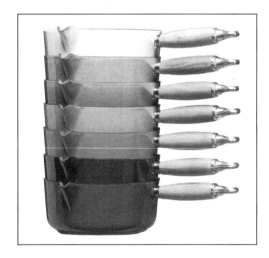

Le Creuset cookware is stylish and high quality but, being cast iron, it needs a strong cook to carry it from the stove to the table.

LACOSTE

René Lacoste, a tennis legend, twice won Wimbledon (in 1925 and 1928), twice won the US Open (in 1926 and 1927) and three times won the French Open (in 1925, 1927 and 1929). He was also one of the French team who won the Davis Cup in 1927 and describes the origin of the Lacoste Alligator emblem as follows:

I was nicknamed Alligator by the American press, after I had made a bet with the Captain of the French Davis Cup Team about a suitcase in alligator skin.
He promised to give it to me if I won a very important match for our team. And the public must have been fond of this nickname which conveyed the tenacity I displayed on the tennis courts, never letting go my prey! So my friend Robert George drew an alligator which I then had embroidered on the blazer I was wearing on the courts.

In 1933, René Lacoste and André Gillier, owner of a French knitwear firm, set up a company to make tennis and golf shirts designed by the champion and bearing his logo and a legend was born, particularly as most sports shirts of the time were woven,

long-sleeved and starched.

Today, more than fifty years after the company was created, over thirty-five million articles are sold annually in over eighty countries under the Lacoste trademarks. The originality of the La Chemise Lacoste Company, and one of its strengths, comes from the fact that it has always licensed out the manufacturing and distribution of its products to carefully selected partners in each market. The Company registers and directly defends the trademarks it owns throughout the world and it also specialises in styling, new product development and in marketing co-ordination, paying particular attention to promotion, publicity and advertising.

The alligator device demonstrates convincingly how, in certain circumstances, a device mark can reinforce a powerful brand property.

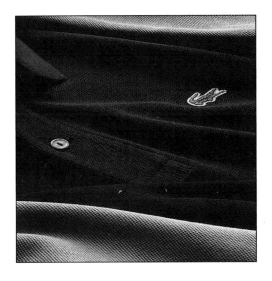

NOUVELLES FRONTIÈRES

Nouvelles Frontières ('new frontiers') is France's largest travel company. It was founded in 1967 and now covers travel agencies, charter flights, hotels, tours, special events etc. Much of its activities are, indeed, concerned with 'new frontiers' – India, Nepal, Indonesia, Africa, West Indies etc – and in France the Nouvelles Frontières company has developed a unique cachet and market positioning.

The travel industry is extremely fragmented and necessarily seasonal. It is also particularly subject to economic conditions, oil prices, etc. Brand building can therefore be especially difficult.

RICARD

Ricard is a pastis, a generic term in French for all aniseed flavoured spirits, but unlike its near cousin Pernod it also contains liquorice which gives it a distinctive colour, bouquet and taste. The use of aniseed in drinks goes back centuries and traditional elixirs from all round the Mediterranean laid claim to its restorative and digestive powers. In this century pastis became most widely used as an aperitif drunk along with water, particularly in the South of France. The most famous pastis brand is Ricard, a brand which, it is claimed, is Fance's most successful pastis, Europe's top selling spirit and the world's third best selling spirit brand.

Most of the sales of the brand are achieved in France and its neighbouring countries

where Ricard has universal recognition, aided in large part by the Ricard motor racing circuit, the sponsorship of world famous yachts and yachtsmen and the huge research programmes into agriculture and oceanography which are financed by the Ricard family. Ricard also currently sponsors Ligier Formula One motor racing cars.

The Ricard brand is particularly strong in the South of France but it now has a strong international following.

MOËT & CHANDON

Moët & Chandon are the largest champagne producers in France (and hence, by definition, in the world since champagne can only come from France's champagne district) and Moët & Chandon is the leading brand in the French home market (with a 6.3 per cent market share) and in export markets (23.8 per cent market share). (The Group also, however, produces Mercier, a strong number two in France, as well as Ruinart and of course, Dom Pérignon.)

The House of Moët dates from 1743 and became Moët & Chandon in 1832 when Jean-Remy Moët, the founder's grandson, handed over the business to his son Victor and his son-in-law Pierre-Gabriel Chandon.

To many people both in France and abroad Moët & Chandon and champagne are synonymous. Much of the credit for popularising yet, at the same time, maintaining the exclusivity of this superlative product must rest with Moët & Chandon.

Moët & Chandon is the most powerful and respected champagne producer in France and hence, of course, in the world.

YVES SAINT LAURENT

Though the Groupe Yves Saint Laurent makes almost 80 per cent of its sales outside France it is still, nonetheless, a quintessentially French brand with powerful associations of elegance, style and sophistication.

The Yves Saint Laurent group started off as an *haute couturier* but this activity now contributes less than 10 per cent of its sales. Boutiques contribute a further 15 per cent but the bulk of the company's income now comes from brand licensing activities in such areas as fragrances (YSL brands include Opium, Paris, Rive Gauche, Kouros and Jazz), make up, accessories and leatherware.

The company has controlled its core asset, its brand, skilfully and maintains strict control over licensees in so far as quality, distribution and pricing are concerned.

Yves Saint Laurent is regarded as the greatest *couturier* since Chanel and the embodiment of French *chic*.

BACCARAT ○

Baccarat was founded in 1764 as a glassworks and began making crystal in 1867. It now produces 40 per cent of France's hand-made crystal and prides itself on producing the finest crystal in the world. The company is also able to supply any design it has produced in over 200 years of existence.

The Baccarat name stands head and shoulders above others in France as a brand of crystal and glassware due to the use of excellent raw materials, highly skilled craftsmen and superb designs. The product is distributed through leading stores worldwide and also through seven company-owned stores: two in Paris, one in Baccarat itself and one each in New York, Tokyo, Osaka and Hong Kong. Even those who cannot afford the product sometimes visit a store to gaze fondly upon Baccarat's beautiful products.

Baccarat crystal is quite beautiful and much prized. It is also very, very expensive.

PERNOD ○

Pernod was invented in Switzerland in the late Eighteenth Century by a French doctor fleeing from revolutionary France and gained the nickname 'La Fée Verte' – The Green Fairy. In the 1850s (by which time the Pernod brand was firmly established) it came to be given to French soldiers to protect them from the perils of malaria and tens of thousands gained a taste for the distinctive, anise flavoured drink, a taste which soon permeated the whole of French society.

By the 1890s Pernod was the preferred drink of Parisian Café society and the Pernod bottle and the distinctive Pernod carafe were painted by Degas, Manet, Picasso, Toulouse-Lautrec and others.

Until the 1970s Pernod's sales were largely confined to France but strong export markets have now been developed in Britain, Germany and the rest of Northern Europe – its sister brand Ricard, on the other hand, is strong mainly in the Mediterranean area.

Pernod – and its sister brand Ricard – are quintessentially French though other Mediterranean countries, for example Greece and Turkey, also favour aniseed-flavoured drinks.

PERNOD ®

CHANEL N°5

 CHANEL NO. 5 ☆ ▢

Chanel No. 5 is the classic French fragrance brand – it is elegant, timeless and indelibly associated with style, sophistication and luxury.

It was created in 1921 by *parfumier* Ernest Beaux and takes its name from the fact it was the fifth sample submitted to the legendary Coco Chanel for her approval.

The perfume industry has developed its own highly communicative language to describe fragrances. Chanel No. 5 is considered a complex floral perfume with a strong aldehyde base. Its components are:

Top Notes:
'Floral-Fresh': Ylang Ylang from the Comores – Neroli from Grasse.
Middle Notes:
'Floral': Jasmine from Grasse – Rose de Mai from Grasse.
Lasting Notes:
'Woody Notes': Sandalwood from Mysore – Bourbon Vetyver.

Even a description of the make-up of the product reflects its mystery and sophistication!

Though fashions in fragrances come and go Chanel No. 5 is timeless – it is distinctive but not vulgar, long-lasting and beautifully packaged.

DIM ○

Everyone rejoices in someone else's 'funny' brand name – the Japanese brands Creap (coffee creamer), Pocari Sweat (sports drink) and Cedric (motor car) cause great amusement in English-speaking countries as do British brands such as Fairy Liquid (detergent) in the US and Irish Mist (liqueur) in Germany.

Dim is the leading French brand of hosiery and underwear and is now part of the Sara Lee Group. Though the brand name is a source of mild amusement outside France, within France the brand has a near awesome reputation – the products are of high quality, are well distributed, and powerful, original

French advertising is frequently far from coy and Dim's advertising is no exception.

advertising has been consistently used to build the brand's reputation. Dim's advertising agency is Publicis who has worked closely with the brand owner to build a powerful brand image.

COINTREAU

Cointreau is a cognac-based orange-flavoured liqueur. It is sold in distinctive, chunky, square bottles, a style which became popular in the mid-Eighteenth Century and which therefore lends the brand desirable associations of both tradition and mild idiosyncracy. (The Vligenthart, a Dutch East Indiaman which sank off the coast of Holland in 1743, has recently yielded hundreds of wine bottles which bear a close resemblance to the modern Cointreau bottle.)

Cointreau is a high quality, tasty product with wide distribution and strong and distinctive packaging. For generations the brand has remained in the Cointreau family and has maintained close family links with Remy Martin. Recent family disputes have served to disturb these old relationships but, in the French tradition, family wars have been kept largely out of the public eye and the brand's esteem and popularity has not been threatened. Now it seems that the Rémy Martin and Cointreau businesses are to come together again with the participation of Grand Metropolitan, further evidence of the increasing concentration of powerful drinks brands into the hands of a few major world companies.

In France observers have followed with interest recent family disputes over the future of Cointreau. These however have done little to damage the brand.

GITANES

For many people the merest whiff of smoke from a Gitanes cigarette is sufficient to conjure up images of France and all that is French. Gitanes, and its sister brand Gauloises, are owned by Seita, the state-owned tobacco monopoly which holds over 50 per cent of the French tobacco market. However, both Gitanes and Gauloises, with their traditional dark tobacco and high tar content are coming under pressure from health lobbyists, from French and EEC legislators and from public opinion. But it is not just the Gitanes product itself which is idiosyncratic and distinctly French – the packaging is unmistakable combining both nostalgia and sophistication, brand qualities which the promotion for Gitanes has, over the years, sought to reinforce and develop.

The essence of France is still, for many people, the unmistakable smell of a French cigarette, most probably Gitanes.

PEAUDOUCE

Disposable nappies are the brand developer's dream – a huge, relatively homogeneous market; strong interest in the product by the purchaser, if not the consumer; and advertisements full of beautiful, cuddly, gurgling babies. On a world basis Procter & Gamble's Pampers brand is dominant (and, indeed, P & G pioneered the superabsorbent materials used in nappies) but in France and, to a somewhat lesser extent, elsewhere in Europe Peaudouce helps ensure that P & G does not have things all its own way.

French mothers and, occasionally, fathers change some 2.7 billion nappies a year and over 20 per cent of these are Peaudouce, a brand which has received strong promotional support as well as constant product innovation – elasticated legs and waists, superstrength middle sections, tailored nappies and now environmentally sensitive bleach-free nappies. In 1988 Svenska Cellulosa, owners of the Molnlycke brand, bought Peaudouce for FF 1.6 billion (US $346 million) from Financière Agache, a French holding company, a realignment which confirmed the increasing concentration of disposable nappy brands into the hands of a few key players.

The market for disposable nappies is huge but bitterly contested. Peaudouce is a strong competitor to P&G's all-purpose Pampers brand.

SPONTEX

Société Française de Viscose, founded in 1903 to produce artificial fibres for use in garments, came to recognise the absorption qualities of certain fabrics and the production of synthetic cellulose sponges was then only a small step away. The Spontex brand name was first registered and used on an international basis in 1933 and today Spontex is a world leader in household cleaning products including sponges, sponge cloths, non-woven wipes, scourers and mops. Some 50 per cent of the company's turnover is derived from the French market, the rest from overseas production and export, and the brand's success is due to innovation, quality and strong marketing – in 1990, for example the British subsidiary won a major television advertising award for its Handimop advertising.

Natural sponges have always been rare and expensive objects. Environmentalists, too, objected to their removal from the sea bed. Spontex products presented an attractive alternative and still do today.

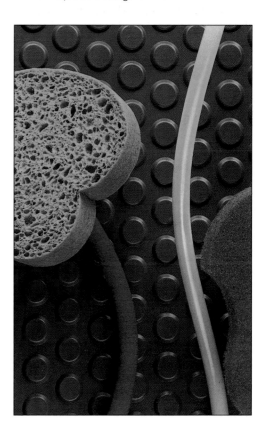

GERMANY

GERMAN BRAND OWNERS suffered expropriation of certain valuable trademark rights after both World Wars and this factor, combined with a clear sense of property, has made German companies acutely aware of the importance of brands and of the value and power of trademark rights. Indeed, companies around the world complain bitterly that Germany is the hardest jurisdiction in the world in which to acquire statutory trademark rights due both to the practices followed at the Registry and near-routine objections from the owners of existing trademarks. (Defenders of the German system, on the other hand, retort that at least one can be sure, having acquired a trademark in Germany, that it is worth more than the paper it is written on.)

In Germany, too, private companies predominate and publicly held corporations have a much lesser influence than in countries such as the USA, UK and France. Privately held businesses with close links with major banks are able, it is argued, to take a much longer term view than public companies subject to the tyranny of a stock market, investors and financial analysts and are better able to invest in and develop brands without the pressures for short-term returns.

German brands are renowned for their high quality. Apart from areas such as automotive, many German brands are, however, relatively unknown outside Germany (indeed, only three of the world's top fifty brands are German) though European companies are anticipating increased competition after 1992.

GERMANY

BRAND	LEADERSHIP	STABILITY	MARKET	INTERNATIONALITY	TREND	SUPPORT	PROTECTION	TOTAL
BAHLSEN	□	●	●		□	●	●	○
BLAUPUNKT		□	□		○	●	●	
BOSS	○	□	○	○	●	□	●	○
BRAUN	○	□	○	○	○	●	●	○
CHIO		○	□		○	○	●	
DER SPIEGEL ★	●	●	●		□	○	●	□
8 × 4		○	□		□	○	○	·
GOLDPFEIL		□	□		□	□	●	○
GRANINI	□	□	●		□	●	●	□
HB	○	△	○		○	●	●	
JACOBS SUCHARD	□	○	●	○	○	□	●	○
MAGGI	●	□	●		○	□	●	○
MELITTA	□	●	●	○	□	□	●	□
ROSENTHAL	□	□	○	○	○	□	●	○
SALAMANDER	○	●	○		○	○	●	
SCHWARZKOPF	○	●	●		□	●	●	○
TEEKANNE	○	□	●	○	○	●	●	○
UHU	●	□	○		□	●	●	○
WELLA	□	●	●	○	□	●	●	○
WIENERWALD	□	○	○		□	□	●	○

KEY ★★ Top Ten brand ★ Top Fifty brand ● exceptionally strong □ very strong ○ strong △ problem area

8 × 4

8 × 4 was developed over thirty years ago as a line of deodorants. It is now brand leader in its country of origin, Germany, and has also been successfully exported. The unusual name has its roots in the original chemical formulation for soap which has thirty-two molecular components: 8 × 4 = 32!

8 × 4, in the consumer's eyes, has become synonymous with quality and reliability as well as offering product performance at an acceptable price. With a distribution that covers supermarkets through to the local corner shop, it has become a tried and trusted brand, well-liked and respected by users.

Opinion is divided as to whether the unusual name assisted, or hindered, the brand's success.

MAGGI

Maggi, the food manufacturer, has been operating in Germany for over a hundred years.

The company was actually founded in 1872 by a Swiss, Julius Maggi, whose concern for the social welfare of his fellow citizens, combined with his entrepreneurial spirit, prompted him to investigate the concept of nutritious foods which were both easy to prepare and affordable. By 1886, he had managed to develop the first instant soup product – a dried pea and bean flavoured compound. That same year he also developed the now internationally famous 'Maggi Würze' – a spicy sauce which can pep up even the most tasteless of soups.

In 1887, Maggi moved to Singen in Germany which was well placed to take advantage of the expanding railway network and Julius Maggi's enthusiasm and energy soon led to other manufacturing sites in Paris, Milan, Prague and Amsterdam. His creativity and foresight were not only responsible for new product development but also the creation of a press and advertising department, the first of its kind, headed by none other than Frank Wedekind, later to become a famous dramatist. Maggi was himself responsible however for the enduring design of the four-sided brown sauce bottle for Maggi Würze; he also chose yellow and red as the colours for Maggi labels, today the Maggi house colours.

Now Maggi produces about 200 items ranging from spices, sauces, consommés, broths, soups in tins and dry powdered soups, through to pasta and potato based dishes. They all remain true to the original criteria of being affordable, nutritious and easy to prepare.

Even today the company still follows principles developed in the past; for example, all staff are 'co-workers', valuable assets to be rewarded and given a sense of ownership. Maggi's future is therefore bound up in traditional principles but its success in adapting to changing market conditions and consumer requirements and its investment in new product development and food technology have made it an enduring brand name and a true market leader.

Maggi is one of Germany's, and Europe's, major food brands.

GRANINI

'granini', the fruit drink company, was founded in 1964 and has been part of the Melitta Group since 1967.

When 'granini TRINK GENUSS' fruit nectars were first introduced, consumers were won over by this premium drink offering a genuine, fruity taste. It was the product idea – a new way of 'making fruits drinkable' – which gave the brand its unique quality and the features which the consumer has come to associate with 'granini' – fruit pulp content, rich consistency, top quality and a wide selection of fruit and vegetable varieties – give the brand a clear advantage over the competition. 'granini's' brand identity has also been strengthened by its presentation and packaging: the wide necked, dimpled glass bottle is ideally suited to presenting the contents directly to the consumer and is an excellent way to show off a quality product.

Under the 'granini' umbrella name, the company has rapidly become a market leader and important sub-brands include Trink Genuss, Vitamin-10-Plus, Labamba, Trink-Leicht and Garten Ernte.

Innovation is a rule at 'granini'. The brand image is a result of innovative and creative marketing. This, together with distinctive products and distinctive presentation are of immediate appeal to the public.

The phrase 'fruit nectar' is delicious in itself and 'granini' products live up to the promise.

BAHLSEN ○

Bahlsen as a brand combines quality as well as tradition and these consistent values have supported its position as a market leader in the biscuit and confectionery market.

It was Bahlsen who, over thirty years ago, first produced a chocolate flavoured 'Lebkuchen' – a type of ginger bread biscuit. They remain the market leader in this particular area and have extended their repertoire to include numerous variations on a traditional recipe. Bahlsen's excellent milk and dark chocolate flavoured products have also engendered enormous consumer loyalty over the years – yet another example of how product quality and excellence can provide sustainable differentiation over the competition.

The Bahlsen product range now includes nibbles and snacks and, on an international basis, Bahlsen has built up an excellent reputation for its products.

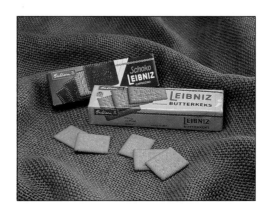

Bahlsen has developed a formidable reputation for high quality products and constant product innovation.

CHIO

Founded in 1962, this manufacturer of fresh and piquantly flavoured nibbles has quickly built a reputation for quality, taste and product variety.

Started by the family members Carl, Henrietta and Irmgard von Opel (hence the name) in the Pfalz, the company was bought in 1977 by Convent which undertook to modernise the manufacturing plant.

No artificial ingredients are used in Chio's products and its oil, corn, peanuts and spices are of top quality while its potatoes are still specially chosen and grown for the company in the Pfalz.

Chio's new product introductions – Chio Jumbo Flips and Chio Pick-up – are proving highly successful in the growing snack market, offering fun and taste, the consistent qualities of the Chio brand appeal.

Manufacturers around the world have discovered markets for premium snack-food products. Chio's position in the German market is particularly strong.

Jacobs is particularly well known for its coffee and Suchard for its chocolate. Now part of Philip Morris, Jacobs Suchard is strengthening its position across the whole of Europe.

JACOBS SUCHARD

Jacobs Suchard is one of the most important food producers in Europe. Its operations include coffee, confectionery and drink products and Jacobs Suchard, the product of a merger in 1982 of Suchard/Tobler and Jacobs, embraces three major brands: Milka from Suchard, Toblerone from Tobler and Jacobs Krönung from Jacobs.

Jacobs Suchard's leading position is not only maintained through its ownership of three top brands in the coffee and chocolate market but also through its commitment as a company to serve the consumer. This approach, combined with the company motto – 'Jacobs Suchard ist ein Unternehmer der Unternehmer', 'Jacobs Suchard – an entrepreneur amongst entrepreneurs', underlining the entrepreneurial and innovative attitude to market development, will ensure the continued lead of the brands in their market-places.

WIENERWALD

If you asked anyone in Western Germany where to go for a quick bite to eat, something like chicken 'n' chips, the answer would have to be Wienerwald.

One of Germany's largest restaurant chains, Wienerwald specialises in poultry. Its restaurants are regarded as solid, middle-class eating places which, over the years, have consistently served good, wholesome food.

Its recent acquisition by Grand Metropolitan has provided the impetus to branch out. Expansion throughout Continental Europe and Eastern Europe is planned and the need to attract a wider clientèle than previously, to include younger people, families with young children and the business-lunch market, has been clearly recognised. The new-look Wienerwald restaurant, unveiled in May 1990 in Munich, provides a more attractive and modern setting for customers. The menu has been expanded to cater for any mealtime occasion, from the traditional coffee and cake, to the more substantial two- or three-course lunch or dinner as well as a variety of snacks. A take-away service is also available.

High disposable incomes in Germany have provided Wienerwald with a strong home base from which to expand.

With a new, clear brand identity, a long-standing involvement in the restaurant business and the support of Grand Metropolitan, Wienerwald is well placed to become one of the leading restaurant businesses in Europe.

BLAUPUNKT

Since 1925 the 'blue dot' from Blaupunkt has stood for progress and quality. The blue dot was originally used by engineers of the founding company, Ideal, to denote their most technically advanced earphones – and so a world renowned brand and trademark was born.

Blaupunkt's product range now covers stereos, hi-fi equipment, car radios and business communications equipment. Not only are quality and reliability part of the brand's philosophy – the first box radio set from Blaupunkt survived a crossing of the Sahara desert in 1932 – but Blaupunkt's

engineers are always on the look-out for ways to harness the power of electronics for the benefit of others, in either leisure or safety areas. An example of the latter is Blaupunkt's development of a car radio which picks up a signal and automatically switches on the radio so as to alert drivers to traffic problems ahead.

Blaupunkt firmly believes that electronics can enhance our quality of life. It is this attitude which makes it a brand well placed for the future.

Blaupunkt is one of the relatively few European electronics companies to preserve its brand reputation intact in the face of Japanese competition.

MELITTA

Not many women were immortalised at Berlin's Imperial Patent Office but one woman did manage to penetrate this bastion of traditional male dominance. In 1908 Melitta Bentz, wife, housewife and mother of two, handed in her application to patent the world's first coffee filter machine and coffee filter paper. Not being able to enjoy her cup of coffee due to the unappetising residue left at the bottom of the cup, she experimented with a new coffee making system using a piece of blotting paper from her son's school exercise book and a perforated tin can. The rest is history.

With its distinctive red and green colours, adopted by the company as early as 1925 to sustain and protect their point of difference from increasing competition, the Melitta brand name has, over the years, become a trusted friend in households in Germany and around the world. What started off as a small family concern has, over the years, through skilful management, grown into a major corporation. Melitta has also successfully pursued a policy of brand extension, counting such names as granini among its company brands, and is actively pursuing a policy of international market development as far afield as the US and Japan. The company's philosophy could be 'Nothing is impossible' and this determination, combined with its strong work ethic, tenacity and thriftiness, have all contributed to its success.

The Melitta brand is particularly associated with coffee filter machines and filter papers though it is also a powerful force in branded coffee.

TEEKANNE

Teekanne (or 'teapot') started a hundred years ago in Dresden as a small business selling Japanese and Chinese teas. Since then it has grown into one of the largest tea brands in Europe and into the largest manufacturer of herbal tea bags in the world.

The qualities which transformed this small firm into an international business are just as valid today as they were at the turn of the century: high product standards, customer education about tea, public relations programmes and good relationships with suppliers all play an equal part in the brand's success.

Teekanne products such as 'Pompadour' and 'Teeflott' also enjoy a quality reputation with the catering trade and products

developed for the catering market have significantly raised tea-making standards in restaurants, canteens and the like – probably much to the relief of the customer! Tea drinking is now on the increase in Germany and tea is proving popular with young consumers.

Herbal teas are very popular in Germany and Teekanne is the clear market leader.

SALAMANDER

SALAMANDER

Nowhere in Western Germany will you find a busy shopping centre without a branch of Salamander, the shoe retailer and manufacturer which caters for the needs of all Germans of all ages.

The company, which has adopted the name and logo of a small black and yellow lizard, has come to represent quality and comfort in footwear. Not only that, Salamander shoes also manage to introduce a fashion element into this successful equation. An extremely strong brand in the footwear sector, Salamander enjoys both high consumer awareness and great popularity.

Integrated manufacturing and retailing exists, it seems, more in the footwear sector than almost any other.

UHU

This household glue product must have one of the most unusual and memorable brand names of any product. Although the name bears no relation to the actual product – it is, in fact, the popular name for an owl in the Black Forest area – UHU has over the years become a near-generic in Germany for any type of household glue.

Meagre means did not stop the founder, Hugo Fisher from realising his product's potential. Over a period of fifty years, the farsighted and creative marketing programme implemented by the company has made UHU one of the most successful and universally known brand names.

Schools and kindergartens were supplied with UHU glue at no cost, thereby ensuring that the word 'UHU' became more familiar than the word 'glue' from an early age. The memorable advertising campaign *'Im Falle eines Falles . . . UHU' 'In the event of an emergency . . . UHU',* targeted at the amateur modelworker, sent sales soaring.

They have done so ever since.

This unusual brand name is derived from that of a bird which in turn is named from its call.

BOSS

Boss, the men's designer and clothes manufacturer, was founded in 1923 by Hugo Boss. The early years concentrated mainly on raincoats, plain dark suits and dustcoats. With the arrival of Eugen Holy, Boss's range became less utilitarian and extended to include suits and jackets. International expansion followed with Austria and Switzerland as the first export markets in 1972, with Benelux, Scandinavia and the UK following soon after.

A new era began at Boss in 1974 with the introduction of fine, lightweight Italian fabrics and a modern and design orientated approach became the order of the day. Shirts, poloshirts, sweatshirts and knitwear were added to the collection.

In 1977, by which time the USA had been added to the list of export markets, Boss was chosen as the wardrobe suppliers for the popular TV shows Miami Vice and L.A. Law, a move which confirmed the company's reputation as a major international men's designer.

The last few years have seen the extension of the product range into men's cosmetics and sunglasses. The company has also exchanged shareholdings with the Japanese enterprise, Leyton House. With its combination of classic and sporty designwear, Boss has become a popular and desirable brand for consumers.

BOSS
HUGO BOSS

In the last two decades Boss has emerged as one of the world's leading menswear brands.

GOLDPFEIL

Goldpfeil is a brand of luggage and the name was taken from the 'Golden Arrow' – a luxury train which the founder's son, Heinrich Krumm, used in 1929 to travel from London to Paris. This concept of quality is of central importance and perfect quality is something that Goldpfeil strives for, not only in its selection of raw hides but also in the design of its bags, luggage and business items as well as in the exceptional quality of its craftsmanship. (Even today, all Goldpfeil products are still hand sewn.)

However, tradition does not hold Goldpfeil back; the company is receptive to new ideas as witnessed by its innovative product designs and its international orientation with a presence on all five continents. It has also

adapted to changed market requirements and has developed and up-dated its traditional trademark, the golden arrow.

As a brand it has remained resilient and successful in an industry where fashions are fickle and quality is often sacrificed for profit.

Goldpfeil, or 'Golden Arrow', is Germany's leading brand of luxury luggage.

GOLD / PFEIL

BRAUN

Braun, the electrical appliance manufacturer, was founded by Max Braun in Frankfurt in 1921. Its initial products were radios and other audio equipment but the company quickly branched out into the manufacture of kitchen appliances as well as electric razors. In 1962 Braun became a publicly quoted company and expanded its international network.

Still based in Frankfurt, Braun's major international markets are Japan, North America, the UK, Italy and Spain. The company's biggest selling items are the Braun electric shaver and household machines such as coffee-makers, mixers, toasters, irons etc. Other product areas include oral hygiene and haircare as well as clocks and watches.

For all its diversity in production, the one trait that is common to all Braun items is the element of quality design which lies at the heart of this brand's appeal. Indeed, high quality design is central to the brand image and reputation of Braun.

Braun's brand image is based particularly upon very high quality product design.

SCHWARZKOPF

The Hans Schwarzkopf company is a leading manufacturer of haircare products and toiletries. Founded at the turn of the century in Berlin, the name Schwarzkopf, its logo of a small head coloured in black (which is a literal translation of the name) and its slogan 'It's only the genuine article if it comes from the small black head' have all contributed to making the name a quality brand.

Schwarzkopf lists shampoos, special haircare products, medicinal shampoos and styling products in its product range. Well-known product names from Schwarzkopf include Schauma Shampoo, Dare Deo, Gliss, Drei-Wetter-Taft hairspray, Bac and Kaloderma as well as Hattric, Prestige and Rodeo for men. A successful policy of product

and brand extension and the simple but effective logo and name have ensured Schwarzkopf's position as a market leader.

The Schwarzkopf ('black head') logo relies upon a graphic representation of the company's brand name.

WELLA

Wella is the second-largest producer of haircare and hairstyling products in the world. Founded in 1880 by the Stöher family in Sachsen and Thuringen, the business today operates in thirty-five countries from Brazil to Japan. A successful policy of line and brand extension has increased the product range to some 300 items, mainly used in hair salons.

One area of particular success has been Wella's entry into the hair fashion area with products such as styling cremes, mousses, gels and sprays. The newest product range on the market is 'Design' which has enjoyed the support of a co-ordinated marketing drive using a multi-media advertising campaign. This uses young, dynamic imagery to support the brand positioning. This theme is carried through into the packaging and the slogan 'Design – you've either got it or you haven't' has become a catchphrase for the fashion-conscious.

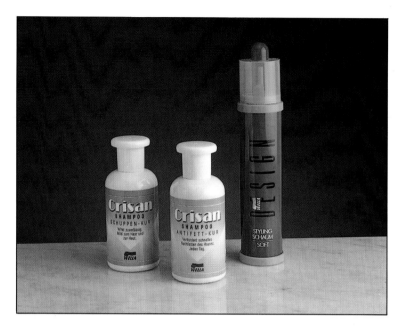

Wella products are sold internationally, particularly in the world's hairdressing salons.

DER SPIEGEL

Der Spiegel's subtitle 'A German news magazine' aptly describes this publication – a weekly magazine covering the political and economic scene, culture, sport and today's way of life.

The forty years of *der Spiegel* ('the Mirror') are inseparably linked with four decades of the Federal Republic of Germany: the West German partial state was founded in 1949 and *der Spiegel* was first published in 1947. Then, it was published on meagre, grey paper, had twenty-six pages and a circulation of 15,000 copies. Today over a million copies are printed every week on high-grade paper, with an average of 226 pages.

Yet despite the turbulent changes in Europe and Germany over the last forty years, *der Spiegel* has maintained continuity. As in 1947, *der Spiegel* is still the only German news

DER SPIEGEL
DAS DEUTSCHE NACHRICHTEN-MAGAZIN

magazine; as in the past, it is pledged to a form of journalism which does not restrict itself to printing facts, but also throws light on backgrounds and names the people involved in events. The image of the publication has remained what it was when conceived by Rudolf Augstein forty years ago: an incorruptible, critical publication of high quality, answerable to no-one and entirely independent of political or economic institutions.

With over five million readers, *der Speigel* is one of the most widely read magazines in Germany and it has a quality readership with high purchasing power and decision-making capability.

Few newspapers or journals have the authority or readership of *der Spiegel*, Germany's leading weekly news magazine.

![Rosenthal logo]

ROSENTHAL

Rosenthal is Germany's leading manufacturer and retailer of innovative, design-led and exclusive cutlery, porcelain and glass products.

Over the years Rosenthal has gained international fame for its 'Rosenthal-Studio' line and the 'Classic Rose Collection' – as well as for its collaboration with famous artists, painters and sculptors. The porcelain division accounts for the majority of the firm's operations; it is also the oldest, dating back to 1891. The glass and cutlery divisions were started within the last twenty years.

Design, innovation and exclusivity are the hallmarks of Rosenthal, qualities that are found in their products and in the layout of their shops, their promotional literature and packaging. The result is a dominant brand name that will continue to lead its sector of the market.

Rosenthal products are known for their style and their quality.

HB

Created thirty-five years ago and brand leader for twenty-five years, the HB story is not only one of the most enduring success stories of post-war Germany but also a textbook example of consistent and successful brand marketing.

Filter cigarettes with American-style blended tobaccos initially proved unsuccessful in the German market. Accustomed to old-style, strong Oriental tobaccos, smokers complained that these new cigarettes 'tasted of nothing'. Therein, however, lay the opportunity which B.A.T. seized: in 1955, after test marketing, HB emerged, a quality filter cigarette with a blend of Oriental and US tobaccos, supported by attractive packaging and a clear and motivating communications programme. HB captured the, by then, optimistic mood of post-war Germany and its 'Wirtschaftswunder': 'Happy, carefree enjoyment'. By 1959, HB had already achieved a 16.7 per cent market share as well as the No. 1 position in the market.

Advertising has continued to play an integral part in the brand's success. The cartoon character of the little HB man who lets the little niggly things in life get the better of him, became one of the best loved figures in German advertising history. By presenting HB as the problem solver, a strong emotive brand positioning was maintained in an increasingly competitive and cluttered market place. Over the years, however, advertising and packaging have moved with the times, taking account of a younger target market, while still maintaining the core brand value of enjoyment. This consistency, maintained throughout a period of change, has ensured that HB has retained its position as market leader.

HB successfully combined traditional Oriental tobacco blends with lighter US tobaccos to produce a cigarette which met German post-war tastes.

ITALY

ITALY HAS TAKEN ITS PLACE alongside the leading industrialised countries of the world as home of some of the world's finest and most sought after brands. Italians and non-Italians often speak of *Lo Stile Italiano* (the Italian Style) — both reality and myth have succeeded in creating in the minds of consumers worldwide an association between Italian products and a certain 'designer' style.

Of course, this is reflected in the *haute couture* labels that have emerged from Italy in recent decades and have, at times, eclipsed the French houses in setting the trends in international fashion: Gucci, Valentino and Missoni have become household names. This reputation for the best in modern design has further extended not only to high-street fashion — witness the

phenomenal success of Benetton and Stefanel — but also to high-tech, industrial and household products. Brands such as Martini and Ferrari have always maintained an international high-life *cachet* but other long-established brands such as Alessi, Fiat and Olivetti have also been able to capitalise on the renaissance of Italian Style.

But not all Italian brands are designed for export. Retail brands like Standa and Alpitour and food brands such as Saiwa, Barilla, Lavazza and Cirio may not be well-known outside Italy but are part of the every-day fabric of Italian life. In Italy such brands remain potent signs of national identity while Italy's international brands have become strong symbols of national pride and achievement.

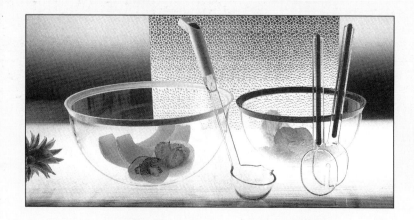

BRAND	LEADERSHIP	STABILITY	MARKET	INTERNATIONALITY	TREND	SUPPORT	PROTECTION	TOTAL
ALESSI	○	○			○	□	●	
ALITALIA	○		□	○			●	
ALPITOUR	□		□				○	○
BARILLA	●	●	○	○	□		●	○
CANDY	□	○	□	○	○	○	●	○
CIRIO	□	●	○			○	●	○
FERRARI	●	●	○	□	□	○	●	□
FIAT	□	●	□	□	○	□	●	□
GUZZINI	○	○	○				●	
LA RINASCENTE	○	□			○	○	●	
LAVAZZA	□	□	○		□	□	●	○
MARTINI	□	●	○	□		●	●	□
MISSONI		△		○	○		●	
OLIVETTI	●	□	□	□	□	□	●	□
PIRELLI	○	○	○	□		□	●	○
PRÉNATAL	□	○	○		□	□	●	
SAIWA	○	□	○				●	
STANDA	○		○		□	□	●	
STEFANEL		△		○		○	●	
VALENTINO	○			□	□	□	●	○

KEY ★★ Top Ten brand ★ Top Fifty brand ● exceptionally strong □ very strong ○ strong △ problem area

GUZZINI

The cutlery, bowls, plates and other kitchenware items exported around the world under the Guzzini name symbolise the ancient and the modern. They are created in a workshop but are then manufactured by robot.

Guzzini's business started at the turn of the century with craftwork items made of ox horn. In the 1930s they began using a revolutionary new material: plexiglass. The range of products grew and concentrated more on household objects. In the 1960s Guzzini made another technological leap forward with the introduction of high quality thermo-plastic injection moulding.

Guzzini products have become familiar household objects; they are known for their excellent design, attention to functional detail and use of brightly coloured plastic.

Italian product and furniture design is rightly praised. Guzzini is at the forefront of design in the kitchenware and houseware areas.

CANDY

Candy is Italy's leading brand of household domestic appliances (known as 'white goods') and Candy products are exported across Europe. Candy has a particularly consumer-oriented approach to appliances tailoring them to customers' requirements and emphasising this factor rather than technological wizardry. One example of this is the use of light-hearted brand names making the products more friendly and approachable.

The advertising treatment also aims at un-

dramatising the technological aspect and concentrating on Candy's straightforward competence; the slogan is *'Candy sa come si fa'* ('Candy knows how').

Though the brand is facing increased competition from Spain, Turkey and the Far East its market stature remains high.

Italy's domestic appliance manufacturers enjoy a strong position across the whole of Europe. Candy is Italy's leading brand.

MARTINI

For over a century the Martini & Rossi company's range of vermouths has been synonymous internationally with cocktails and apéritifs. The range comprises three main types of vermouth – rosso, bianco and secco – but it is the last of these that has achieved the greatest fame as part of the Martini Cocktail: gin, dry Martini, ice, perhaps an olive, shaken not stirred (as James Bond would have it).

Over the years the company has succeeded in maintaining unchanged a strong and distinctive visual image: the bottle label with its intricate rococo motifs and gold medals from the Nineteenth Century exhibitions is instantly recognisable. But despite this traditional label design Martini is advertised in a young, upbeat and upmarket way. In the 1960s and '70s Martini commercials set the standard for aspirational advertising – beautiful people living the high life in the world's great cities drinking Martini 'The Right One'. The long-legged waitress on roller skates carrying a tray of Martinis through St Tropez or New York became famous as the 'Martini Girl' and the slogan 'Anytime, Anyplace, Anywhere' symbolised the flexibility of Martini as a drink

for a variety of occasions and a variety of lifestyles.

For several years Martini has also been used on a range of sports clothing.

Martini is a versatile drink which is neither very expensive nor very strong, virtues to which Martini & Rossi has added sophisticated, contemporary associations.

VALENTINO

Having started from the humblest of origins, Valentino Garavani now enjoys one of the greatest reputations of any fashion designer on the international scene. But this was only achieved after a rigorous grounding in the basic principles of tailoring and a laborious apprenticeship in Paris learning about materials, cuts and colours.

In 1960, in his *atelier* in Via Condotti in Rome, Valentino presented his first collection revealing the full fruits of his experience gained while working in Paris. The first to recognise his great talent were the American buyers who had no hesitation in calling it 'a true revelation'. Leading women wanted to be seen in items bearing the Valentino signature, from Farah Diba and Jackie Kennedy to Elizabeth Taylor. In 1967, he presented his 'White Collection' with, for the first time, the 'V' trade mark. From that moment it became a symbol not only of the House of Valentino but also of 'the Italian Style'.

Valentino received the Neiman Marcus award, the 'Oscar' of the fashion industry and in 1969 he proposed his first ready-to-wear collection for the modern woman who did not want to sacrifice true elegance. His name was then extended into men's fashion. Since then Valentino has established himself more and more as the maestro of expensive, prestigious and uncompromising elegance.

The Valentino brand has also been broadened to include a fragrance with the name 'V', fashion accessories, lingerie and home furnishings such as decorated tiles. Valentino has designed costumes for La Scala, Milan, and some of his works are on permanent exhibition at the Metropolitan Museum of Art in New York.

Valentino is widely regarded as one of the most exciting and talented fashion designers and has done much to establish the reputation of Italian fashion design.

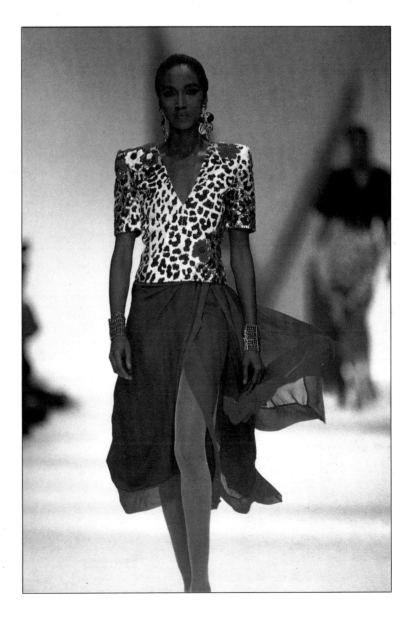

MISSONI

The New York Times has written of Missoni: 'For the wools used and the workmanship employed they are probably the best jumpers in the world'. Ottavio and Rosita Missoni created their first collection in 1966 and by the following year they were already being shown in Paris. They were then invited to New York by Vogue for the launch of their new line 'put together'. Their playful use of colours, as if on an artist's easel, marked a new era in knitwear fashion. The Missoni brand was born and the company moved from the Missoni's native city, Florence to Milan.

In 1973, Missoni won the Neiman Marcus

MISSONI

Missoni's skills with colours and unique designs have given the brand a distinctive market positioning.

award and the name now symbolises everything that is prestigious about the city of Milan. The 'modo Missoni' – their way of mixing colours – has set trends from the start. They have recently diversified into other areas such as non-woollen clothes, sportswear, fragrances, stage costumes (for La Scala) and even interior decorating and customising cars.

OLIVETTI

Founded in 1908 by the engineer Camillo Olivetti, Olivetti is today the leading European company in the area of office automation, equipment and Information Technology. With almost 60,000 employees throughout Europe, Olivetti is also involved in software and computer education. The company has supplied systems and equipment to industry, commerce and the public sector (including Scotland Yard in London) and is responsible for the automatic teller machine network in Italy and the system that controls Italian traffic lights.

Apart from technical excellence Olivetti is also known for the attention it pays to design. Not only is the equipment æsthetically and stylishly designed but also ergonomically sophisticated to ensure the best possible inter-face between humans and machines. It is this idea of co-operation and dialogue between Olivetti machines and their users that lies at the heart of the brand's positioning. This is captured in the slogan: *'La nostra forza è la vostra energia'* ('Our strength is your power'). Olivetti is one of the 'power brands' of Italy and contributes to securing its financial ties with the rest of Europe.

Information technology brands sometimes appear remote and somewhat 'non-human'. Not so Olivetti: the brand stresses the interface between human and machine.

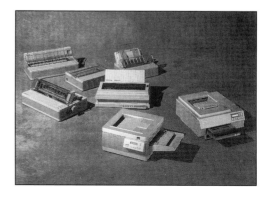

olivetti

ALITALIA

Alitalia is Italy's state-owned airline operating 122 aircraft on European and intercontinental journeys. Alitalia also runs a comprehensive domestic network through its sister company ATI. In 1989, the Group carried more than sixteen million passengers and 230 million kilos of goods. Alitalia flies to 102 destinations around the world and has over 4700 flights scheduled each week. Alitalia could also probably boast the longest flying tradition of any airline in the world. After all, Leonardo da Vinci – an Italian – was publishing designs and diagrams of people in flying machines in the fifteenth century! It is appropriate, therefore, that Alitalia's home airport, Rome's Fiumicino, should be named after him.

Alitalia

Alitalia's brand image has been adversely affected by strikes and other industrial relations problems.

The airline aims to create 'brand values' by emphasising hospitality, friendliness and Italian quality in all its activities. In the 1980s it adopted an integrated marketing strategy bringing together such features as the interior design of aircraft, customer care programmes and targeted advertising. However, the airline has been badly hit in recent years by strikes, both by its own personnel and Italian airport staff and these have damaged Alitalia's reputation.

ALPITOUR

Since the beginning of the 1960s, Alpitour has been the leading brand in the Italian travel industry. 'Luxury travel at half the price' was the slogan under which Alpitour launched its 'Inclusive Tour' and created the market for individual all-inclusive holidays to the main European tourist destinations. Alpitour has also helped to sell Italy as a holiday venue.

In 1985, Alpitour was a founder member of SHANA, a collaboration of some of the most important tour operators in Europe. These companies are already developing a pan-European strategy and Alpitour is well placed to take advantage of 1992 and the creation of a single European market.

Approximately 15 per cent of package holidays taken by Italians are from Alpitour and in 1988–89 they carried 350,000 passengers. Alpitour was awarded the Oscar of the European travel industry in 1989.

Alpitour has prospered as a result of Italy's growing economic power.

CIRIO

Cirio is a brand of tomato-based products that has become a symbol of Italy and Italian cooking. The products range from skinned tomatoes to sauce bases as well as related products such as vinegars and jams. It is a brand of long standing and has strong associations with the Italian pasta tradition. Advertising campaigns of recent years have been designed to consolidate the image of Cirio as the essential ingredient to the favourite Italian dish of pasta with sauce. Cirio has become synonymous with tomatoes, and synonymous too with Mediterranean cooking.

The brand is owned by Cirio-Bertolli-de-Rica, the processed foods division of SME. SME operates in two principal areas: food manufacturing and food distribution (through the supermarket chain GS and the motorway restaurants Autogrill).

Sauces play an important rôle in Italian cooking and Cirio is synonymous with such sauces.

STANDA

Standa, a well-known name since the 1930s, is today one of the largest Italian self-service retail chains. The chain comprises, at present, 263 outlets, some selling food only, some non-food and some mixed, as well as 250 affiliated stores. The brand's success over the years has been determined by a careful choice of merchandise and a good balance between quality and price, appealing first and foremost to the middle market of Italian consumers.

The Standa image had, however, been in decline up until 1988 when the company was bought by Berlusconi's Fininvest Group. This marked the relaunch of the brand and stores were updated and new services, such as travel agencies and financial advice centres, were introduced. But most importantly the acquisition provided a synergy between Standa and the brands stocked by Standa through shared advertising time on the Berlusconi channels.

'Standa – la casa degli italiani' ('Standa – the home of Italians') is the advertising position that the company has taken as its own and which it has continued to follow in recent years.

Italian retailing is still exceptionally fragmented with hundreds of thousands of small owner-managed stores. Standa, a major chain, stands out in the retail scene.

BARILLA

This private company is the Italian market's leading pasta brand.

The commercial history of Barilla, or rather of the Barilla family, began in 1877 with a little shop selling pasta and bread. The first factory dates from 1910 and the family only stopped baking bread in 1952. The current managing director, Pietro Barilla, belongs to the third generation of Barilla entrepreneurs and the family tradition is destined to continue as his sons are already involved in the business. In 1971, the company was sold to the American Grace Corporation but it was bought back by the Barilla family in 1979.

One result of the 'Grace Period' was the launch of a range of baked goods grouped together under the name Mulino Bianco ('The White Mill'). This is now the market leader in its sector in Italy and has contributed greatly to the growth of the company in recent years.

Pasta is central to Italian cuisine and Barilla is Italy's leading brand of pasta.

SAIWA

The somewhat Japanese sounding name Saiwa is actually one of Italy's largest biscuit brands, the name being an acronym derived from the original wafer manufacturer based in Genoa (*Società Anonima Industria Wafer Affini*). The brand is best known for Vafer Saiwa, its cream-filled wafer biscuits, and for Oro Saiwa, a golden-coloured breakfast biscuit that can be found in almost every Italian kitchen. Oro Saiwa is Italy's best-selling biscuit and 16,000 tonnes of it are sold every year. But these are only part of a wider range of products including salt biscuits (Premium Saiwa), chocolate biscuits (Urrà Saiwa) and well-known international brands like Ritz and Chipster that appear under the Saiwa endorsement.

Saiwa has a reputation for product quality with one of the most modern biscuit factories in Europe. Although it is a very traditional brand, Saiwa has also been aware of the need to respond constantly to changes in consumer tastes and has therefore introduced wholemeal and low-fat variants of its most popular products.

The Saiwa brand of biscuits is the strongest in Italy and Saiwa has a reputation for quality and innovation.

ALESSI

In 1921, Giovanni Alessi, a skilful metal worker from Novara, founded in Omegna, on the edge of Lake Orta, a workshop for turning, pressing and fusing metal and producing mainly metal objects for the table and the kitchen. The coffee pots and tea sets made by Alessi are now world famous and their highly distinctive shapes and colours have made them a must for the designer kitchen. Since the 1950s Alessi's work with Italian architects has also played its part in creating the 'legend' of Italian design. The Alessi catalogues have carried objects created not only by Alessi but by more than eighty international designers and some are on display in the permanent collections of the most important museums in the world.

The 1980s saw Alessi partially shift its attention away from metal objects for the home to other related areas such as objects made of wood and china, small items of furniture, and ovens and cooking apparatus,

Alessi's beautiful objects for the kitchen and the table, mainly made from metal, are world famous.

either under the original brand name or under new names such as Twergi and Tendentse. The *Officina Alessi* was formed in 1983 with the aim of resuming Alessi's experimental work in different types of metal.

PIRELLI

Pirelli is the world's fifth biggest tyre producer and has a reputation for manufacturing the best and the most technically sophisticated road tyres, especially low-profile steel-braced radial tyres. As well as being used on some of the world's best sports cars and saloon cars, Pirelli tyres have also had a close association with Formula One motor racing. Moreover, by not competing at the lower priced commodity end of the tyre market Pirelli has managed to minimise its losses in years when other major tyre manufacturers have suffered badly from cut-price competition. Pirelli sells tyres worldwide and is a particularly strong brand in South America and even Japan.

Pirelli Group activities are not, however, limited to tyres. It is also Italy's largest manufacturer of cables and fibre optics and

produces sports shoes under the Superga name.

The elongated 'P' that distinguishes Pirelli has become a trade mark in its own right and was originally designed to express the elasticity of the rubber that goes into the tyres. But Pirelli's most celebrated marketing device is the notorious Pirelli calendar sent out each year to suppliers and customers. Some of the world's best photographers have been commissioned to take shots of the world's most famous models, topless, in beautiful locations that have no more than a passing association with tyres or rubber technology.

The dominant brand in its Italian home market since the time of the Cinturato Pirelli has enjoyed a world-wide reputation for high performance tyres.

FIAT ◻

The *Fabbrica Italiana Automobili di Torino* or FIAT, founded in 1899 by the senator Giovanni Agnelli, has shown since its beginnings, a particular interest in overseas markets.
In 1909, exports to the United States were begun and by 1915 FIAT was also exporting to Melbourne and Sydney, Australia. In 1907, the first cars manufactured under license from FIAT were produced in Austria.

By 1945 the FIAT name was present in over 150 countries, from China to the United States, from the USSR to Africa, from South America to Australia.

From its origins in motor car manufacture, production has moved also into other sectors: industrial and agricultural vehicles, aeroplanes and public transportation. Today

FIAT worldwide comprises over 700 companies and 270,000 employees.

The group strategy of innovation and internationalisation continues to produce strong results. Great importance is placed by FIAT upon applied research and its factories already contain more than 1800 robots employed in the more tiresome and dangerous production processes.

The FIAT name and the names of its cars have become part of the lives of every Italian. FIAT's range of small, inexpensive cars have brought car ownership within the reach of all.

FIAT is a colossus of Italian manufacturing industry producing a wide range of automotive, aerospace and industrial products.

FERRARI ◻

Founded by Enzo Ferrari in Modena in 1929, Ferrari is the renowned brand leader in Formula One motor racing and produces sports cars recognised throughout the world as undisputed status symbols.

The greatest coachbuilders in Italy, from Pininfarina to Bertone, have supplied ideas and designs and made an essential contribution to the defining of the unique Ferrari style. But the company's products – which since 1965 have been part of the FIAT portfolio – are not just prestigious symbols of Italian style: they are the results of expensive research and rigorous testing both in the laboratory and on the track and are constructed after endless hours of dedicated research into aerodynamics, manœuvrability and technical design.

The factory at Maranello counts among its accolades: ninety-three international Grand Prix wins; eight victories in the *Mille Miglia* (the thousand mile race around Italy); and nine in the Le Mans twenty-four hours. The Ferrari

stable has also produced nine world champion motor racing drivers.

The non-racing sports cars are without doubt some of the most coveted products that the Italian market can offer the world. Time and again classic Ferrari cars have set new record prices for cars sold at auction. Meanwhile, the same Ferrari name has, in recent years, been used as a brand name for other products such as wrist watches and clothes. *'Il cavallino rampante'* (The Prancing Horse of Ravenna) has become an instantly recognised symbol of technical efficiency and style.

Ferrari combines Italian style and elegance, and Italian engineering know-how in a unique fashion.

LA RINASCENTE

Founded in Milan soon after World War II, La Rinascente (meaning 'Rebirth' or 'Renaissance') rose like a phoenix to become the city's premier department store. It stands in a building at the side of the Galleria Vittorio Emanuele facing Milan's magnificent cathedral. Its luxurious atmosphere and attentive service make it a pleasure to shop in and La Rinascente attracts not only Milanesi but also the many visitors to the city.

The name is also applied to a range of non-food items sold in the store, while food lines sold by La Rinascente are branded SMA. Recently La Rinascente has started to move onto the international scene, setting up a series of joint ventures in major European countries.

Milan's *La Rinascente* department store is rapidly developing an international reputation.

PRĒNATAL

In spite of its French sounding name Prénatal is actually an Italian brand. The idea of a shop catering specifically for mothers and babies, though revolutionary, was clearly attractive and since the first shop opened in Milan in 1963 a chain of 300 shops across Italy, Germany, Spain and other European countries has developed.

Prénatal's success is not due just to the comprehensive range of products it endorses but also to the level of service that lies behind these. The Prénatal service to mothers and women during pregnancy is designed to provide them with advice, information, assistance or just reassurance. Moreover, the experience gained in day-to-day contact with mothers or mothers-to-be enables Prénatal constantly to improve its service. Prénatal funds a study centre whose book *The Prénatal Guide to Birth* has run into five editions and has sold 500,000 copies to date.

Alongside this scientific and serious approach to childbirth is an appreciation of the 'fun' side of motherhood and babies. Thus, Prénatal does not rely on stereotypes of what a good mother should be. Instead of pictures of sedate conservative mothers pushing babies in prams its advertising shows pregnant women on trapezes, playing electric guitars, dressed as mermaids or punks, skiing and even in wedding dresses.

Italian babies are some of the most beautifully dressed in the world, a factor which Prénatal has benefited from, and contributed to.

STEFANEL

Stefanel's success has been built on distributing high quality, factory-made knitwear through its own tightly woven chain of outlets. The shops succeed in combining the two concepts of a 'boutique' and a 'high street' store. Over the years, as well as expanding its own network of shops, Stefanel has also broadened its range of merchandise, initially limited to clothing for men and women, to include the Stefanel Kids brand for children's clothes.

To ensure that the brand values of Stefanel clothes are maintained, the positioning of the brand has shifted from the concept of designers and fashion shows to the broader and more marketable concept of clothes that are 'fun to wear'. To this end, press and TV advertising adopts the strategy of associating Stefanel items with an enchanting and evocative natural landscape or with a significant and decisive emotional moment in the lives of its wearers.

Stefanel, like its great rival Benetton, has been one of the great fashion successes of recent years both in Italy and internationally.

LAVAZZA

Founded initially as a chemist's shop in Turin in 1925, Luigi Lavazza's company began to specialise in products from the Far East. After the Second World War Lavazza introduced the first coffees to be packaged in tin wrappers, but the brand's great boom can be firmly linked with the television commercials that it ran in the 1960s through which Lavazza gained a 50 per cent share of the Italian coffee market. Lavazza has recently extended into decaffeinated coffee where it has around a 22 per cent share. Today it is the clear market leader in coffees and its packs are a symbol of high quality combined with low price.

Advertising remains a very important part of Lavazza's marketing strategy; it was used in the 1980s to update completely the brand's image as a superior quality, family coffee.

Lavazza dominates the Italian coffee market through a combination of price, quality and strong brand support.

The brand is just beginning to extend into other European countries and in the UK, for example, its slightly unusual and rather suggestive name is the focus of an advertising campaign that aims at establishing brand recognition.

UK

IN THE LATTER PART OF THE 1980s most European Community countries initiated programmes designed to remind local businesses that 1992 was imminent and that, with the completion of the European Single Market, huge new opportunities would open up for them. Companies were urged, therefore, to prepare for a single market of 350 million consumers – and were warned of the dangers of missing out.

However, many managers in Britain and the rest of Europe have found it difficult to translate worthy Government exhortations into actionable initiatives. Though commitment to the concept of a single European market has been consistently high, companies have found difficulty in formulating specific plans to take advantage of the alleged opportunities.

Nowhere does the Single Market offer more opportunities than in the area of branded goods. Indeed, so acute has the interest in brands and branding become in Europe that some companies in Britain and France are now entering brands in their balance sheets as intangible assets so that the true underlying value of the business is reflected more accurately in the financial accounts. Equally significantly, many major companies are now undertaking detailed 'brand audits' so that they understand with precision the profitability of their brands as well as their strengths, weaknesses, capacity for extension, potential opportunities for licensing and so forth.

Companies are also looking hard at their brand portfolios and are seeking both to acquire brands, especially international and Europe-wide brands and, in certain instances, to divest themselves of unwanted brands. Thus Nestlé of Switzerland acquired Britain's Rowntree for £2.5 billion, Cadbury-Schweppes of Britain has acquired a host of brands from Procter & Gamble (US), and Perrier (France) and SmithKline Beecham have divested themselves of unwanted food brands to CPC Corporation.

But at the same time as companies have been developing and adjusting their brand portfolios to take advantage of new European realities a growing realisation has taken place that Europe is a far more difficult market than it appears at first sight.

There seems little chance, therefore, that there will be homogenisation of branding in Europe and that international 'esperanto' brands will replace local brands. There will, no doubt, be a crystallizing out of brands in Europe and it is certain that powerful international brands will continue to make ground at the expense of local brands. Large-scale brand diversification will, however, continue.

The owners of virtually all British brands recognise that they are now at something of a crossroads – the opening up of Europe provides not just opportunities for British brands abroad but for foreign brands in Britain. How will Britain's indigenous food brands fare when British housewives have ready access to the high quality food brands already available to the French housewife? Will British grocery retail chains survive in the face of competition from the huge German chains who seem able to survive, even prosper, on much thinner margins? Will the British insurance industry be over-run by foreign competitors?

Just as the political map of Europe is changing so too is the branding map. Britain has, to a large extent, been shielded by geographical and political factors from full-blown competition in the branded goods area. Rapid change is, however, taking place and will hit the branding area as hard as any other.

UK

BRAND	LEADERSHIP	STABILITY	MARKET	INTERNATIONALITY	TREND	SUPPORT	PROTECTION	TOTAL
ANDREX	○	●	□		□	□	●	○
BASS	□	●	□		○	●	●	○
BBC	●	●	●	○	□	○	○	□
BISTO	●	●				○	●	
BOOTS	□	●	●		□	□	●	○
BUPA	□	●	●		□	○	○	
CADBURYS	○	●	□	○	□	●	●	○
DULUX	□	□	□		○	●	●	○
DUREX	□	□	●		●	□	●	○
ELASTOPLAST	○	□	□		□		●	
FAIRY LIQUID	○	●	□		□	□	●	
FLORA	○	□	●		□	○	●	○
HAMLEYS		□	□		○	○	●	
HOVIS	○	●	●		○	□	●	○
KALIBER	○		○		□	○	●	
KITKAT	□	●	●		□	●	●	□
LAND ROVER	□	●	□	○	□	○	○	□
LIBERTY		●	○		○		●	
LUCOZADE	○	□	●		□	●	●	○
MARKS & SPENCER (ST MICHAEL) ★	●	●	●		●	○	●	□
MARMITE	●	●	●		○	●	●	○
OXO	□	●	□		□	□	●	○
PHILEAS FOGG	○	○	●		●	○	●	○
SAINSBURY'S	●	●	●		●	○	●	□
SELLOTAPE	□	●	□		□	○	●	○
SWAN VESTAS	○	□	○		△	○	●	
TETLEY'S	○	●	●		□	●	○	

KEY ★★ Top Ten brand ★ Top Fifty brand ● exceptionally strong □ very strong ○ strong △ problem area

DULUX

Dulux is Britain's major brand of paints. It is owned by ICI and the brand has virtual universal recognition among adults in Britain.

The reasons for the brand's success are many: a high quality, sensibly priced product; very wide distribution; strong advertising support; and well directed product innovations – Dulux has been particularly skillful in anticipating and moulding changing consumer tastes in colours and finishes, for example through its Harmonies and Gentle Whites ranges.

The major challenge currently confronting the brand is the rapid concentration of retail buying power in the hands of a few major 'do-it-yourself' chains including B&Q (owned by Kingfisher, formerly Woolworth Holdings), Homebase (J Sainsbury) and Do-it-All (a merged group owned jointly by W H Smith and Boots).

Until the mid 1970s the do-it-yourself market was very fragmented and consisted mainly of builder's merchants, small local stores selling timber, electrical goods, curtain rails etc and a few general purpose high street chains such

as F W Woolworth. Then the 'D-I-Y explosion' took place – large out of town warehouses sprang up all over the country and quickly coalesced into five or six major chains who now own the lion's share of the market.

These chains have enormous purchasing power and have, no doubt, put pressure on Dulux's margins. More importantly, all such chains have introduced 'own label' ranges of paints which are keenly priced and prominently displayed in-store. ICI has always declined to manufacture own label paint products yet has found its own brand, Dulux, facing increasing pressure.

Dulux illustrates well the competition which exists in some markets between manufacturer's brands and own label brands.

FAIRY LIQUID

Fairy Liquid is Procter & Gamble's main brand of washing-up liquid in the UK and though the brand name causes much amusement among visiting Americans, in its home market it is a very serious brand indeed and clear leader in its sector.

Fairy Liquid has been around since 1960, although the Fairy brand name has been used on such products as Fairy Snow and Fairy Toilet Soap for much longer. Fairy Liquid is ranked Britain's twenty-fourth grocery brand by Nielsen. Its positioning is one of 'strong but gentle', a message which the brand's owners have communicated powerfully and skilfully.

Fairy Liquid's highly successful positioning is one of gentleness combined with efficiency.

LAND ROVER

The first Land Rover was introduced in 1948 as a multi-purpose, all-terrain four-wheel-drive vehicle mainly for farmers and agriculturalists. It was quickly recognised as 'the world's most versatile vehicle' and by 1989 1.5 million had been built of which over 70 per cent were exported. Most are still in service.

Land Rover's reputation is based on ruggedness, longevity and 'fitness for purpose' and the Solihull-based company offers an enormous range of specifications and extras to cope with almost any conceivable application. The company also produces two 'first cousins' to the original Land Rover: the Range Rover, a stylish, luxury four-wheel-drive vehicle which has achieved enormous popularity in Europe, North America, Australia, the Middle East and Japan; and the newly introduced Land Rover Discovery which is aimed at the rapidly growing market for high-performance leisure vehicles.

Though Land Rover by no means has the four-wheel-drive market to itself – Japanese competition is especially strong – the Land Rover brand possesses unique associations of quality, performance and reliability in this specialist sector.

In the face of increased Japanese competition Land Rover has developed new products less particularised to agricultural and military applications.

LUCOZADE ◯

Lucozade, a brand from SmithKline Beecham, was developed in the 1920s as a glucose drink for invalids and convalescents, especially children. Until the early 1980s the brand

In the 1980s Lucozade has become a product more for healthy adults than sick children.

continued to be positioned essentially as a drink for sick children but, since 1983, the brand has been fundamentally repositioned with considerable success.

It was in 1983 that Daley Thompson, the British Olympic decathlon gold medallist, was first used to promote Lucozade as a sports drink. Since then, one-drink bottles and cans have been introduced as well as Lucozade glucose tablets, flavour variants (e.g. lemon barley and orange barley) and most recently, Lucozade Sport isotonic drink.

In less than ten years Lucozade has thus been successfully repositioned from being a drink for sick children to a drink for healthy people of all ages and now represents something of a textbook case of good, sensible brand management.

MARMITE

Marmite, recently sold by SmithKline Beecham to CPC International along with Bovril and Ambrosia in a £157 million deal, is the archetypal local, niche brand. Marmite is a dark brown, sticky, strong smelling, savoury paste. It looks and tastes like meat extract, but in fact is 100 per cent vegetarian as it is a yeast extract, made from a by-product of the brewing industry.

Marmite is part of the fabric of British society. It is rich in Vitamin 'B' and scores of British children have been weaned on Marmite and hence have come, almost from birth, to appreciate its finer qualities. Those who come to the brand later in life, however, often find its taste far from appealing. The heyday of the brand was probably during the First and Second World Wars when food was rationed and vitamins and dietary supplements, including Marmite, received Government support. Many people born during the Second World War and the post-war baby boom are still loyal users today.

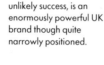

Marmite, a somewhat unlikely success, is an enormously powerful UK brand though quite narrowly positioned.

The brand's current positioning is enormously strong but, at the same time, its very narrowness makes the job of brand development a difficult one. Users of the brand know it intimately – it's an old friend – and may not appreciate change. Non-users of the brand, on the other hand, also have a clear, though sometimes negative, image of the brand and have steadfastly resisted its blandishments. The task of repositioning or extending the brand will not be easy.

DUREX

The most popular of all condoms sold in the UK are Durex brand condoms produced by LRC Products. In recent years the AIDS crisis

The Durex brand name is almost synonymous with condoms in the UK, a market strength which brands such as Mates have yet to harm.

has led to a resurgence of interest in such products and considerable growth for the Durex brand.

The Durex name (from DUrability, REliabilty, EXcellence) has existed since the early 1930s and is used on nine different types of condoms as well as on diaphragms and spermicides. Until the early 1970s public attitudes towards contraception meant that brand promotion was necessarily undertaken in a discreet, low key fashion – opportunities for advertising and point of sale display were strictly limited. Now, however, the brand is highly visible and is promoted through advertising, public relations campaigns and sponsorship – motor cycling and hot air ballooning have both been used extensively in recent years.

HOVIS ○

In 1886, Richard Smith developed a flour containing vitamin-rich wheatgerm at a time when the usual practice was to remove the wheatgerm as it soured the flour. He took his new discovery to S Fitton & Sons and they marketed it as 'Smith's patent germ flour'.

It did not sell well and in 1890 a national competition was organised to find a better brand name. The £25 prize was awarded to a London student for the name Hovis, derived from the Latin *'hominis vis'* meaning the strength of man. And so a major new brand was born.

Advertising campaigns, competitions in the national press, and bakery shop promotions increased brand exposure dramatically, such that by 1906 the following verse appeared in a competition in the Daily Mail.

Hovis and Clovis are words that rhyme Clovis was King in olden time. Alas! poor Clovis is long since dead but Hovis still reigns! as King of Bread.

Widescale exposure to television in the mid-fifties provided Hovis with new advertising opportunities and the famous slogan 'Don't say brown say Hovis' was first used at this time, together with the image of a boy pushing a bike up a hill.

Recent recognition of the benefits of wheatgerm has led to renewed consumer interest in Hovis, Britain's leading brand of wheatgerm flour and bread.

In the 1980s the Hovis range was extended from its base as a wheatgerm loaf into wholewheat and stoneground wholemeal loaves, and a new organic stoneground Hovis loaf has recently been launched nationally. For 100 years Hovis has been the leading British brand of brown bread, a position which the brand seems certain to retain in the 'healthy 90s' and beyond.

BBC ▢

The British Broadcasting Corporation – the BBC or, sometimes, 'the Beeb' – still has for many listeners in Britain and abroad inescapable associations with Bakelite radios (wireless sets, as they were then known), wartime broadcasts to occupied Europe ('London calling') and TV coverage of the Queen's coronation in 1953. It is therefore widely seen by people in Britain as part of their heritage and is held in deep affection.

The BBC was formed in 1922 and made its first radio broadcast in 1923 and its first (and

the world's first) regular, high definition television broadcast in 1936. In 1938, the first BBC foreign language service began, in Arabic, and the BBC World Service now broadcasts in English and thirty-six other languages.

The BBC radio and TV services are financed through a licence fee and are therefore free of advertising. The BBC has also maintained, over the years, an impartiality and a concern for standards and quality which has earned, and retained, public respect.

Britons are said to be mightily fond of their institutions – the Monarchy, MCC, famous regiments etc. The BBC is a British institution which retains enormous respect and affection.

SELLOTAPE

Sellotape dominates the UK home and office markets for adhesive tapes with a market share of around 65 per cent, five or six times greater than its largest competitor Scotch. Indeed, in the UK home market over 96 per cent of consumers recognise the brand and, in a recent survey, some 80 per cent had bought a Sellotape product within the previous three months.

Outside the UK, however, the brand has achieved only limited success, partly due to the formidable marketing and distribution strengths of 3M, the world's leading tape producer and the owners of the Scotch brand, but also due to a specific decision on the part of the brand owners to focus on the brand's core market, the UK, and not risk diluting effort elsewhere. Having said that, Sellotape has made strong progress in Northern Europe.

The brand is now over fifty years old but it is only in recent years that major efforts have

In the UK, the name Sellotape is a semi-generic term for adhesive tapes.

been made to extend the brand into new product lines in related areas. The brand is now in a transitional phase from being a fairly narrow product brand to a wider umbrella brand providing endorsement in new and related areas.

Andrex is an excellent product which has received powerful, consistent promotion and support.

ANDREX

Toilet paper might be considered as merely a functional commodity item yet in the UK Andrex toilet tissue is, according to Checkout magazine, Britain's fifth largest grocery brand. It comes behind Persil, Nescafé, Whiskas and Ariel but, with sales of around £165 million, outsells such powerful brands as Coca-Cola, Heinz baked beans and Kellogg's Corn Flakes.

Andrex is owned by Scott Paper Company and sells more than three times as much as its nearest rival. The brand has, consistently, been innovative (it was, for instance, the first to introduce coloured tissue) and has always maintained product quality and a value for money image. The brand was the first to use TV advertising for toilet rolls in 1972 and its much loved 'puppy' campaign has reinforced the brand qualities of softness, strength and value.

FLORA

Flora is a fine example of a brand which has greatly benefited from changing lifestyles. It was launched in 1964 as a sunflower oil margarine high in polyunsaturates. At that time the role of polyunsaturates in preventing heart disease was well known to doctors but not to the general public and by 1971 Flora's share of the UK yellow fats market was still below one per cent. Slowly, however, the brand took off: in the mid-70s several influential TV programmes focused on coronary heart disease and the benefits of polyunsaturates and the brand owners (Van den Berghs, part of Unilever) initiated new advertising campaigns to promote the brand and to capitalise on this new awareness.

Throughout the 1980s Flora's market share grew steadily though, by 1985, it was still only a relatively modest 5.6 per cent. Yet by the end of the decade it was three times as high. Why? Much work was done during the late 1980s to broaden the brand's positioning so as to include women and also to extend the range by the addition of an extra light product, dressings, cheese products, low salt margarines and Flora products for baking. The major factor, however, seems to be mainly one of achieving consumer familiarity. Clearly, companies developing new brands need to be persistent and determined as brand success is seldom achieved overnight, even in 'fashionable' market sectors.

Flora has benefited from changing lifestyles and increased consumer interest in 'healthy eating'. It is also a tribute to persistent, singleminded brand management.

HAMLEYS

Hamleys bills itself as 'the finest toyshop in the world'. It can trace back its roots to 1760 and a visit to Hamleys on Regent Street is a 'must' for many visitors to London. In the weeks before Christmas the numbers trying to get in to Hamleys are so great that there is an 'in' and an 'out' door and the Police ensure that Regent Street is not completely blocked by the crowds.

Despite the power of the brand name, owners of Hamleys have found that wider exploitation of the name is not as easy as might at first appear. In 1986, for example, the Harris Queensway retail group bought Hamleys and quickly expanded the provincial chain of smaller Hamleys stores from three to ten. They proved far from successful largely, it is thought, because these smaller stores could not deliver the Hamleys promise of enormous range and choice; they were, in effect, little differentiated from other toyshops. Hamleys is

The new owners of Hamleys are seeking to translate high brand recognition into high profits.

now under new management and the Regent Street store is to be completely remodelled to provide an even greater range of toys; plans are also in hand to develop own label toys and licensing.

ELASTOPLAST

Elastoplast is Britain's leading first aid dressing brand and the choice of millions of parents to dress children's wounds. It was originally developed to treat varicose veins and ulcers in bedridden patients but became more widely used by doctors when Horatio Nelson Smith, the 'nephew' in the corporate name T G Smith & Nephew, the company which developed and still owns the brand, circulated information on clinical efficacy to 40,000 doctors.

Though the brand is now sold internationally it is particularly strong in the UK and is both a hospital and a retail brand. The brand has also been subject to constant development and there are now waterproof, clear and special 'character' (i.e. printed) versions of the product.

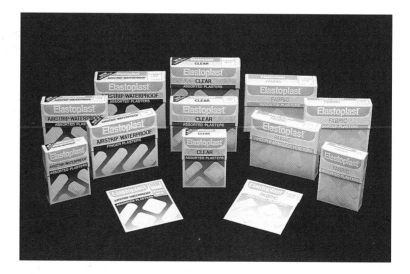

Elastoplast

Elastoplast enjoys in the UK market the same level of recognition as that of Band-Aid in the US.

SWAN VESTAS

Swan Vestas, a brand which dates from 1883, is still Britain's number one match with a 29 per cent market share. It is also the only brand of matches consistently asked for by name.

One of the key features of the brand is its highly distinctive packaging and, in particular, the flat box shape. In fact, the packaging design has changed eight times over the last 100 years though each change has been relatively subtle and consumer recognition and affection for the brand has never been challenged through dramatic repackaging.

The strength of the Swan brand has also been carried through into a range of complementary smoker's sundries. In 1984, the Swan range of smokers' requisites was launched, including gas refills, gas fluid, flints and pipe cleaners. The range tidied up a previously fragmented market and is now the leading player in this market.

The Swan Vestas brand has been heavily supported over the years by high profile above and below the line activity, including the Swan Vestas Celebrity Angling Classic, the biggest sporting event in the world in terms of the number of participants.

Pipe smokers — who should know about matches as they seem to spend most of their time lighting their pipes — swear by Swan Vestas.

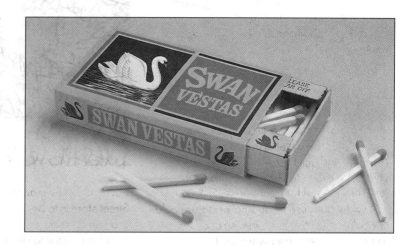

BASS

Bass have been brewers since 1777 so when in 1876 they obtained the first registered trade mark in Britain under the new 1875 Act for their red triangle device, they were already almost centenarians. Indeed, by that time Bass beers were to be found all over the world — Manet in 1882 immortalised two bottles of Bass in his famous painting 'Bar at the Folies Bergères' and the Union Pacific Railroad served Bass in its dining cars.

Bass is now a broadly based brewing and leisure group whose beer brands include, besides Bass, Tennent's, Worthington, Stones and, in Britain and Europe, Carling Black Label. The Group also now owns the Holiday Inn chain. The Bass brand is, however, still of key importance and Bass Ale is recognised around the world as the No 1 British ale.

Bass pale ale is one of Britain's leading beer brands though British ales have never enjoyed the international success of lighter beers.

1905

1915

1923

1933

1940

1951

1961

1971

1978

TETLEY'S

Tetley's is a powerful, regional brand of British beer, 'bitter', as it is known. The loyalty and dedication that Tetley's beer commands is unparalleled. It is talked of as the one thing – apart from Yorkshire County Cricket Club – that Yorkshiremen most miss when they are away from home. The Huntsman logo on the side of a pub or on a draught beer font is as evocative a visual image of Yorkshire as Ilkley Moor or the ruins of Fountains Abbey.

The Tetley's brand has now spread across the Pennines to neighbouring Lancashire and down to the South of England. This good honest Yorkshire beer brand is even available as far afield as Melbourne, Australia. The

British bitter is best drunk on draught; Tetley's is one of the leading brands and is particularly strong in Yorkshire.

canned version of Tetley's is regarded by connoisseurs as a minor distraction – it is the draught bitter that is the true brand and dedicated Tetley's drinkers are insistent that their pints are properly drawn.

Tetley's attention to quality means it cannot be shipped around the world or brewed under license as easily as its upstart lager cousins. But wherever there are Yorkshiremen there will be a demand for Tetley's.

But what of Tetley's tea? This, curiously, is also an Allied Lyons brand, with a Yorkshire heritage and a devoted following among the British public. But there's certainly no danger of confusing the two.

CADBURY'S

Cadbury Ltd, the chocolate and confectionery arm of the Cadbury Schweppes Group, is a large, broadly based company with a wealth of strong brands, among them Dairy Milk, Roses, Milk Tray, Wispa, Creme Eggs, Flake, Crunchie, Fruit & Nut, Wholenut and Double Decker.

Cadbury's, however, uses branding differently from its major competitors: whereas Rowntree and Mars have more or less free-standing brands with little corporate endorsement, Cadbury's uses its corporate name powerfully on all its products. Thus, whereas most consumers would not know, or perhaps care, that Rowntree makes After Eight and Mars makes Twix, they would have little doubt that Milk Tray, Dairy Milk and Flake are all brands from Cadbury's.

Cadbury's, as a result, has remarkably wide exposure as a brand, but conversely, the wide scope of usage and the fact that the name is normally used together with a product brand means that the management of the brand is a particularly delicate task.

Cadbury's

Britons consume more chocolate and confectionery than people from most other countries. Cadbury's, one of the most powerful brands in the UK, benefits from its strong home base.

KITKAT

KitKat is a formidable brand; it, and the Mars Bar, are the only two brands which sell more than £100 million at r.s.p. in the British chocolate confectionery market. It was launched by Rowntree in 1935 and within two years was the company's best seller.

KitKat is a moulded wafer bar consisting of three layers of crisp wafer biscuit with a praline filling, shaped into fingers which are easily broken from the bar, and covered in milk chocolate. It is essentially a snack product and

KitKat is positioned part way between a snack and an indulgence – it is, in fact, both.

the 'Have a Break, Have a KitKat' slogan has become widely known through consistent advertising on TV and in other media.

In 1988, after a desperate tussle with Swiss rivals Jacobs Suchard, Nestlé bought Rowntree for £2.5 billion, two and a half times the pre-bid capitalisation of Rowntree and many times Rowntree's tangible net asset value. It is certain that a significant part of the intangible asset value of Rowntree can be attributed to the KitKat brand.

MARKS & SPENCER ☆ ☐

This British-based retailer is the only retailer in the world afforded an AAA financial rating. Certainly, in Britain the company is near legendary – it has a 16 per cent share of all UK clothing sales and 5 per cent of UK food sales and its flagship store near Marble Arch is reckoned to have 'the fastest moving stock in the world'.

Many of the business principles pioneered by Marks & Spencer have been widely copied by others – no-quibble exchange of goods, meticulous buying and quality control procedures, only limited use of advertising, sophisticated staff welfare programmes etc.

One curious policy is that of using dual brands – the corporate brand is Marks & Spencer, yet, even though the company sells no manufacturer's brands at all, only own label, it uses a separate product brand name, St Michael, on its goods.

The reasons for this policy appear to be largely historical: though the company can trace back its origins to 1882, the St Michael

trademark was not used until 1928. At that time a separate trademark was chosen as the company wished its own label products to enjoy the same 'free standing' status as the manufacturers' brands which, at that time, predominated in the company's stores. Over the following years, however, manufacturers' brands were steadily eliminated in favour of the company's exclusive brand until only own label products were sold. All of these bear the St Michael trademark, the exclusive brand of Marks & Spencer.

Marks and Spencer, the UK's most profitable retailer, is actively looking to expand its operation on an international basis.

LIBERTY

Arthur Lazenby Liberty, who trained in the lace business, was much influenced by the section devoted to Japanese art at the 1862 International Exhibition in Kensington, London. This was one of the earliest exposures of a cultural tradition so different from that of Victorian England and when, in 1875, he opened his own store, Liberty specialised in exotic Oriental artefacts and silks and quickly attracted the attention of famous members of the Pre-Raphaelite Brotherhood including artists such as D-G Rossetti, Leighton and Burne-Jones and designers such as William Morris.

Liberty now has retail stores throughout the UK as well as a wholesale company and the company is famous worldwide for its superb

range of dress and furnishing fabrics and for its furniture, wallpaper, clothing, jewellery, metalware and ceramics. Liberty products all have a certain distinctive 'Liberty Style', still heavily influenced by Oriental designs, and reflect too Arthur Liberty's passion for providing the public with beautiful things at affordable prices.

The distinctive Liberty 'look' has survived for well over a century.

O X O ○

The brand name Oxo first appeared on a jar of liquid beef extract in 1900 when it was positioned as synonymous with health, strength and endurance. At the 1908 London Olympics the company was the official caterer and supplied the runners in the marathon with drinks of Oxo. It also managed to persuade the entire British team of athletes to recommend Oxo in a special souvenir brochure for the Olympics.

Great explorers of the time also took supplies of Oxo on their expeditions, notably Shackleton in 1907 and Scott (to the South Pole) in 1911.

Liquid Oxo was a resounding success but a two ounce bottle was still quite expensive for many people. The company searched for something that would retail for a penny and the Oxo cube was born in 1910.

Oxo cubes went with Alcock and Brown on the first transatlantic flight and to the top of Everest in 1953 but by the mid-1950s the brand was facing a crisis – it had come to be associated with wartime austerity not with post-war Britain. The brilliant and highly successful 'Katie' TV campaign which started in 1958 and ran for eighteen years changed all that. Katie, a recognisably good cook, demonstrated the product's versatility and also that it fitted into contemporary lifestyles. Similar campaigns still run today, and the brand is now seen, despite its heritage, as a young, up-to-date product closely associated with good cooking and family values.

The short, powerful Oxo name is both memorable and impactful.

OXO IS BRITISH · MADE IN BRITAIN · BY A BRITISH COMPANY WITH BRITISH CAPITAL & BRITISH LABOUR

Oxo, like many such great brands, is woven into the fabric of British society and is thoroughly familiar and reassuring.

BOOTS

Boots the Chemists is a British institution. Founded by Jesse Boot in Nottingham at the end of the nineteenth century, Boots now dominates UK retailing of pharmaceuticals, healthcare products, toiletries and personal care products. Boots is also a major force in photographic products, garden chemicals, baby products, home brew and home winemaking products.

But Boots is more than just a retailer, though retailing is still the single most important part of the company. Boots is also a major pharmaceutical company (it developed an anti-inflammatory drug known as ibuprofen shortly after the war, a product which is sold in its prescription form as Brufen and in its OTC form as Nurofen in the UK and Nuprin in the US) and has its own soap factories and other 'tied' production facilities. Boots has also recently become a major force in the UK in car accessories and do-it-yourself retailing through its acquisition of Ward White, owners of Halfords and of Payless.

Boots the Chemists so thoroughly dominate the UK chemist shop scene that for many new products a Boots listing is essential to success.

Boots is, however, most visible as a retail brand and falls fairly and squarely into the category of a traditional, reassuring, honourable British retailer. It generates enormous confidence in, and is much liked by, consumers and its brand appeal, coupled with its superb retail sites on Britain's high streets, assure its continuing succcess.

BUPA

BUPA is the acronym of the British United Provident Association, Britain's leading independent private health care company. It is properly pronounced 'boopa' and currently has a spontaneous awareness among British adults of some 75 per cent.

BUPA, a non-profit making organisation, has successfully established itself not just as a name which is synonymous in Britain with high quality private health care, but also as an employee benefit which is on many a job hunter's checklist. In particular, since 1979, the Association has used television advertising to build its brand awareness and brand image and it now quite clearly dominates its sector.

Mrs Thatcher's encouragement of private medicine has led, in recent years, to much wider acceptance in Britain of the concept of private health insurance.

BUPA
Britain feels better for it.

SAINSBURY'S

Sainsbury's is Britain's leading grocery chain – it does a difficult job very well – and is particularly renowned for the quality of its fresh food.

Sainsbury's also clearly demonstrates the need to update brands so as to keep them contemporary and appealing in a constantly changing world. Sainsbury's has paid particular attention to growing public concern about the environment and has formed a senior level management committee to keep environmental issues under constant review. Sainsbury's has, for example, specifically addressed the issue of ozone-damaging chlorofluorcarbons and has stopped using them wherever possible in its business, for instance in its refrigeration plants and in the polystyrene trays it uses for meat packaging. The company is also taking the lead in the retailing of 'green' products.

Sainsbury's brand image is so strong and its customer base so loyal that being a

'Sainsbury's shopper' is a clear socio-economic statement in itself.

PHILEAS FOGG

Phileas Fogg is a range of premium snack foods produced by Derwent Valley Foods, a company set up in 1982 in Consett in North-East England, a community devastated by the closure of the local steel mill.

Phileas Fogg is a character in Jules Verne's *Around the World in Eighty Days*, a Victorian classic made into a popular film in the 1960s starring David Niven. Phileas Fogg brand snacks come from around the world and include tortilla chips, Shanghai nuts, Punjab puri, zakuski (light corn wafers from Southern Russia) and *mignons morceaux*, mini-garlic breads for aperitifs. The products are of high quality and beautifully packaged with lively, colourful graphics. These factors, combined with a quirky and distinctive brand name, give the brand great personality and have led to its considerable success in the British market.

Phileas Fogg's success in a highly competitive market dominated by major, well-resourced competitors has given great heart to other, aspirant brands. It has also helped to transform the British snacks market – since the arrival of Phileas Fogg other manufacturers have become much bolder and more innovative and the overall market has grown considerably in size and consumer interest. Indeed, ten years ago potato chips and salted peanuts made up virtually the entire market but now there is an almost bewildering choice of products.

Phileas Fogg demonstrates that bold, skilful brand development can still lead to success, even in today's crowded markets.

BISTO

Bisto was launched on 4 February 1910 by Cerebos Limited, now part of Ranks Hovis McDougall. It was a revolutionary gravy salt which replaced existing methods of making gravies with a convenient all-in-one solution.

In 1919, the Bisto Kids, invented by William Owen, first appeared and they dominated Bisto advertising until 1989. Bisto has led its market continuously since its launch and it was not until own label gravy makers first appeared in the 1970s that Bisto's market share dropped below 75 per cent for the first time.

In 1979, a modern instant version of Bisto was introduced using granular technology and this perked up the market dramatically. During the 1980s Bisto continued to win back

Bisto dominates an important niche market in the UK. The brand's owners are now considering whether brand extension is feasible.

market share in an enlarged market until, by 1989, a market share of 75 per cent had again been achieved.

The year 1989 also saw the first significant extension of the Bisto brand away from the gravy maker market into cooking sauces with the launch of Bisto Casserole Saucery.

Bisto has virtual universal recognition in the UK and has been managed carefully and conservatively over many decades. In an age when 'brand extension' is all the rage it will be interesting to see whether Bisto's owners will continue to settle for their current strong performance in a relatively narrow segment or whether they will attempt to use the brand more widely, possibly risking, in so doing, the brand's core franchise.

KALIBER

Kaliber, Guinness's alcohol-free beer, is a brand to watch. It started life as an initiative of Guinness Ireland and was originally intended mainly for the Irish market (though sales in the UK were not ruled out) – Bass's Barbican brand was starting to make some inroads into the Irish market and, as the dominant Irish suppliers of stouts, ales and light beers, Guinness was determined to resist the intruder, even though sales of Barbican were modest.

The problem when developing a new brand of alcohol-free beer in the early 1980s was what market to aim it at – sportsmen, teetotallers, reformed drinkers, lunchtime drinkers, drivers, Muslims (not a large market in Ireland, but a sizeable one in Britain) or what? How then should the new beer be positioned – as a sports drink, an adult soft drink or as a real beer which happened to have no alcohol?

Research indicated that the product should have genuine beer characteristics – the brand identity should be strong, incisive and related to a mainstream European beer culture – and the alcohol-free nature of the product and the possible occasions of use should be communicated through advertising and labelling rather than through a semi-descriptive brand name. Hence the selection of the name Kaliber.

Shortly before Kaliber was launched in Ireland it was spotted by Guinness's new Chief Executive, recently recruited from Nestlé, one Ernest Saunders. He had been brought in by the Guinness family when the company was in what seemed to be terminal decline with a brief to revive its fortunes. In due course he bought Bell's Whisky and Distillers, the latter deal later the subject of a notorious legal case, but one immediate decision which he made was to insist that Kaliber should be developed as a worldwide brand and not merely as a brand for Ireland.

This change of strategy necessitated an international trade mark registration programme as well as some redesign of the packaging. Kaliber has now been launched in the UK, parts of Continental Europe and in certain Pacific Rim markets. Though it is meeting strong competition (for example from Heineken's Buckler brand) the underlying market for alcohol-free beers is growing strongly throughout the developing world and Guinness is 'quietly optimistic' that Kaliber is a baby 'mega brand'.

Kaliber is the leading alcohol-free beer in the UK and is being steadily introduced to export markets.

IN JAPAN BRANDS AND BRANDING serve precisely the same function as in any other country. Cultural and language influences, however, have had a powerful influence on how Japanese companies choose brand names. While many of the Japanese brands which are most familiar in the West are long-standing corporate brands derived from family or place names or the names of the major industrial conglomerates, very many Japanese product brand names used in the home market are in fact taken from Western languages. The Japanese term for words borrowed from other languages is *gairago*; the language has thousands of these borrowings, and adds hundreds more each year. However, these words are absorbed into the Japanese language, defined and written in the syllabic alphabet called *katakana.* Loanwords in this category have their uses in consumer marketing, but it is the unadulterated *gairago* — the brand names and slogans in their original Roman spellings — that really move the merchandise. They get attached to cars and soft drinks and toiletries with an exuberance unmatched anywhere in the world.

The use of *gairago* is not a recent trend. The first product in Japan with a foreign name was a pharmaceutical called Kindorusan, introduced in the 1860s. The name itself was a hybrid. Kindoru- was written in *katakana*, while the -san suffix used the Chinese character for powder. The label, however, showed a picture of an elderly, heavily bearded gentleman carrying a child in a kimono, thus unequivocally proclaiming Kindorusan to be an imported or foreign product. Having just emerged at this time from a long period of self-imposed isolation, the Japanese were unable to match the quality, innovativeness and sophistication of the foreign goods that were beginning to appear on the market. Hence foreign goods developed a distinct cachet and by extension any product with a foreign name came to have a special appeal, a mystique, an implied presumption of quality.

Although the increasingly sophisticated Japanese consumer has come to realise that foreign products are, in terms of quality, now quite often inferior to those produced domestically, foreign language brand names have lost none of their appeal and mystique. However, with the high exposure of Japanese products in foreign markets, coupled with the huge numbers of overseas visitors coming to Japan each year, companies are finding that they must be increasingly careful in the selection of brand names in languages other than their own.

The Japanese approach to branding now is to attain a level of 'foreign-ness' that would not necessarily be easily understood by the foreign buyer, but that would be as readily recognisable to the non-Japanese sophisticate as to the Japanese. Take, for example, Nissan's Cefiro, a sporty model aimed at a young, educated buyer who still has 'fire' in his (or her) stomach. Subliminally, the name Ce-FIR-o suggests to non-Japanese people fire and a devil-may-care approach to life. The majority of Japanese purchasers, however, are probably not aware of the origins of the name and are only attracted by its melodious sound. Nissan's branding team can explain in minute detail exactly how the name was reached and what are its genuine Latin roots.

Other recent examples of the penchant for Latin-sounding names is Aera, a new magazine from Asahi, which though sounding sophisticated, simply means 'Asahi-Era' a pun that many Japanese would appreciate now that they see this company taking up the reigns of world leadership in marketing and branding. Another example is Mono, a Japanese-language catalogue-style magazine which, though sounding like the Latin for 'one' is, in fact, the Romanised version of the Japanese word for 'object'; and that is exactly what Mono is — a magazine about gadgets and gizmos to attract wealthy young people.

The move toward coined brand names with obscure roots in classical or European languages is unsurprising when the Japanese meaning-based approach to branding is taken into account.

In Japan, ordinary words are seldom considered emotive enough. For example, very few Japanese would want to be seen driving a car called Samurai. It would not be seen as progressive. That vehicle, therefore, is sold in Japan under the Jimny brand. It does not make any sense to the Westerner, but to the Japanese the name suggests Western ruggedness. And that is exactly the image Suzuki wanted for its four-wheel-drive vehicle.

This example also illustrates another problem peculiar to the Japanese market: that of which sounds appeal to Japanese ears. This is of course a problem which is only fully understood by those who understand the language. However, it is a problem faced by all those who launch products with foreign names in Japan because these names are always written in both Roman letters and in *katakana*. This writing system is composed of forty-eight characters, representing five vowel sounds, a nasal 'n' and an array of consonant/vowel combinations, all with fixed pronunciation. This makes them a useful pronunciation guide for Japanese faced with foreign words, but it also forces foreign words into an often unfamiliar consonant/vowel pattern. While this is not such a great problem for a language like Italian, it quite often renders English pronunciation rather odd, and makes French generally unrecognisable.

Added to these are the other famous Japanese pronunciation problems, as reflected in *katakana:* no distinction between the sounds 'l' and 'r', 'b' and 'v', and 'h' and 'f', and no 'th' sound. It is these phonetic differences that give rise to such transliterations (rendered from English to *katakana* and back) as *teburu* (table), *Shekusupia* (Shakespeare), *baiorin* (violin) and *rabureta* (love letter).

Even though many Japanese brand names may sound nonsensical to Western ears, you can guarantee that they have a meaning that has been carefully worked out by the naming teams in Japan. That this meaning may not be in any way apparent to the average consumer is not considered a problem, in the same way that Japan's 'mood' TV advertising often leaves the viewer in doubt as to what the product is until the very end. Whereas in the West, most brand names have clear, intended meanings, such as Ford's soaring Sierra, or Land Rover's confident Discovery, such directness is alien to modern-day Japanese branders.

It is unlikely that either Ford or Land Rover took their dealers into account when naming their respective vehicles. In Japan, however, manufacturers like to give dealers a conversational opening with prospective clients. Thus, when branding a product, the option of manufacturing a name that, though not easily recognisable, can be quickly explained to the buyer, is often chosen.

The reason for this is that the relationship between dealer and customer in Japan is much more complicated than in the West. Customers like to feel they are being pampered and given preferential treatment. A purchase is not simply a matter of the exchange of goods for money. If the retailer sits down with the customer and explains, for example, the meaning of a brand name, the customer feels as if he is being let into some exclusive club. If, therefore, a brand has a simple, self-explanatory name, it is unlikely to meet several distinctly Japanese criteria. It will not offer the foreign-name sophistication; it will not be seen as progressive and, perhaps, worst of all, it will not enable the dealer/retailer to strike up a relationship with the potential purchaser.

The secret of branding in Japan is simply to understand that foreign words carry a certain cachet. The meanings do not have to be clear, but must be readily explainable. One recent marketing success clearly demonstrates this point.

Japan, with its hard working and often tired armies of white-collar workers, is a mecca for manufacturers of caffeine and glucose-based 'health' drinks that give an immediate energy boost. A recent entry to the market is 'Turtoise', a name that to Western ears sounds remarkably like Tortoise, not the image of health and speed that most foreign manufacturers would choose for a similar drink. However, when the Japanese-language explanation on each bottle is read, it turns out that tortoise is exactly what the manufacturer meant.

The blurb clearly states that for centuries *suppon* (the Japanese word for tortoises) have been famed for their longevity and an ability to overcome the hardships of life. At a time when *polluribyo* (sudden death from overwork) is a growing problem in Japan, what better aim, the manufacturer suggests, can workers have than extending their lives? This typifies the Japanese approach to branding. Develop a brand name that has certain recognisable sounds, but not necessarily with a distinct meaning. Then explain it, either on the product or via a salesman, in the way that will be most likely to give the purchaser a feeling that the product holds a certain exclusivity.

A problem that will continue to plague Japanese manufacturers, however, is how to accommodate the vastly different brand naming requirements of the domestic and overseas markets. Despite the high visibility of Japanese products in world markets, it is the domestic market which continues to be of paramount importance. Products are almost always launched in the domestic market first, and those that succeed are then taken overseas. It is often at this point that problems with brand names first appear. Lack of originality often means that the name is unavailable in the markets of interest. Those that are available are frequently so idiosyncratic as to be unusable.

Pocari Sweat is a sports drink (a soft drink containing electrolytes, etc. for use after exercise) which was introduced on the Japanese market in 1980. By 1984 it had gained a 36 per cent share of the market in Japan, and generated considerable competitive interest and response from manufacturers such as Suntory and Coca-Cola. Obviously to the Japanese consumer there was nothing particularly strange or unusual in drinking a beverage called Sweat. When test-marketed overseas, however, the response was predictable and ranged from hilarity to repulsion. Naturally, although somewhat reluctantly, the name had to be changed and the product is marketed overseas as Pocari.

For the connoisseur of brands and branding Japan is a paradise; not only are many of the most powerful new world brands Japanese in origin, but Japan is a spawning ground for innovative, exciting new products and exotic, even hilarious brand names — the Japanese consumer is perfectly happy to eat Germ bread, while drinking Blendy coffee laced with Creap non-dairy creamer. He wears Trim Pecker trousers, uses Blow Up hairspray and puts Skinababe on the baby's bottom. He eats at restaurants with names like My Dung and Le Macquereau (The Pimp), and cultivates his garden with Green Pile fertiliser. The branding vocabulary in Japan is in a class by itself but Japan is also a country of amazing vivacity and energy and it is clear that just as the West has, in the past, substantially influenced Japanese branding practices, Japan will have an increasing influence on branding in the West.

JAPAN

BRAND	LEADERSHIP	STABILITY	MARKET	INTERNATIONALITY	TREND	SUPPORT	PROTECTION	TOTAL
AKAI		○	□		○	○	●	○
ASAHI	○	□	□		□	●	●	□
BRIDGESTONE	□	●	□	□	□	□	●	□
BROTHER	□	●	□	○	○	□	●	□
DIAMOND		●	□		□	●	●	○
FUJI PHOTO FILM	●	●	●	□	□	●	●	□
GEKKEIKAN		□	□		□	□	●	
HONDA	○	●	●	□	●	●	●	□
JAPAN TOBACCO	●	○	●		□	●	●	□
KAO	□	●	●	○	●	●	●	□
KIKKOMAN	□	●	□	○	□	●	●	□
MITSUKOSHI	○	●	□		□	□	●	○
NORITAKE	○	●	□		○	□	●	
PENTEL	□	●	□	□	□	○	●	□
PILOT	□	□	○		○	●	●	○
SEIKO	●	●	●	○	□	□	●	□
SHISEIDO	□	●	●	○	□	●	●	□
SNOW BRAND	□	●	□		□	●	●	□
SUNTORY	○	□	□	○	□	●	●	□
WACOAL	●	●	●		□	●	●	□

KEY ★★ Top Ten brand ★ Top Fifty brand ● exceptionally strong □ very strong ○ strong △ problem area

AKAI ○

Akai was founded in 1929 to make electrical equipment for cars. In 1950 the company started to produce components for record players and similar products and in 1954 launched a tape recorder under the Akai brand name. It was a major success and Akai is now a leading producer of VCRs, electronic musical instruments, learning laboratories, miniaturised microcassette players, electrocardiographs, hi-fi systems, CD players and recording equipment.

The Akai brand is well respected internationally in the electronics market.

AKAI

JAPAN TOBACCO

Japan Tobacco (JT) was established in 1898 as Japan's government bureau tobacco monopoly and in 1905 its activities were expanded to include salt. The Company was privatised in April 1985, when Japan's tobacco market was liberalised (largely due to intense US pressure) but JT still holds over 87 per cent of the domestic market, making it the world's fourth largest tobacco company.

Tobacco brands owned by JT include Mild Seven, Caster, and Cabin all of which have a substantial market share in Japan. In addition to its tobacco operations, JT is rapidly diversifying into pharmaceuticals, systems engineering, physical fitness, agriculture and beverages.

Interestingly, brands such as Mild Seven, Caster and Cabin are known outside Japan mainly from their presence in duty-free stores and city centre outlets favoured by Japanese visitors. The brands are also recognised from sponsorship – Cabin, for example, has sponsored Formula One motorsport though few motoring enthusiasts outside Japan know

what Cabin is or have any opportunity to purchase the brand. The strongly entrenched position of JT's brands in their home market and of overseas brands in their home markets does little to encourage brand wars in a sector which is relatively undifferentiated and under increasing regulatory pressure.

The Mild Seven cigarette brand is one of Japan Tobacco's leading brands yet it is little known outside its home market.

SEIKO

Hattori Seiko make timepieces and the Seiko brand is a household word and is synonymous with fine watches around the world. Hattori Seiko views marketing as a challenge to its creativity and has developed a multi-brand strategy, including the Seiko, Jean Lassale, Lassale, Pulsar, Lorus and Alba brands.

Less than twenty years ago the electronic watch was virtually unknown – 99.9 per cent of all watches were mechanical and it seemed inconceivable that within a few years inexpensive watches accurate to a few seconds a year would be available to all. Seiko, which has provided world firsts in quartz watches, TV watches and LCD colour TVs, is in large part responsible for this

timekeeping revolution. At one time, too, it looked as if Seiko, virtually singlehandedly, would extinguish the bulk of Switzerland's watch-making industry though eventually the Swiss rallied and have, in part at least, held off the Japanese challenge.

SEIKO

Seiko is now one of the best-known and most respected brands of watch in the world.

DIAMOND

Established in 1913, Diamond is the leading publisher in Japan and, together with its subsidiary companies, Diamond publishes a large number of books and magazines, with an emphasis on industrial and economic publications. The group's flagship publication, *Diamond,* is a weekly magazine covering economic issues and President, a monthly publication, also ranks among Japan's leading economic and business publications. The company also produces a number of English-language publications, such as Diamond Directory and Industria, which support the foreign business community in Japan and the company has formed tie-ups with overseas companies to offer Japanese-language versions of a large number of Western journals ranging from *Car and Driver* to *Harvard Business Review,* a lucrative business in Japan where fluency in Western languages is still quite rare but interest in things Western intense.

Diamond dominates publishing in Japan, particularly in the industrial and economic area. The company also has strong international links.

ASAHI

Asahi, best known for its beers but a producer too of foods, soft drinks and pharmaceuticals has shown sales growth in recent years averaging 70 per cent. The major reason for this is Asahi Super Dry beer, a product which annually sells nearly seventy-five million cases in Japan.

Asahi Super Dry is a light beer with a particularly 'clean taste'. It was first introduced in 1987 and within two years over one third of all Japanese beer sales were of dry-type beers. It says much for the strength of the Asahi Super Dry brand that despite massive competition and the launch of scores of new dry beers Asahi Super Dry has maintained a near 50 per cent share of this competitive market sector.

Curiously, Western breweries have apparently taken little interest in the dry beer phenomenon. Heineken is one company thought to be looking at a dry beer, as are certain US brewers, but there is little sign in the West of any rush to emulate Asahi's success.

Asahi dominates the dry beer market in Japan but, as yet, this type of beer is relatively unknown outside Japan.

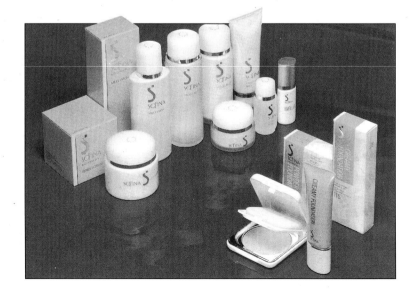

WACOAL

Wacoal, founded in 1946, is not a mining company but is Japan's recognized leader in the body fashion industry, particularly women's lingerie. Headed by Koichi Tsukamoto the Company's products include brassières, girdles, body suits, bra slips, slips, petticoats, shorts, negligées and pyjamas.

Wacoal, like all successful Japanese businesses, takes its responsibilities very seriously and has a clear sense of mission. In Wacoal's case its mission is to make products which are loved by their wearers and which help women to become more beautiful.

Wacoal concentrates on producing body fashion products that combine style and design with comfort the wearer.

KAO

Kao Corporation is a leading manufacturer of personal care, laundry, cleansing and hygiene products, as well as fatty chemicals, speciality chemicals and floppy disks. With annual net sales of over ¥572 billion ($4 billion approx) Kao boasts a large number of leading brands. In personal care products Sofina cosmetics, UV Care, Make Clear Gel, Biore, Essential and Success are just a few. In laundry and cleansing products, Kao's domestic market share is 70 per cent in certain sectors (e.g. bioconcentrated detergents) and Attack and Touch are two of the company's brands. Hygiene products include Merries diapers (nappies), Bub therapeutic bath tablets, Actibath and Sanina.

Kao is frequently called 'the Procter & Gamble of Japan', a comparison which neither company likes but which is apt – the product lines of both companies are similar as are their internal cultures and their passion for their brands. They even share a similar 'Man in the Moon' corporate symbol though there are differences in the visual execution.

Recently, Kao purchased Andrew Jurgens, a US personal care products manufacturer located in Cincinnati, Ohio just a few hundred yards from Procter & Gamble's head office. The competition between the two companies is clearly hotting up!

The Sofina cosmetics and skin care brand is just one of Kao's successful product lines.

KIKKOMAN

In 1917, the Mogi and Takanashi families merged their businesses and the Kikkoman brand was born. Kikkoman is best known for its soy sauce and in recent years the brand has expanded outside its huge home market and, due to the growing internationalisation of eating habits, now enjoys a strong niche positioning in many Western markets.

Kikkoman has also profited by discovering new flavours and bringing them to Japan: Del Monte juice and tomato products, Lea & Perrins Worcestershire Sauce and Coca-Cola are a few of the brands that Kikkoman markets in Japan. Kikkoman has also developed low-salt soy sauces, the Beyoung brand of vitamin and protein supplements and other nutritious foods and has even established a number of swimming schools in Japan.

In 1989 Kikkoman announced that it had set aside a fighting fund of $1.7 billion and would use this to expand into Western markets through acquisition as, clearly, its own domestic brands have only limited appeal outside Japan. Though few Japanese companies would consider making a contested bid for another company and much prefer more gentlemanly alliances, clearly Kikkoman is likely to become, through friendly acquisitions, a major force in world food markets. Kikkoman has already started its acquisitions policy with the purchase of Del Monte's US food processing businesses.

The growing internationalisation of Japanese food has led to export opportunities for Kikkoman. Its main overseas drive, however, will be through acquisition.

SNOW BRAND

As Japan's largest dairy company, Snow Brand Milk Products produces milk, butter, infant formulas, cheese, ice creams, and margarine and is particularly strong in the butter and cheese markets, with a more than 50 per cent market share.

Snow Brand's high popularity is supported by strengths in production, technology, marketing and distribution, with the company's marketing capabilities being described by the Nihon Keizai Shimbun, Japan's leading economic publisher, as the best in Japan.

Snow Brand's operations centre on foods, especially those that are beneficial to health and the company has entered such growth areas as 100 per cent fruit juices, where it has formed a joint venture with Dole. Other partners include Quaker Oats and eight other companies from around the world.

Snow Brand, already a market leader in Japan, is looking to expand its business by forming strong links with overseas brand-owning companies.

BRIDGESTONE

The success of Japan's motor industry has contributed to the success of component suppliers such as Bridgestone.

Bridgestone, established in 1931, was thought by many consumers in the West (where its products first started to appear in volume in the mid-1970s) to be tied up with Firestone, an altogether more familiar brand. Ironically, the Firestone brand was acquired by Bridgestone in 1988.

Bridgestone is now one of the world's great tyre manufacturers but the company is rapidly diversifying into new fields where technological and marketing synergies can be found. Examples of such new products include DeoraFlow air deodorizers for automobiles and rest rooms, all-rubber optical fibre, pressure gauges and spray-culture systems. Bridgestone also produces bedding and furniture lines created in co-operation with prominent designers as well as tennis rackets, tennis balls, golf clubs and golf balls. Bridgestone Cycle, another subsidiary, is also the largest manufacturer of bicycles in Japan.

SHISEIDO

The major international successes of Japanese companies have, to date, been in such areas as automotive and electronic products. Many companies around the world, however, are expecting to meet increasing Japanese competition in entirely new areas. Cosmetics and toiletries is one such area: Japanese products are of outstanding quality and are beautifully packaged.

Shiseido is the leading Japanese manufacturer of cosmetics and toiletries. The company's brand image is extremely strong with a powerful presence in leading department stores in the major cities. (The big city department stores have a potent influence on consumer behaviour.) Shiseido has also successfully targeted new growth areas, for example men's toiletries – the toiletries habit did not come naturally to Japanese men and even today subtle fragrances are preferred. In the 1970s Shiseido introduced their Tactics range for men, a brand which is still market leader.

PILOT ◯

Namiki Manufacturing changed its name to Pilot in 1939 to underscore the Company's role as a guide to culture, information and intellectual pursuits.

The Pilot brand of pens and mechanical pencils is recognized as among the world's finest and the brand is also used on notebooks, gift products and a host of related items.

Pilot's marketing strategy centres on flawless after-sales service, direct contact with and feedback from customers, use of Pilot's own staff in key department stores and other sales outlets, and the development of satellite shops to provide information on customer preferences and trends.

Japanese consumers demand high quality, not just in products but also in packaging, promotional material, point-of-sale displays etc. Shiseido leads the Japanese toiletries market, largely on the basis of quality.

Pilot's pens and mechanical pencils span the entire range from inexpensive disposables to presentation items which are objects of great worth and beauty.

FUJI PHOTO FILM

Fuji Photo Film was founded in 1934. The full title is necessary because there are hundreds of unconnected companies in Japan all bearing the name Fuji due to the Japanese near reverence for Mt Fuji, the beautiful volcanic cone which, on a clear day, is visible from downtown Tokyo. It is now one of the world's major manufacturers of photographic film and paper as well as cassette tapes, floppy disks, home video tapes, cameras, colour copiers and commercial, medical and industrial products. Sub-brands used in association with the Fuji house brand include Reala (film), Velvia (professional quality film), Quicksnap (cameras) and Axia (tapes). These product lines reflect the company's principal theme of I & I: 'Imaging and Information'.

Fuji's annual sales amount to ¥1,000 billion ($7 billion) and Fuji is a major world competitor to the mighty Kodak. Indeed, rivalry between the two companies is intense with each trying to gain a marketing or product lead over the other: for example, official sponsorship of the Los Angeles Olympics was given to Fuji; a major victory –

Fuji Photo Film, with its distinctive green livery, is now Kodak's major international competitor.

and on Kodak's home turf. However, Kodak has been particularly successful in introducing improved ranges of colour film.

PENTEL

Pentel is best known as a brand of writing implements but the full product range now extends into specialised high tech sectors.

Pentel, founded in 1946, is a world leader in stationery products for school, office and personal use. Indeed, the company claims that two thirds of all the important developments in writing instruments since the Second World War were made by Pentel, as evidenced by the company's winning of the Deming Prize in 1976.

Pentel brand products now cover pens, pencils, felt pens, paint, notebooks, erasers and correction fluid as well as hand held terminals, graphic digitizers and precision assembly robots. Through a combination of innovative, high quality products, strong distribution and aggressive marketing the brand has come to dominate sectors of the stationery market both in Japan and internationally.

Brother is a typical example of a Japanese company using a Western-sounding name — indeed this may well have helped the brand to become established internationally.

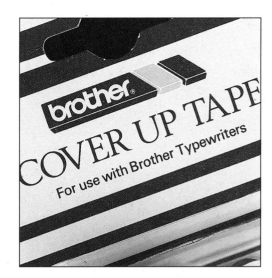

BROTHER

Brother Industries, established in 1934, is a global company with operations in twenty countries. The Brother brand is a household name in Japan and increasingly, around the world and is best known for its sewing machines and electronic typewriters though the brand now extends to word processors, colour copiers, facsimile machines, knitting machines, microwave ovens and other household appliances and machine tools.

Like many Japanese companies, Brother is anxious to establish a positive international reputation and is particularly proud to be the official typewriter supplier to the Olympics.

SUNTORY

Suntory, founded in 1899, is the dominant force in the Japanese beverage and liquor market and one surprise which many first-time visitors to Japan experience is the range, quality and diversity of Japanese whiskies, many of them bearing the Suntory trademark.

Suntory was the first Japanese producer of wine and whisky and now has a broad line-up of alcoholic and non-alcoholic beverages, processed foods, and pharmaceutical products.

In addition to its own Suntory beer label, the company also markets Budweiser and Carlsberg beers and has acquired a number of distinguished wine labels.

In non-alcholic beverages, Suntory markets teas, including sugar-free oolong tea, Perrier and Volvic mineral water from France, and a full line of carbonated drinks and fruit drinks.

In top-quality foods, Suntory operates Häagen Dazs Japan Inc. and First Kitchen restaurants. Other activities include co-operation in the publication of *Newsweek* in Japan, Tipness sports clubs, the operation of Suntory Hall, and the management of Cambridge English School. Suntory is also

Though Suntory is best known for its whiskies, wines and soft drinks, the company now has activities in sectors as diverse as publishing and sports clubs.

becoming widely known outside Japan, partly as a result of sports sponsorship (e.g. the Suntory World Matchplay Championship at Wentworth) but also due to acquisitions — Suntory recently purchased, for example, the Pacific Region food manufacturing businesses of Britain's Ranks Hovis McDougall.

SUNTORY

NORITAKE

The Aichi and Gifu prefectures in the Nagoya area of Central Japan have been the centre of Japan's ceramics industry since the Eleventh Century and it was here that Noritake, Japan's leader in china and tableware, was established in 1904. In 1932 Noritake produced the country's first bone china and in 1934, it developed the tunnel and kiln conveyor production system.

The Noritake brand is now used on fine china, cutlery and glassware as well as on stoneware, earthenware, cutting and grinding systems, vacuum fluorescent displays, ceramic components, thick film-printed circuit boards and other industrial products.

But it is for its fine china that Noritake is best known. Noritake is establishing a growing reputation for its designs and now competes head on with the European brands in international markets.

Noritake designs used to echo traditional Western designs. Now however Noritake is establishing a growing reputation for innovation in the design of china and tableware.

Noritake

HONDA

Honda is famous for its automobiles, motorcycles and power products. It currently produces three million motorcycles a year ranging from the 50cc Zook scooter to the astonishing 1500cc Gold Wing machine and two million motor cars including models such as the Accord (the number one car model in the US), Vigor, Integra, Ascot and Legend. The company's power products include engines, tractors, lawn mowers and snow throwers.

Honda has developed a powerful reputation for product engineering and innovation and the Honda brand is often compared to high quality German marques such as BMW and Mercedes-Benz. In the important automobile sector, in particular, Honda is a specialist, up-market brand which derives particular benefits from its participation in Formula One motor racing. Only ten or a dozen years ago Honda's brand reputation in important markets such as the US was, it seemed, inextricably linked to motorcycles and lawnmowers. Now the brand has successfully made the transition to that of a high quality motor manufacturer capable of competing with the best on a world basis.

Honda motor cars, motorcycles and power products enjoy an enviable reputation for advanced engineering, superb design and high quality manufacture.

MITSUKOSHI

Mitsukoshi Ltd. was established in 1673 and incorporated in 1904, making it one of Japan's oldest and most prestigious retailers. The company has a domestic network of fourteen major department stores, including major locations in Tokyo and Osaka, ninety-four satellite shops and overseas activities in nineteen major metropolitan centres worldwide.

Mitsukoshi's activities include department store operation, wholesaling, importing and exporting, real estate agency activities, construction, travel agency operation, life and non-life insurance, consumer finance, promotion and others.

All of the Company's department stores rank among the leading retailers in their respective areas, with the Nihonbashi Main Store in Tokyo being particularly noteworthy.

Mitsukoshi is expanding rapidly with plans to construct 92,600 square metres (one million

Mitsukoshi is Japan's leading retailing and department store group and the support of Mitsukoshi is frequently central to new brand success in Japan.

square feet) of new floor space during the next five years. Mitsukoshi is also entering new businesses, such as marine resort development and mail order sales. This aggressive investment activity and the Company's excellence in merchandising and planning are sure to keep Mitsukoshi in the forefront of Japanese retailing for years to come.

GEKKEIKAN

Gekkeikan, founded by Rokuroemon Okura in 1637, is a leading Japanese brand of sake. The process for producing sake is based on rice which is polished, washed, steamed, mixed with water and other ingredients and then pressurized, filtered, sedimented and blended. Sake has the alcoholic strength of a fortified wine and is normally drunk warm in small china cups. Bars and sake shops have sake delivered in traditional, heavily decorated barrels but sake for home consumption is sold in bottles like other alcoholic beverages.

The Gekkeikan brand is applied not just to sake but also to plum wine, shochu and other traditional alcoholic beverages and the company also distributes German and French wines, beers and brandies in Japan.

The growing internationalisation of Japanese business has led to large expatriate Japanese communities in many major cities around the world and this has led in turn to growing export opportunities for the Gekkeikan brand. Indeed, the company has recently formed its first overseas subsidiary, in the United States.

French brandy, Scotch and Japanese whiskies, beer and, of course, sake are the favourite alcoholic drinks in Japan. Gekkeikan is the leading Japanese sake brand.

AUSTRALIA AND PACIFIC

WHEN BRITAIN JOINED THE EUROPEAN COMMUNITY in 1971 and, in effect, threw in its lot with its European neighbours thus largely severing traditional colonial ties with countries such as Australia and New Zealand such countries had fundamentally to reappraise their place in the world and even their sense of national identity. Australians and New Zealanders, brought up on a diet of English public school heroes, traditional white Christmases (even with temperatures outside of perhaps 40°C) and the British Monarchy, had to work hard to develop a new set of loyalties, a new orientation, a new sense of national pride.

Though old ties have been far from severed (Australian and New Zealand lamb, wool and dairy products, for example, still look to the UK as one of their major markets) a heightened sense of nationality has grown up. This awareness of nationality stops well short of narrow-minded nationalism and has its roots in influences and behaviour which can be traced back through generations. Nonetheless, a non-apologetic pride in being an Australian or a New Zealander is evident in each country's leading national brands.

The Australian culture favours 'mateyness' and straightforward, honest, look 'em in the eye, no-nonsense values and this is the positioning taken by many of Australia's leading national brands. Curiously, however, for all their 'Australian-ness' several of the archetypal Australian brands featured are owned by foreign companies, among them Holden (by General Motors of the US) and Vegemite (by Kraft of the US, now part of Philip Morris). (The same is true, of course, of 'national' brands from around the world; Britain's Marmite is now owned by CPC, Jaguar by Ford and Lea & Perrins by BSN of France.)

The brands of Hong Kong, Singapore and Philippines which we feature demonstrate further that branding is a practice which can be used in virtually all countries with all types of cultural backgrounds. Indeed, it is anticipated that, as a result of the energy and entrepreneurial flair of countries in Asia, world markets can expect to see a growing number of successful international brands from countries such as Malaysia, Taiwan, Korea, Hong Kong, Singapore, Philippines and Indonesia.

AUSTRALIA & PACIFIC

BRAND	LEADERSHIP	STABILITY	MARKET	INTERNATIONALITY	TREND	SUPPORT	PROTECTION	TOTAL
AEROPLANE JELLY	○	○				○	●	
ANCHOR	□	○	○	○		○	●	
BUNDABERG	□	□	●		○	□	●	○
CANTERBURY OF NEW ZEALAND		○	○		○	○	○	
CASTLEMAINE XXXX	○	□	●	○	○	□	□	□
CHESTY BOND	□	□	○			□	●	○
DOLL	○		□		○	○	●	
DRIZA-BONE	●	○	□			○	●	○
FOUR 'N TWENTY	□	○	○			○	○	
HOLDEN	○	□	□			□	●	○
JAG		○				○	○	
JUST JEANS	○				○	○	○	
MALVERN STAR	○	○	○			○	●	
MEADOW LEA	□	○	□			□	□	
QANTAS	□	●	●	□	□	□	●	□
ROSELLA	○	○	□		○	○	●	
SAN MIGUEL	□	●	●	○	□	○	●	□
STEINLAGER		○	●	○	□	□	●	○
STUBBIES	○	○					●	
TIGER	●	●	●	○	●	○	●	□
TIGER BALM		●	□	○	○		●	○
UNCLE TOBYS	○	□	●		○	○	●	○
VEGEMITE	●	●	○		○	○	●	□
VITASOY	□	□	○		□	○	□	○

KEY ★★ Top Ten brand ★ Top Fifty brand ● exceptionally strong □ very strong ○ strong △ problem area

DRIZA-BONE

Driza-Bone oilskin riding coats were invented in the Nineteenth Century by a Scottish emigrant to Australia who manufactured waterproof coats for sailors from used lightweight sails treated with linseed oil. Farmers and drovers also used these new garments but specified a longer coat, a fantail to put over the saddle, wrist and leg straps.

The trademark Driza-Bone ('Dry as a Bone') was first registered in 1933, by which time the linseed oiling process had been replaced.

The brand is perceived in Australia and, increasingly, abroad as thoroughly Australian and Driza-Bone oilskin coats have an outstanding reputation for comfort and toughness. In Australia its heritage and association with the outback allows it to be both a fashion garment and a work garment.

The brand name is so thoroughly Australian it even has to be said with an Australian accent.

DRIZA-BONE®
The legend of the bush.

VITASOY

Vitasoy is a Hong Kong based soyamilk product which is positioned as a nutritious, reliable beverage and which is particularly popular with Chinese consumers. Though Vitasoy was first launched over 50 years ago, current interest in 'healthy eating' products has led to continued strong growth for the brand – it now has over 90 per cent of the market in Hong Kong, it continues to grow at 5–10 per cent a year in volume terms and it is available in all supermarkets, grocery stores, fast food outlets, soft drink outlets and schools. Vitasoy is also spreading outside Hong Kong due, in part, to former residents of Hong Kong emigrating to cities such as Vancouver and London – as they have moved they have taken the 'Vitasoy habit' with them.

Vitasoy is a brand which is more or less unique to Hong Kong but which, in our increasingly health conscious world, has good international prospects.

DOLL

Doll, a Hong Kong based brand, started as an importer of instant noodles in 1968 and is now one of Hong Kong's most imaginative and innovative food processors whose range includes frozen foods, snack foods and the ubiquitous 'Doll' instant noodle.

Doll produces high quality products which are closely adapted to suit local tastes. In Hong Kong the Doll brand has a prompted awareness of 98 per cent and the company's products have won prestigious Hong Kong Quality-Mark Awards in both 1986 and 1989.

The Doll brand has, since 1968, established a reputation in Hong Kong for fine quality food products.

TIGER

Tiger Beer, first brewed in 1931, is the national beer of Singapore and is also drunk around the world. Tiger Beer is described as a 'premium quality gold medal beer' and it can truly justify this description – it has a highly distinctive taste and has won no less than twenty-three international gold medals for quality in Paris, Geneva, Rome, Lisbon and Madrid. Moreover, the Asian Wall Street Journal rated Tiger 'the best among eighteen brands'; the London Sunday Times praised Tiger, out of a field of 250 brands, for its 'balance, clean taste and aroma', the New York Times attributed Tiger's success to its 'careful brewing process'; and the Washingtonian Magazine, in a blind taste-test involving several hundred brands, unreservedly voted Tiger 'positively the best beer in the world'.

Tiger beer's taste and quality makes it popular among beer enthusiasts around the world and its international reputation leads to enormous pride and affection for the brand in its home market where it has a market share of over 50 per cent – Tiger Beer is, for Singaporeans, a tangible symbol of their maturity and success and of their ability to compete in world markets with world-beating local products.

Tiger demonstrates strongly that fine beer can be brewed even in countries with a relatively young brewing tradition.

VEGEMITE

Vegemite, a Kraft brand, is the Australian first cousin of Britain's Marmite and, like Marmite, is considered by those not initiated into its subtle appeals to be every bit as 'strange'.

Vegemite is a concentrated yeast-based spread. Its taste is highly distinctive but those who are weaned to it become thoroughly addicted. It is also natural and extremely nutritious – it is full of vitamin B.

Vegemite is quintessentially Australian and is as much a part of Australia's heritage as kangaroos and Dame Nelly Melba. It is extremely widely distributed and is available not just in food stores and supermarkets but also in hotels and restaurants, even on Qantas flights. The use of individual size catering portions has provided opportunities for trial by everyone in Australia thus increasing the customer base, a policy which has not been followed by Britain's Marmite and which, it is argued, has restricted the number of new Marmite users entering the market.

Only the Australians and the 'Poms' seem to appreciate concentrated yeast extract spreads.

Vegemite has been available since the 1920s and is carried by Australian expatriates to all corners of the world. It has also given Australia a second national song, the 'Happy Little Vegemites' jingle, which continues to put a rose into every patriotic cheek.

HOLDEN ○

Holden, a General Motors company, is Australia's No. 2 car company with a 20 per cent market share; Ford is currently market leader. Holden however holds a special place in Australian hearts – starting in 1948 with the first locally-made car, Holden provided a sorely needed solution to Australia's motoring needs: a powerful, rugged, well designed, six cylinder family car with a suspension system developed in Australia with Australia in mind. The Holden helped conquer Australia's 'tyranny of distance' and the previous staple of Australian motoring – British designed four cylinder cars – virtually disappeared. Today there are more Holdens in use in Australia than any other brand, some two million.

Australian motorists need a car which is tough and reliable and which can take distance in its stride – a car like a Holden.

MALVERN STAR

The Malvern Star brand started life in 1885 as a bicycle shop in Malvern, a suburb of Melbourne. In 1920, the shop was bought by Bruce Small who developed a bicycle manufacturing business and today Malvern Star, Australia's oldest bicycle brand, continues to lead the field.

To many Australians Malvern Star is part of growing up and the brand is regarded as reliable, trustworthy and thoroughly Australian. In a market where there is little brand knowledge and where consumers find it difficult to differentiate between product features Malvern Star enjoys a well-known and positive image.

For many years Hubert Opperman, the Australian world champion cyclist of the 1920s and '30s helped promote the brand but more recently billboard advertising and joint promotions (e.g. with McDonald's) have been used.

Malvern Star has been, for generations of Australian kids, the bicycle of choice.

Bushranger.

CHESTY BOND

Chesty Bond athletic singlets and the Chesty Bond cartoon character were first launched in 1938 – Bonds wanted an identity for their 2/6d singlet and Popeye, a favourite cartoon character of the day, inspired the idea for Chesty.

Since 1938, over 200 million Bonds cotton athletic singlets have been sold, thanks largely to Chesty's early feats of triumphing over Headlock Hector, sinking a Nazi submarine, subduing a marauding bull and escaping from Black Rita the pirate woman. Chesty's appearance coincided with the start of World War II and Chesty, of course, joined in the fighting, rescuing damsels in distress and saving Australia from the invaders. He was a superhero who always subdued the sinister forces of evil, usually relying on the magical properties of his trusty singlet.

Now Chesty Bond athletics wear represents quality, value, affordability, dependability and good, honest all-Australian 'fair dinkum' values. The brand has an 80 per cent share of the athletic singlet market and Chesty himself is an Australian institution.

Athletic singlets are part of the unofficial national dress of Australia and Chesty Bond dominates the market.

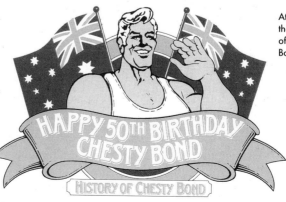

HAPPY 50TH BIRTHDAY CHESTY BOND

HISTORY OF CHESTY BOND

MEADOW LEA

The Meadow Lea brand of margarine was launched in Australia in the 1930s but in its polyunsaturated form first saw the light of day in 1963. Since 1973 it has been market leader.

Meadow Lea is positioned as a premium polyunsaturated spread that is distinctly Australian. It has broadly based appeal and has never tried to apologise for not being butter. Rather, the family is pivotal to Meadow Lea's positioning and the role of 'Mother' is an essential component of this.

In Australia, margarine accounts for 70 per cent of the yellow fats market with polyunsaturates dominating. Meadow Lea is the outstanding brand in its sector and its advertising message 'You Ought to be Congratulated', is now part of the Australian vernacular.

Despite its 'dairy feel' Meadow Lea is a margarine – a premium polyunsaturated spread – and is market leader in Australia.

FOUR 'N TWENTY

Four 'N Twenty is the 'great Australian taste' in meat pies, pastries and sausage rolls. Four 'N Twenty products are available across Australia and are now virtually part of the cultural landscape. The brand enjoys near 100 per cent awareness in Australia and the brand's owners, Petersville Industries, claim that Four 'N Twenty is the largest producer of meat pies in the world.

The Four 'N Twenty story started in Bendigo in the late 1940s and it was not long before a large percentage of the company's pie production was being sent to Melbourne – at first for special events like the 1948 Royal Melbourne Show, and then to local retailers. Demand expanded quickly and the company opened its first Melbourne factory in a pavilion in the showgrounds.

The company attributes its success to cost-effective production, extensive distribution, strong advertising support, particularly on television, and clever use of sports sponsorship, especially Australian Rules football.

In the nursery rhyme 'four and twenty blackbirds were baked in a pie'.

FOUR'N TWENTY PIES
The Great Australian Taste

AEROPLANE JELLY

Aeroplane Jelly, a family owned business, is famous across Australia. The company was founded in 1927 by Herbert Adolphus Appleroth who coined the name Aeroplane and the company slogan 'Above All'. During the Depression one packet of Aeroplane Jelly would feed a family of four at a cost of only five cents and the product's low cost, combined with Appleroth's flair for publicity resulted in wide awareness and acceptance.

The most successful publicity stunt Appleroth devised was the competition to find the best child singer for the Aeroplane Jelly song. Kids of all ages were taken into the studios of 2UW in 1937 to sing the song live on air. This meant the song was heard on air up to 100 times a day! The winner was a pretty girl of five years old, Joy King, (now living in Queensland) and the original recording is still being used today.

Today the desserts market does not consist only of jelly and ice cream and the jelly crystals market has been static. The company has however diversified into a broad range of grocery goods as well as into own label.

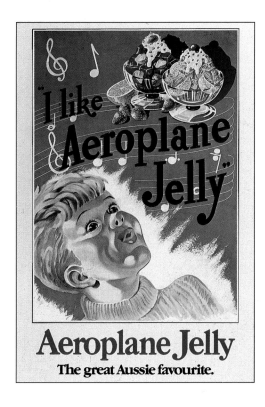

When Americans discovered Jell-O, Australians discovered Aeroplane Jelly. Both are major brands in their respective markets.

TIGER BALM

Tiger Balm is a soothing camphor and peppermint-oil based ointment first produced by a Chinese herbalist called Aw Chu Kin in his dispensary in Rangoon, Burma. His two sons Aw Boon Haw and Aw Boon Par set up a company to produce Tiger Balm which now has annual sales of over US$100 million.

Tiger Balm is produced mainly in Singapore and is used all over Asia for arthritis, backaches, even headaches and flatulence. It is also used by athletes and has become well established in Switzerland, Holland and in specialist stores in the US. Tiger Balm's packaging and positioning is unequivocally

Tiger Balm, based on traditional Chinese herbal remedies, has a strong following in the Far East.

exotic and Eastern and this in large part explains its success – Tiger Balm is quite clearly differentiated from its competition and as, too, it contains only natural oils it can also claim a distinct product advantage.

BUNDABERG

The Bundaberg Distilling Company started production in 1889 and now Bundaberg Rum, with sales of some 700,000 cases, is the largest spirits brand in Australia, ahead of brands such as Johnnie Walker, Jim Beam, Southern Comfort, Bacardi and Smirnoff. In world terms, however, the brand is quite small – its volume is some 3 per cent of Bacardi's.

Bundaberg (Bundy as it is affectionately known) is a smooth, flavoursome rum with a distinctive taste which mixes well with colas and citrus juices. The particular flavour of Bundy is such that many Australians would not accept a substitute and the brand is promoted as youthful, vigorous and fun-loving.

Bundaberg has a particular flavour and a young, fun-loving brand personality.

ROSELLA

Rosella is the most authentically Australian brand of soups and sauces. The Rosella Preserving Company was formed in 1895, initially as jam and pickle manufacturers, and takes its name from the Eastern Rosella, a colourful Australian bird. The brand has around a 25 per cent share of the Australian canned soups and sauce market and a reputation based on a consistently high quality product and trustworthy Australian ancestry. The brand also has wide distribution and a reputation for innovation (e.g. 'Lite Soups') and is strongly supported by TV advertising and special promotions.

Rosella is the dominant Australian brand of soups and sauces.

JUST JEANS

Just Jeans is a mass-market retailer of good quality, medium priced 'jeanswear' for men, women and children. (The term 'jeanswear' includes bottoms, tops, jackets and accessories; in fact, all forms of casual wear.) The company started in 1970 with just one outlet in Melbourne but it now has a staggering 200 shops nationally and is moving into New Zealand.

Just Jeans is now the leading jeans brand in Australia with a broad appeal to all sectors. The company prides itself on its flexibility, sophisticated reporting systems, restlessness in seeking out new opportunities, 'customer first' sales policy and development of a distinct brand personality, a personality which is reinforced by advertising, strong logo recall and uniform retail outlets.

Just Jeans, a relatively recent brand, has a massive retail presence in the Australian market.

SAN MIGUEL

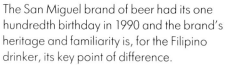

The San Miguel brand of beer had its one hundredth birthday in 1990 and the brand's heritage and familiarity is, for the Filipino drinker, its key point of difference.

Even though San Miguel was the first beer to be brewed in the Philippines there are now thirteen beer brands produced locally and a further ten imports are available in major supermarkets. San Miguel, however, dominates the medium to high price segment as a result of quality, distribution, promotion and constant innovation – recently, for example San Miguel Super Dry and San Miguel Non-Alcoholic beers have been introduced. The company has also put much effort into dealer aids, for example electric coolers and signage, a powerful factor in a market like the Philippines.

San Miguel beer is brewed and marketed under license in Papua New Guinea, Indonesia, Western Samoa and Nepal; there is also a major San Miguel brewery in Hong Kong. In addition, San Miguel is exported to major overseas markets such as the United States, Australia and Japan where it enjoys a reputation for high quality.

San Miguel is the dominant brand of the Philippines. It is also brewed in Hong Kong and certain other markets and is widely appreciated in the US.

UNCLE TOBYS

For successive generations of Australian children Uncle Tobys was synonymous with a hot porridge breakfast and a rush to get to school. Today, however, to most Australian children Uncle Tobys is most familiar for its Crunchy, Chewy and Wrapps Muesli Bars or for Microwave Popcorn, Roll Ups, le Snak and other branded cereal products (e.g. Vita Brits, Weeties, Fibre Plus and Oat Bran).

Uncle Tobys had its origins in the China tea trade and its venture into oat milling dates from 1893. The famous illustration of Uncle Toby standing with a lady (the Widow Wadman) was designed by Nellie Love, daughter of the company's founder, who took as her inspiration *The Life and Opinions of Tristam Shandy* by Laurence Sterne.

As recently as 1983 Uncle Tobys was a niche brand used on a range of slow-selling oat and oat-based products but since then the brand has undergone a transformation – the brand now covers some forty different products and retail turnover has increased

Brands such as Uncle Tobys, built around a particular personality, provide strong promotional opportunities and are particularly appealing to children.

tenfold, to some A$250 million. Indeed, in late 1989 the corporate name was changed to the Uncle Tobys Company.

Uncle Tobys is now a broadly based cereals and 'healthy snack' brand and, through careful development, has become a valuable property with unique associations of quality, taste, health and nutrition, all in an approachable, homely, fun, truly Australian context.

UNCLE TOBYS

Jag is best known for designer denim but is now expanding its base to include sportswear and personal accessories.

JAG

Jag is a fun, status brand, designed by Adele Palmer, which operates in the fashion sportswear and 'lifestyle' market, this latter including fragrances, sunglasses and watches. The brand is particularly strong in Australia but it also sells in the US, South America, Canada and New Zealand.

To most consumers, Jag means designer denim and the brand is particularly known for linked stories – for example trousers, skirt, shirt, jean, singlet and jacket, all themed for multiple sale.

The brand is heavily promoted through leading fashion magazines with high quality point of sale material distributed through a wide account base and strong editorial support in newspapers and 'glossies'.

CANTERBURY OF NEW ZEALAND

Canterbury of New Zealand claims that its sports and leisurewear is 'the world's toughest activewear'. The company's famous rugby jersey was developed in 1918 but became famous when it was worn by the 'Invincibles' All Blacks team in 1924. Now Canterbury of New Zealand garments are sold in New

Canterbury of New Zealand's sports and leisure wear is renowned for its durability and style.

Zealand, Australia, Germany, Sweden, United Kingdom, USA, Canada and Japan.

In New Zealand the brand has a 93 per cent awareness mainly through sponsorship of rugby (e.g. All Blacks, Australian Wallabies, the Fiji rugby team, etc.), yachting (e.g. America's Cup, Whitbread Round the World Race, Admiral's Cup), special events (e.g. Commonwealth Games, the Brisbane Expo) and through advertising. Most of the company's garments are multifunctional and are highly regarded for style, colour, fashion, durability, comfort and attention to detail.

CANTERBURY OF NEW ZEALAND

ANCHOR

The Anchor dairy products brand is operated by the New Zealand Co-Operative Dairy Company within New Zealand and by the NZ Dairy Board, the world's largest trader in dairy products, in export markets.

It promises 'quality – at an affordable price' and consumers perceive it as a brand which they could not better even if they paid more. The brand is sold in eighty overseas markets and is clear brand leader in the UK.

Anchor brand dairy products are one of New Zealand's largest earners of foreign currency.

CASTLEMAINEXXXX

Castlemain XXXX Bitter Ale (or 'Fourex' as it is usually known) is regarded in Queensland, its home state, as 'our beer'. The history of the brand can be traced back to the 1880s and in a country with a strong beer culture and a state with a tropical climate, XXXX Bitter Ale is positioned as bold, gutsy, patriotic, traditional and an outstanding thirst slaker.

Dry, laconic humour is used to promote the brand (e.g. 'I Can Feel a XXXX Comin' On') and in a new country, Queenslanders take particular pride in the sense of continuity provided by the brand. 'It's what I've always drunk. It's what my father and his father before him drank'. The recipe is also reassuringly familiar (it has not changed since 1924), as is the labelling and packaging.

Australians very much enjoy friendly rivalry and competition. Southerners (i.e. people from New South Wales and Victoria) joke that 'Queenslanders call it XXXX because they can't spell beer' but the oddness of the brand name and the opportunities it provides for quips and puns, coupled with a fine product make it a remarkably successful and appealing brand particularly well adapted to a sociable pub atmosphere.

In 1985, agreement was reached with Allied Breweries of the UK whereby they distribute Castlemaine XXXX Export Lager, brewed in Brisbane, and brew and market Castlemaine XXXX Draught Lager.

Australia was first colonised barely two centuries ago, so Castlemaine XXXX has been brewed for more than half of the country's recorded history.

The bond which develops between a beer drinker and 'his' local brew can be very strong, as is shown by Steinlager, the leading beer of New Zealand.

STEINLAGER

Steinlager is New Zealand's best known brand of beer and has gained much international acclaim through its sponsorship of the New Zealand All Blacks national rugby team and the successful Steinlager II challenge for the Round the World yacht race trophy.

The brand is the flagship of New Zealand Breweries (part of Lion Nathan) and has won international awards for taste and quality. In a market which abounds with high quality, distinctive brands Steinlager has succeeded in carving out a niche based upon high product quality and close associations with sport and exciting outdoor activities.

STUBBIES

In Australia, shorts outsell long trousers and Stubbies shorts are Australia's favourite brand.

STUBBIES

Stubbies was first launched in 1973 as a brand of men's shorts and thirty-five million pairs have since been sold. The brand has also now been extended into a complete range of menswear products, mainly in the low to medium priced sectors of the market.

Stubbies is a no-nonsense, down to earth, thoroughly reliable brand which is all-Australian and proud of it. The brand is sold mainly through discount stores and supermarkets and provides consistent quality, good fit and value. The brand has outstanding recall among all Australians and benefits greatly from its unashamedly Australian positioning and matey, friendly brand name.

QANTAS

Qantas started life in 1920 as Queensland and Northern Territory Aerial Services, an air service providing a lifeline in Australia's huge outback. (Qantas began the world's first flying doctor service and ran it for twenty-one years.) By 1934 Qantas had started to fly the Australian leg of the fourteen-day mail service to London and in 1935 Qantas provided its first international passenger service to Singapore. Today Qantas Airways Ltd, the oldest airline in the English-speaking world, has sales of A$3.3 billion (£1.5 billion or US$2.7 billion), 16,000 employees and a worldwide reputation.

Australia's large size and geographical isolation made aviation a natural, both for communications within Australia and in order to provide links with the rest of the world. It has also resulted within Qantas in a tradition of innovation and self-reliance of which the company is enormously proud.

Qantas is an Australian institution; it now operates international air services as the Australian flag carrier and is an integral part of Australian life.

Qantas has one of the strongest – but most memorable – names of any leading airline, a reminder of its origins in the 1920s.

REST OF THE WORLD

IN THIS SECTION WE FEATURE brands from, in the main, Benelux and Scandinavia, parts of the world which have long had a reputation for fine quality products and skills in international trade. But the Caribbean is represented too (with Red Stripe) as is Korea, the Soviet Union, and other countries.

Eastern Europe is currently being viewed with great interest by Western brand owners. McDonald's and Pepsi-Cola have both made well publicised *debuts* in the Soviet market and the opening up of the East German market on July 1st 1990 saw convoys of trucks delivering thousands of tons of branded goods to shops and supermarkets throughout East Germany. Overnight Western brands accounted for 80 per cent of shop sales and only in such areas as fresh produce did local suppliers get a look in.

Branded goods drive out commodities – a principle which has been powerfully demonstrated in East Germany. What will now be interesting to observe is whether East German and other East European producers can develop their own local brands to compete with Western brands or whether the onslaught of Marlboro, Lucky Strike, Tampax, Nivea, Mars and Volkswagen will be irresistible.

REST OF THE WORLD

BRAND	LEADERSHIP	STABILITY	MARKET	INTERNATIONALITY	TREND	SUPPORT	PROTECTION	TOTAL
BOLS	○	□	□	○	□	○	●	○
CARLSBERG	○	●	●	□	□	●	●	□
DOUWE EGBERTS	○	●	●	○	□	□	●	□
GROLSCH		○	●	○	●	●	●	□
HASSELBLAD		●	□		○	○	●	
KERRYGOLD		○	○		○	○	●	
PHILIPS	○	○	□	●	○	□	●	□
RED STRIPE		○	●		●	○	●	○
SAMSON		△	○	□	○	□	●	
SAMSUNG	○	○	●	○	●	□	●	○
SANDEMAN	○	●	□	●	○	○	●	○
STOLICHNAYA		□	●	○	●		●	○
TOBLERONE	○	●	□	□	□		●	○
WOOLMARK	□	●	□	●	○	○	●	□

KEY ★★ Top Ten brand ★ Top Fifty brand ● exceptionally strong □ very strong ○ strong △ problem area

WOOLMARK □

The Woolmark is a Certification Trade Mark owned by the International Wool Secretariat and is applied to pure new wool products which meet the high international quality and performance standards laid down by the IWS. These cover not just fibre content but also colour fastness, appearance retention, durability and so forth. The IWS, in turn, is funded by the Southern Hemisphere wool producers, mainly from Australia and New Zealand and the aim of the Woolmark programme, with its distinctive logo, is to ensure that wool products maintain and build their *cachet* in the face of competition from other natural and man-made fibres.

CERTIFICATION TRADE MARK
PURE NEW WOOL

Woolmark, a Certification Trade Mark, is now applied to over 400 million garments a year.

Certification Trade Marks are also used by groups of peanut farmers in the US, coffee producers in Colombia, cheese makers in the UK (particularly from the Stilton area), sherry producers in Spain and scores of others. Such trade marks are, however, quite rare compared with normal trade marks and service marks. Such trade marks are also notoriously difficult to manage and for many producers IWS's success with the Woolmark is an exemplary story of good practice. The Woolmark is now applied to over 400 million garments a year worldwide as well as to carpets, furnishing fabrics and a host of other products.

SANDEMAN

The House of Sandeman, founded in 1790, is a leading brand of both sherry and port. The English have long had a taste for fortified wines (including Shakespeare's Falstaff) and many of the major shippers of port and sherry were, like Sandeman, founded by Englishmen in the Eighteenth Century.

Sherry is produced in the Jerez region of Spain and port is named after Oporto in Northern Portugal. The Spanish and Portuguese producers have both sought in recent years to prevent the names sherry and port being applied to any product that does not originate from a closely delineated area and which does not have official approval as to origin and quality – thus fortified wines produced in other countries could not use descriptions such as 'Cyprus sherry' or 'Australian port'. Within the European

Common Market much support has been given to the Spanish and Portuguese governments by France and Italy as both countries have regional specialities (e.g. champagne) seeking similar protection. However, even though the concept of protecting specialist regional products is now well accepted within the EC, other countries, who fear for their domestic producers, are less sympathetic.

Sandeman's powerful visual image is the silhouette of The Don (or nobleman) in a black cape, taken from a painting produced in 1928 by George Massiot Brown and purchased by a member of the family for fifty guineas. Now, despite a continuing British fondness for sherry and port, the company's most rapidly growing export markets are Germany (for medium dry sherry) and France (for port).

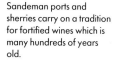

Sandeman ports and sherries carry on a tradition for fortified wines which is many hundreds of years old.

RED STRIPE

Red Stripe is the national beer brand of Jamaica and is to Jamaican beer drinkers what Carlsberg is to the Danes, Heineken to the Dutch and Steinlager to the Kiwis. In recent years Red Stripe has, however, become an important niche brand in the US and UK. In both countries it started to be sold in outlets popular with Jamaican immigrants and rapidly acquired an enthusiastic following among other beer drinkers. In the UK, for example, young white drinkers imitated the habits of black consumers who were seen as 'streetwise' and knowledgeable, so much so that HP Bulmer, the British cider maker took on the brand and now markets it along with Strongbow and Woodpecker ciders, Perrier and Buxton mineral waters and the Orangina brand of soft drink.

Red Stripe is the national beer brand of Jamaica and in terms of consumer loyalty ranks alongside such 'island' beers as San Miguel (Philippines), Kalik (Bahamas) and Tiger (Singapore).

GROLSCH

Although a relative newcomer to British and American markets, the name 'Grolsch' has been familiar to Dutch drinkers for centuries. The origin of the present Grolsche Bierbrouwerij (literally 'brewery of Grol') dates back to 1615 when a Mr Neervelt settled in the town of Grol, now known as Groenlo, and started brewing beer.

For over 300 years the brewery remained a small but flourishing family concern, producing high quality beer for the pleasure and refreshment of the people of Gelderland. Then, in 1922, the brewery merged with the nearby Enschede Brewery and the name 'Grolsch Bier' was adopted as the official brand name of the new business.

Grolsch Brewery has now become a major Dutch company whose products challenge even the mighty Heineken in the home market. No doubt centuries of brewing experience have produced a beer of supreme quality, but the brand has other characteristics which have given it a truly distinctive personality.

In the UK, for example, the arrival of Grolsch in its chunky swingtop bottle with its porcelain stopper was greeted as a breath of fresh air by drinkers bored by an array of poorly differentiated light beers. Grolsch was truly original; it cost more – but it looked and tasted good and soon became the cult beer of affluent young drinkers. The success of Grolsch has spawned a rash of imitators; but it remains a truly authentic brand and this should assure its continued popularity.

Grolsch is a brilliant example of brand marketing.

PREMIUM LAGER

CARLSBERG

The Carlsberg Group owns two of Denmark's – and the world's – best known beer brands, Carlsberg and Tuborg as well as the Hannen Brewery in Mönchengladbach in Western Germany. Carlsberg began exporting beer from its Copenhagen brewery in 1868 and Carlsberg is now brewed overseas in Carlsberg-owned breweries in the UK, Malawi, Malaysia and Hong Kong and under licence in ten other countries.

As a brand Carlsberg is another classic – the company has a passionate devotion to the product and to product excellence, enormous pride in the brand and an unequivocal and unswerving message and positioning. The founders of the business, J C Jacobsen and Carl Jacobsen, declared their purpose to be 'to develop the art of making beer to the greatest possible degree of perfection in order that these breweries as well as their products may ever stand out as a model'. Carlsberg still adheres to the same principles. Indeed in the UK the company's deliberately understated advertising message has been for many years 'Probably the best lager in the world'.

Carlsberg has successfully made the transition from a national brand with a specialist international following to being a true international brand.

BOLS

Bols today is a major international business with subsidiaries across Europe and South America and products which sell throughout the world. Not bad for a company which started life in a wooden shed.

The Bols story starts in 1575 when Lucas Bols built his legendary wooden shed – 't Lootsje' – at Rozengracht near Amsterdam. It was here that he formulated his first liquors using water locally drawn and simple copper kettles heated with turf. These early experiments resulted in the range of liqueurs and *genevers* – the highly distinctive Dutch gins – that are now sold in over 150 countries.

The success of Bols owes much to its ancient craftsmanship and to its obsession with quality. Bols' raw materials buyers have for centuries travelled the world in search of the finest herbs, spices and fruits for the numerous products featuring the Bols brand.

Bols liquors cover a wide range of products; the company has therefore to maintain brand coherence across many applications.

DOUWE EGBERTS

The Douwe Egberts 'D.E. Seal' has become one of the most famous trademarks in Holland and is used across the company's extensive range of coffee products. The brand is a representation of the original wax seal which

Holland is one of the world's leading trading nations with strong early associations with the Dutch East Indies. It is no wonder that Holland has a wealth of powerful brands in such areas as tobaccos, spices and coffee.

was used after the death of the founder in 1806. In those days the seal bore the letters W.D.E., an abbreviation for 'the Widow Douwe Egbert' who, with her sons, had taken over the running of the company. The seal was used on coffee and tobacco bags, on the labels of bottles of spirits and on the company's correspondence – a fine early example of co-ordinated branding!

A brand, of course, can only succeed as long as it continues to provide satisfaction. It says much for the high quality of Douwe Egberts' marketing and manufacturing, therefore, that the brand continues to satisfy an ever-growing diversity of consumer tastes and expectations. The Douwe Egberts 'D.E. Seal' may truly be said to represent excellence in relation to coffee.

STOLICHNAYA

Think of things Russian and vodka immediately comes to mind; Stolichnaya is the Soviet Union's major export brand of vodka and is positioned alongside brands such as Smirnoff and Finlandia as a genuine brand of vodka from the home of all fine vodkas.

White spirits such as vodka, white rum and gin have gained considerable ground in the last thirty years at the expense of 'heavier' spirits such as Scotch, Bourbon and dark rum, due to their versatility.

The Russians were slow to realise the appeal and export potential of their vodkas, (indeed of many of their products, apart from raw materials) but the brand received a huge boost in the US once PepsiCo started to distribute it as part of a barter deal designed to introduce Soviet citizens to the Pepsi habit. Most recently, a premium vodka known as Stolichnaya Cristall has been launched by PepsiCo in the US.

Russian brand names such as Stolichnaya are delightfully resonant and melodic.

Stolichnaya is now exported around the world, (Teacher handle it in the UK) and it enjoys a distinct *cachet* on account of its authenticity, a *cachet* which the somewhat austere packaging does nothing to damage.

TOBLERONE

Toblerone is derived from the name of its Swiss producer, Tobler, now part of Jacobs-Suchard, a company which became part of KGF (Kraft General Foods), the food manufacturing arm of Philip Morris, in 1990 – it is clear that the world's food industries are becoming both increasingly concentrated and increasingly complicated!

Jacobs-Suchard's confectionery brands include Milka, Suchard and Cote d'Or as well as Toblerone and since 1985, the company has increasingly focused on a fewer number of larger, powerful brands. As part of this process, undertaken in response to the completion of the European Single Market and an increased globalisation of brands in the confectionery and chocolate sectors, smaller production plants have been closed (e.g. the Tobler factory at Stuttgart), new high

Toblerone benefits from a high quality, well marketed product and also from its distinctive triangular shape.

efficiency plants established (e.g. the Toblerone plant at Berne) and distribution systems extended.

Toblerone is a high quality brand which continues to grow rapidly, aided in part by its distinctive triangular shape and packaging, wide availability and heavy promotion. It is clearly one of the brands which made Jacobs-Suchard such an attractive acquisition candidate, though it could well be that KGF will sell the chocolate division of Jacobs-Suchard to a third party as their main interest it is said, is in the Jacobs coffee business.

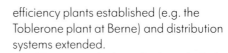

SAMSUNG

Samsung started life as a small export company just over fifty years ago in Taegu, South Korea. Since then it has grown to the extent that it now has some 160 branches in fifty countries, and a workforce of over 160,000 people. In 1987 net sales for the group reached US$21.9 billion, a performance that ranked it thirty-second in the world.

As a trading group Samsung deals in and produces a huge range of goods and services; apart from its extensive range of electronic products and components, its textile and clothing businesses and its interests in shipbuilding, aerospace and the chemical industry, the group owns a number of insurance companies and hotels. The Samsung name is used, however, as a product trademark mainly in high-tech areas such as electronics, semiconductors, telecommunications, aerospace and medical systems.

Samsung, a Korean corporate brand, is now one of the world's leading industrial companies.

KERRYGOLD

Kerrygold is the brand of An Bord Bainne, the Irish Dairy Board, an organisation set up by the Irish Government in 1961 (and, since 1973, a co-operative owned by the dairy manufacturers) to handle the export marketing of Irish dairy products. By 1990 the Board had a turnover of more than I£1 billion and Kerrygold is now powerfully established in Britain, as well as in Benelux, France, West Germany and parts of North America, Latin America and the Middle and Far East.

Ireland is renowned for its rich pastures and lush, beautiful countryside and Kerrygold has drawn strongly on this imagery to develop the brand and promote its product range.

Dairying is one of Ireland's major industries and most of the country's production is sold through the Irish Dairy Board, much of it under the Kerrygold brand.

SAMSON

Samson roll-your-own tobacco is produced by the long-established Dutch firm Theodorus Niemeyer. Samson has for nearly a hundred years been one of Holland's favourite brands and is also popular in Germany, France, the United Kingdom and many other countries throughout the world.

Samson's appeal has always been its unique flavour and high quality and it is these factors, combined with strong imagery, which has contributed to its remarkable longevity. For the first sixty-odd years of its life, however, it was quality allied to a low-selling price compared to the price of cigarettes, which sustained sales. The brand owed its success to unmatched value for money and solid support from working-class smokers.

Then, as tastes and lifestyles changed with the dawning of the sixties, roll-your-own became, quite simply, a cult. And Samson's uncompromising flavour and image appealed to the egalitarian, non-conformist young and a new generation of smokers was introduced to the brand. Smoking roll-your-own was no longer solely a working-class habit. Samson has continued ever since to exert a strong hold on the affections of smokers in all groups of the population, due to its unique flavour and high quality , basic promises which have remained unchanged. This has been supported by powerful and consistent use of pack graphics and advertising which makes Samson a classic of its kind.

Traditionally the brand of the working man, since the 1960s roll-your-own tobacco has enjoyed a much broader consumer base.

HASSELBLAD

The Hasselblad family was first involved in photography as distributors for the Eastman Company, manufacturers of Kodak products. Victor Hasselblad, born in 1906, later developed a special camera for the Swedish Air Force and, in 1941, founded his own company Victor Hasselblad AB.

Hasselblad's cameras quickly acquired a world reputation for quality and in the 1950s were selected by NASA for use in space. What really changed the Hasselblad brand from being a product known only to the professional to one with a much wider reputation, however, was the use of a Hasselblad camera on the Moon in 1969 by Armstrong and Aldrin. Hasselblad became a household name though Hasselblad cameras are still the preserve of the professional and of the 'professional standard' amateur.

Professional photographers, and enthusiastic amateurs, all aspire to owning and using a Hasselblad camera.

PHILIPS

Philips is Europe's largest electronics group; it is headquartered in Eindhoven, Holland, where in 1891 Gerard Philips started his light-bulb manufacturing business and it now manufactures a huge array of electrical and electronic products including lighting, semi-conductor chips, computers, defence electronics, domestic appliances and hi-fi and audio equipment. It also owns Polygram, a major recording group.

The Philips shield logo was adopted in 1938 and this device mark, plus the trade mark 'Philips' are among the most recognised trade marks in Europe and, possibly, the world. In recent years, however, the company has found that mere recognition is not enough: even though brand recognition is high, consumers do not have a clear idea of the 'personality' of Philips or of its values and standards. The company is currently addressing this problem.

PHILIPS

The Philips brand is one of the best known in Europe but is now trying to develop a tighter 'focus'.

POSTSCRIPT

TEN RULES OF GOOD BRAND MANAGEMENT

DOES THIS REVIEW OF OVER 300 OF the world's leading brands suggest any general rules of good brand management? We believe it does and would suggest the following:

1 *Cherish your brands.*
Ensure that your brands are cared for. Treat them as valuable and important assets. Ensure that they have a central role in the organisation.

2 *Take brand management seriously.*
Treat it as a senior function and give it authority and responsibility.

3 *Account for your brands.*
Adopt brand accounting (i.e. brand audit techniques) otherwise you will have no idea as to the financial performance of your brands and will not be able to make informed, brand-related decisions.

4 *Manage your brands conservatively.*
Have a clear idea as to each brand's personality and positioning. Do not tinker with your brands unless there is a good reason for doing so.

5 *Maintain responsibility for your brands.*
It is foolish to surrender responsibility for your brands to an advertising agency. Although agencies are honourable and dedicated they are not brand managers and by no means always share precisely the same objectives as their clients.

6 *Maintain a point of difference in each brand.*
Remember that customers have many brands to choose from; give them a reason to choose yours.

7 *Exploit the equity in your brands.*
Brand extension is a legitimate and sensible activity but care needs to be exercised to avoid brand dilution.

8 *Review your portfolio.*
Brands are increasingly being viewed as separable, transferable assets. You should consider disposing of brands that do not fit your portfolio and replacing them with others that do.

9 *Consider the international implications for your brand.*
The internationalisation of branding makes it important to think beyond national boundaries, otherwise your brand runs the risk of being overrun by a more aggressive foreign competitor.

10 *Protect your brands.*
Trade mark registration affords powerful rights at low cost. You should ensure that you have clear title to your brands in all countries and in all categories of goods and services likely to be of interest.

ACKNOWLEDGEMENTS

The publishers would like to thank all those brand owners and their agents and associates who have supplied information and illustrations for this book. It should be noted that virtually every product or corporate name mentioned in the book is a registered trademark and virtually every logo reproduced in the book is the specific property of a company. The following specific acknowledgements and notices have, however, been requested. **Bacardi** – Reproduced with permission of the trademark owners, Bacardi & Company Ltd, Nassau, Bahamas. **Wrigley's** – Reprinted courtesy of the Wm Wrigley Jr. Company. **Aquascutum** – Reprinted courtesy of Aquascutum. **Levi's** – Provided courtesy of Levi Strauss & Co. **Ray-Ban** – Ray-Ban® is a registered trademark of Bausch & Lomb. **3M** – Courtesy of 3M. **IBM** – Courtesy of International Business Machines. **Harvard** – © 1990 Harvard University. **Hertz** – Reproduced courtesy of Hertz Europe Ltd. **American Express** – American Express Box logo® is a registered service mark of American Express and is printed with permission; photo – American Express Archives Department. **Exocet** – Aerospatiale, France/Mars, Lincs. **Kalashnikov** – Paul Popper Ltd. **AT&T** – © Western Electric News Features. **TGV** – © French Railways – Lafontant. **KitKat** – KitKat is a registered trademark of Nestlé S.A. Vevey, Switzerland. **Elastoplast** – Elastoplast is a trademark of T. J. Smith+Nephew Limited. **Sainsbury** – © J. Sainsbury plc. **Anchor** – Courtesy of the New Zealand Dairy Board. **Vegemite** – Reproduced with permission of Kraft Foods Ltd. **Kerrygold** – Reproduced by permission of Bord Bainne Co-op. **Playboy, Johnson & Johnson, Esso/Exxon, Michelin, Camel, Vogue, Hermès, Scotch, Charlie, Opium, Life Savers, Hoover, Philips** – material supplied by The Advertising Archives, London. Photographic research by Dee Robinson and Sharon Buckley. Project co-ordination by Deborah Taylor. Photography by Zul Mukhida and Walter Gardiner Photography.